In Search of Africa

▲▼▲

W9-BKN-149

In Search of Africa

▲▼▲

MANTHIA DIAWARA

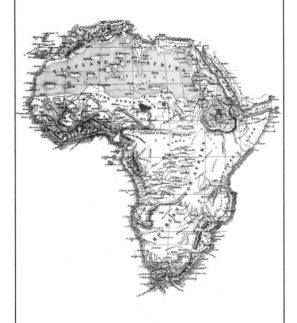

HARVARD UNIVERSITY PRESS

Cambridge, Massachusetts
London, England

Copyright © 1998 by the President and Fellows of Harvard College
All rights reserved
Printed in the United States of America
Second printing, 2000

First Harvard University Press paperback edition, 2000

Situation III originally appeared as "Malcolm X and the Black Public Sphere: Conversionists versus Culturalists," *Public Culture*, 7, no. 1 (Fall 1994). Copyright 1994. Reprinted by permission of Duke University Press.

LIBRARY OF CONGRESS CATALOGING-IN-PUBLICATION DATA

Diawara, Manthia, 1953–
In search of Africa / Manthia Diawara.
p. cm.
Includes bibliographical references (p.   ) and index.
ISBN 0-674-44611-9 (cloth)
ISBN 0-674-00408-6 (pbk.)
1. West Africans—United States—Ethnic identity. 2. Diawara,
Manthia, 1953– —Journeys—Africa. 3. West Africans—United
States—Biography. 4. Afro-Americans—Relations with Africans.
5. United States—Relations—Africa, French-speaking West.
6. Africa, French-speaking West—Relations—United States. 7. Pan-Africanism.
8. Afro-American arts. 9. Arts, African. I. Title.
E184.A24D53   1998
973'.0496—dc21   98-17149

For Regina, Mansita, and Daman

Preface

▲▼▲

I have organized this book into chapters and Situations, borrowing a concept from Sartre. The chapters recount the Sidimé Laye story and my search for Africa. The Situations deal with blackness and modernity, and my own place and role in shaping them. The Situations are designed to provide distance for reflecting on the issues in Africa with which I am concerned. I know that some people will find them obtrusive, or even shocking. They should feel free to skip these pages and continue on with the Sidimé Laye story. I have nothing against the pleasure of the text. Other readers, however, will find connections between what I am saying in the Laye story and what I have tried to theorize in the Situations. Even finding contradictions will constitute a step in the right direction.

Since I have always wanted to produce a work like Erich Auerbach's *Mimesis,* I wrote the entire book in cafés and hotel lobbies in Senegal, Mali, Guinea, Côte d'Ivoire, France, Jamaica, Bermuda, Guadeloupe, Martinique, and the United States. That is, outside of libraries. I would like to thank all the people who tolerated my extended presence, often up to closing hours, in their spaces. My gratitude and thanks go especially to the people at the Teranga Hotel (Dakar), the Café Flore (Paris), Space Untitled (New York), and the Pamela Café and Restaurant (New York). I thank Tahar Ben Jelloun for lending me his apartment on the Boulevard Saint-Germain during the summer of 1996.

New York University provided generous assistance throughout the writing process, and the Center for the Study of Black Literature and Culture at the University of Pennsylvania supported my work in its early stages.

A different version of Situation I appeared in *Black Renaissance / Renaissance Noire* (Fall 1996). A small part of Chapter 4 appeared, in altered form, in *Black Popular Culture,* ed. Gina Dent (Seattle: Bay Press, 1992). Portions of Chapter 5 appeared, in substantially different form, in *The Culture of Globalization,* ed. Fredric Jameson and Masao Miyoshi (Durham, N.C.: Duke University Press, 1998). And part of Chapter 7 appeared, also in very different form, in *Artforum* (November 1997).

I am deeply grateful to all of the people whose friendship and help made this book possible: Sidimé Laye, Seydou Ly, Houston Baker Jr., Clyde Taylor, Walter Mosley, Annette Michelson, Daman Diawara, and Mansita Diawara.

Special thanks go to Christopher Winks, managing editor of *Black Renaissance / Renaissance Noire,* for his valuable advice; and to Fatima Legrand, administrative assistant in NYU's Department of Africana Studies, for helping me with the keyboarding. Valerie Thiers generously took the time to read the manuscript for French accents.

Regina Austin-Diawara was a mainstay from beginning to end. She gave me ideas, encouraged me, and criticized me. All with love.

My editor, Lindsay Waters, believed in me and waited a long time for this book. When I thought I had finished it, he sent it to readers who challenged me to make it better. I am grateful to him and to them. I also feel fortunate to have benefited from the assistance of Maria Ascher. She is a remarkable reader and editor.

Needless to say, I am a very lucky man to have so many people in my corner. I take full responsibility for any errors that may remain.

Contents

▲▼▲

WEST AFRICA

SITUATION I

▲▼▲

SARTRE AND AFRICAN MODERNISM

In the spring of the academic year 1994–1995, I added Jean-Paul Sartre's "Black Orpheus" to the reading list of my course "Introduction to Pan-Africanism." I wanted to emphasize the Harlem Renaissance and the Negritude movement as cultural and political components of Pan-Africanism. It thus seemed to me that Sartre's long essay—introducing the art and philosophy of the Negritude movement, as did Alain Locke's manifesto at the beginning of his book *The New Negro*—would help to set the stage for further discussions of the problematics of race and its relation to culture and universalism.

The class began with W. E. B. Du Bois's *The World and Africa,* which refutes the racist thesis, primarily associated with Eurocentric historians, that Africa was the only continent to have made no contribution to world history and civilization. Du Bois's main objectives in this celebratory book, as in his classic *Souls of Black Folk,* were threefold: to write the history and culture of the people of Africa and African descent; to enable African Americans to identify with Africa as a proud and dignified source of identity that could be placed on an equal footing with Europe, Asia, and North America; and to posit Africa's humanism and rich heritage as a compelling argument against racism and colonialism. Du Bois believed that freedom is whole and indivisible, that black people in America will not be completely free until Africa is liberated and emancipated in modernity. His Pan-Africanism was born from his awareness that freedom was a common goal for black people.

In retrospect, I now realize that the class's initial reaction to *The World*

1

▼

and Africa was aggressive. One student from Africa challenged the very idea of Pan-Africanism, warning us that Africans differed widely across the continent and that African Americans, like white Americans, were ignorant about Africa's complexity. Another accused Du Bois and other Pan-Africanists of the same colonial intentions as white people, and added that race should not be used to justify the paternalism and elitism of African Americans and Caribbeans in Africa. A woman also raised a question concerning the links between Pan-Africanism and sexism. But the majority of the class tended to focus on Du Bois's attempt to raise consciousness about the worldwide exploitation of black and brown people by people of European descent, and on his quest for freedom.

I knew that teaching this class was not going to be easy. I had to find some texts by women and Afrocentrists to add to the reading list. But, one might wonder, why include "Black Orpheus," a text by a dead French white male? Because I find the Du Boisian ideas of race unity especially interesting if they are studied together with and repositioned by other racial theories in time and space, such as the nationalism of the Negritude movement, the Afrocentric movement, and Sartre's thesis of antiracist racism as a basis for combating colonialism and paternalism. I wanted to know what would happen to the core idea of Pan-Africanism if it were taught as a history of often contradictory ideas instead of a chronology of events and historical figures. What were the links, for instance, between Du Bois's statement that the problem of the twentieth century was the problem of the color line and the Diopian (or Afrocentric) theory of the cultural unity of people of African descent? And by extension, how did Du Bois's Pan-Africanism relate intertextually to C. L. R. James's appropriation of the central themes of the French Revolution for black liberation struggles? Or to James's repositioning of the Haitian uprising as the first paradigm of race unity between black and brown people in the modern world? Or to Sartre's call for an antiracist racism? Sartre was important to me in this debate not only because of his role as an intellectual leader who in the 1940s and 1950s was involved in several revolutionary movements in France, including Negritude, but also because of the similarities between his position on antiracist racism and the Diopian essentializing of race.

"Black Orpheus" was written as an introduction to the *Anthologie de la nouvelle poésie nègre et malgache de langue française* (*Anthology of New Negro and Malagasy Poetry in French;* 1948), edited by Léopold Sédar

Senghor. It is the most famous essay on the Negritude movement, serving on the one hand to define the concept for Western audiences, and on the other hand to encourage some of its poets and writers to embrace Marxism in their search for a universal road beyond skin color. For Sartre, Negritude was a separation and a negation in the existential sense; it valorized a word which until then had been an ugly and dirty word in the French language. A French dictionary, *Le nouveau Petit Robert,* gives the word *nègre* (from which Negritude is derived) the following meanings: a person of the black race, a slave; to work like a *nègre* is to work hard without earning the right to rest; to be a *nègre* in the literary world is to be a ghostwriter for famous authors; to speak *petit nègre* is to express oneself in a limited and bad French. In other words, a *nègre* is a person without a soul or a mind; a dirty person; the opposite of a white person, of a human being. For Sartre, Negritude derives its authenticity from the unhinging of the word *nègre* from these traditional connotations in the French language; from the destabilization of the meanings embedded in the roots of the concept; from its revelation that "there is a secret blackness of the white, a secret whiteness of the black, a fixed flickering of being and nonbeing" (Sartre, 1976: 29).

Sartre defines Negritude as an operative power of negation, an antiracist racism, which unites black people in their struggle to reclaim their humanity. In the poetry of Aimé Césaire, Senghor, Léon Gontran Damas, and many others from the French West Indies and Francophone Africa, he finds an authentic élan driven by a new meaning of blackness; an existentialist affirmation liberated from fixed and atavistic connotations in the French imaginary; an obsessive energy sending the black poets after their Negritude. Sartre is reminded of Orpheus' descent into hell to rescue his Eurydice. The black poet, too, will leave no stone unturned, will invert the meaning of every French word which had contributed to his subjugation, and will rescue his Negritude with positive values. Sartre sees another analogy in the manner in which the Negritude poets defamiliarize the French language: that of Prometheus stealing fire, the symbol of knowledge, from Jupiter. This leads the French writer to declare Negritude a *poésie engagée,* "the sole great revolutionary poetry" in French in the 1940s.

At first, Sartre's celebration of Negritude's racial essentialism seems to allow no room for criticism. Like the poets, he sings the African's closeness to nature. He speaks of the synthetic African versus the analytic European;

the capacity of black people to display emotion, in contrast to the cold rationality of white people; and the Africans' blameless role in modern history's catalogue of genocide, fascism, and racism. For Sartre, the white worker is incapable of producing good poetry because he has been contaminated by his materialist culture and its penchant for objectivity. The black man, on the other hand, is subjective and therefore authentic; his poetry is evangelical. The black man, as Sartre puts it, "remains the great male of the earth, the sperm of the world" (45). The Negritude that Sartre describes here resembles that of Cheikh Anta Diop and Léopold Sédar Senghor, who believe that black people live in a symbiotic relation with nature, unlike white people, who dominate and destroy their environment.

But Sartre is not content to define Negritude as only an antiracist racism uniting people around race consciousness to combat French colonialism, paternalism, and imperialism. He also sees Negritude as a becoming, a transcendence of blackness into a future universalism. For Sartre, there are two ways of constructing racial concepts: one is internal and the other external. Those who internalize their Negritude and make it an irreducible difference are mobilized by their desire to compose a unique history, and to shield themselves from outside contamination. They are traditionalists. On the other hand, there is the vanguard that deploys blackness as an antiracist racism, or uses racial consciousness as a social movement, because it "wishes the abolition of racial privileges wherever they are found; solidarity with the oppressed of all colors" (59). Here, Sartre concurs with the blackness of C. L. R. James, who discovered that black unity coincided with the quest for liberty, fraternity, and equality, the French Revolution's central themes, which Toussaint L'Ouverture appropriated for Haiti; of Aimé Césaire, who wrote *Discours sur le colonialisme* (*Discourse on Colonialism*); and of Frantz Fanon, who stated that "a nation which undertakes a liberation struggle rarely condones racism."

Sartre, too, sees the ideal of the French revolution in Negritude:

The black contribution to the evolution of Humanity is no longer a flavor, a taste, a rhythm, an authenticity, a cluster of primitive instincts; it is a dated enterprise, a patient construction, a future. It was in the name of ethnic qualities that the black was recently claiming his place in the sun; at present, it is upon his mission that he bases his right to life, and this mission, exactly like that of the proletariat, comes to him from his historical situation. Because he has, more than all others, the sense of revolt and the love of liberty. And because he is the most oppressed, it is the liberation of all that he necessarily pursues when he labors for his own deliverance. (57)

"Black Orpheus" brought to the surface the ideological divisions among my students. There were those who felt invigorated by Sartre's call for a common struggle on behalf of a universal humanism. They agreed with Sartre that Negritude was about class struggle, that racism and colonialism themselves were conditions of class antagonism. Others felt that this movement toward the universal was disempowering to the black struggle in its effort to define its own agenda for freedom and recognition; they felt that Sartre was diluting the meaning of Negritude.

I asked the class to think seriously about the passage quoted above, and to put into brackets, in a Husserlian sense, the words "it is a dated enterprise, a patient construction, a future." With this phrase, I felt that Sartre had historicized Negritude into a grand narrative, and had conferred upon it a significance equal to that of Christianity and Marxism, two of the most important teleological social movements in modern history.

Negritude's utopia would be a society without racism or class division. Sartre placed his hope on Negritude, which he believed would create the society that Europe had failed to realize at the end of the Second World War. Richard Wright, too, believed that Europeans had abandoned the spirit of modernity by refusing to give up racism and xenophobia. Thus, when it came to ending the evils of humanity and bringing the grand narrative to closure, who could better carry out this mission than blacks, the victims of so much racism and suffering? Negritude propounds the romantic idea that the oppressed would not persecute their brothers and sisters, because they know how it feels to be oppressed; that the excluded would know the meaning of ostracism; and that those who have been the targets of systematic violence would teach the world to love. Confident that decolonization was the most important revolution of the latter half of the twentieth century, the Negritude poets would identify with suffering, as Christ did, in order to end all suffering.

This Sartrean view is worth pursuing in Pan-Africanism; it universalizes black struggle by positing that Africa and other continents involved in the fight against colonialism and racism are the future of the world. Negritude and other decolonizing movements, before being coopted by the Cold War and forced to align themselves with NATO or the Soviet bloc, held the promise of world renewal: black and brown people would have the right to shape their own destinies; and white people would rid themselves of the guilt accumulated through centuries of racism and paternalism. Modernity would finally be fulfilling its true mission, in the Habermasian sense: it would go beyond the visible difference of skin color and save humanity from obscurantism and oppression.

Suddenly, this new perspective changed the goal of Negritude into something larger than the black poets who had conceived the movement. Negritude would not be limited to Africa and turned inward into a narcissistic contemplation of the self, or fixed as a blinding determinism of skin color. Its poets would seize the leaven of life from those who hate and exploit, in order to provide energy to those in need of freedom and emancipation. The mission of Negritude was now universal freedom, which encompasses not only the colonized subjects of Africa and the Caribbean, but also the exploited working classes of Europe, America, and Asia. Clearly, the struggle for black rights in Negritude was congruent with Sartre's Marxian analysis of the condition of the working class in France, and with the aims of the civil rights movement in America. The role of the black poet, like that of a demiurge, was to create a new man and a new woman in a new World, not to ghettoize the muse. Fanon, a young writer coming out of the Negritude movement, was the first to agree with Sartre. In his pathbreaking book *The Wretched of the Earth,* he warned against the pitfalls of racial identification: "The unconditional affirmation of African culture has succeeded the unconditional affirmation of European culture" (Fanon, 1963: 212).

I wanted my students to know what this meant to some of us who had grown up in Africa in the 1950s and 1960s. The idea that Negritude was bigger even than Africa, that we were part of an international moment which held the promise of universal emancipation, that our destiny coincided with the universal freedom of workers and colonized people worldwide— all this gave us a bigger and more important identity than the ones previously available to us through kinship, ethnicity, and race. It felt good to be in tune not only with Sartre but with such world-renowned revolutionaries as Karl Marx, Leon Trotsky, Albert Camus, André Malraux, Fidel Castro, Angela Davis, Mao Tse Tung, Martin Luther King Jr., Nelson Mandela, and Frantz Fanon. The awareness of our new historical mission freed us from what we regarded in those days as the archaic identities of our fathers and their religious entrapments; it freed us from race and banished our fear of the whiteness of French identity. To be labeled the saviors of humanity, when only recently we had been colonized and despised by the world, gave us a feeling of righteousness, which bred contempt for capitalism, racialism of all origins, and tribalism. In fact, the universalism proposed by Sartre became for some of us a new way of being radically chic — of jumping into a new identity in order not to deal with race, which went unmentioned except during discussions of racism. It was not until the mid-Sixties, when we became sufficiently immersed in black American popular culture, that race reappeared as a significant element of culture.

Ironically, this awareness of common struggle, of worldwide demand that human rights be granted by white supremacists and capitalists, seemed to undercut Negritude's first claim to authenticity and singularity. As some students in the class pointed out, it may not be possible to take everyone in the direction that Sartre was taking Negritude. The desire to appear universal may cause Negritude to forget or to ignore some of its constituent elements, and therefore to disintegrate. The students were concerned about Sartre's setting the agenda for the Negritude poets — a white man telling them what to do and how to do it — and thus diluting the radical ideas of the movement.

In this sense, it is true that Negritude was based primarily on poetry by black people about black people. It is also true that every movement has its own internal coherence, which is kept alive by the specific way it sets its constitutive elements in motion and maintains a specific relation among them. This internal autonomy of relation gives a movement like Negritude its singularity, enables it to shine among other movements and even to be admired and imitated by them. If we emphasize too quickly the similarities between Negritude and the proletarian movements around the world, we risk making these constitutive parts invisible.

But, I asked the class, was the movement toward the particular necessarily a move away from the universal? Or, to put it in another way, was the movement toward the universal a selling out of black culture? My own answer is no in both cases. When the particular is successful, its central themes begin to illuminate other struggles and creative projects. And conversely, when the universal is truly universal, it takes away from the particular the need for resistance and ghettoization and brings freedom to the elements that used to constitute the particular. This is what Sartre saw in Negritude, a movement which he thought capable of shedding new light on the meanings of freedom, love, and universal beauty. The light coming from Africa and from black poets, visible enough to influence liberation struggles elsewhere and to unleash energies in other parts of the world against racism and exploitation, is what constitutes the universality of Negritude. It is important, therefore, to distinguish Negritude from the radiance emanating from it. The universality of a thing is not the thing itself; it is what the thing reveals or teaches to others. It is external to the thing itself. Sartre emphasized what is external to Negritude: the black poet's gift to the world—in other words, the lesson of freedom.

Some of my students said that Sartre's universalism was Eurocentric; his sources—Orpheus, Prometheus, the Bible, the proletariat—were all from a European scholastic tradition, not from Egyptian or ancient Sub-Saharan sources. It did not permit the Negritude poets time enough to digest what their blackness meant to them, and what they wanted to do with it. Negritude, as part of decolonization, was important because it gave black people in France their first opportunity to assert themselves in the political, psychological, and artistic spheres. This would later lead to the independence of several African countries, with Negritude writers among the heads of state. Negritude enabled Africans and Caribbeans, for the first time, to deploy blackness as a positive concept of modernization: be proud of your ancestry, discover the beauty of blackness, and let Negritude unite you against colonialism. It is because the Negritude poets turned inward to develop an awareness of their own historical situation that they discovered a truth bigger than themselves. It is because they sang their love song from within this specificity that it echoed worldwide and inspired other liberation songs.

It was time, then, for me to make an argument exposing certain ethnocentric definitions of universalism. I explained to the class that I understood the need to celebrate Negritude on the ground of particularism. I myself might not have been their teacher that day if it had not been for the nationalism of the Negritude poets. My generation had been drawn to Negritude because it promised to make us equal to white people, to lift us above the tribe and the clan, and to provide us with our own nations. Many children of my generation, overlooked by the colonial system, had gone to school and learned to read and write only because of Negritude and independence. It is in this sense that we say that Negritude invented us, taught us how to think in a particularly modern way, and put us inside history. It is easier to ask those who would have known modernity without Negritude to forget about it than to demand those of us who owe our modernity to Negritude to abandon it for the universal. As Sartre himself says, "From the man of color and from him alone can it be asked to renounce pride in his color" (1976: 62). The universalist tendency carries with it and against the separationist tendency a threat of destruction of identity, a shift of priority, an aggressive attitude which leads the separationist to feel anxiety about being cast aside and neglected.

It is important to remember that the universal is always a gift or revelation to the world. The modes of actualization of this gift lead, under certain social conditions, to control, resistance, or disempowerment. First of all, the universal may take on particularist or racist features whenever people, in order to control it, choose a selective means of dissemination. Aimé Césaire was right in calling the colonial experience in Africa a controlled gift system, because it educated native Africans only selectively and Christianized them only partially, and was never interested in letting them take full advantage of the universal potential of education and Christianity.

People still give selectively, and there remains an essentialist tendency which links whiteness to such universal practices as scientific inquiry and classical music. For example, the reluctance to give generously, or to let go, leads some scholars to keep referring to the novel as solely a Western narrative form, as opposed to a form invented in Europe at a particular moment in history. Clearly, to write a novel today one does not have to be a European or subscribe to a European way of life. A parsimonious gift system colors our vision of the United States, which is called a Western society. But despite the existence of many Americans of European descent, and despite the development of certain ideas and practices that originated in Europe, the fact remains that the identities of Americans owe as much to a flight from Europe and its monarchist, Victorian, and religious cultures as they do to Africa and Asia. The United States is not culturally interchangeable with Europe, just as it cannot be with Africa and Asia.

Interestingly enough, reference to America's Western identity is no more than an expression of European Americans' desire to insert themselves permanently in the very image of Americanness, and to maintain the power to reproduce themselves as the ideal and universal Americans. This type of essentialism remains a problem, as people continue to lay claim to certain universal elements discovered by their ancestors at a particular time in history; obviously they are still suffering from separation anxiety. The inability to cope with the loss of an originary country and the psychological split that occurred in the flight from Europe to America lead first to a denial of the new American identities, then to a permanent misrecognition of these new identities as Western, and then to racism and xenophobia. A gift must be total if it is to have positive cultural significance.

The desire to control the universal element in Negritude, or to give selectively, likewise haunts some black people in Africa and the diaspora. Here, though, social agents are faced with a different problem of universalization, because—unlike Euro-Americans, who possess the means of disseminating what is universal and of exercising control over its deployment—they have no mechanism for distributing their Negritude in the public sphere and therefore are unable to control its definition universally. Faced with a dearth of political, cultural, and scientific resources with which to orient audiences toward their category of the universal, black people, who cannot stimulate or impose reality through their representations, either rely on Euromodernisms such as Marxism or Christianity to define their Negritude for them, or retreat into narrow particularism and resistance. For example, Afrocentrists define their Negritude by resorting to the binary oppositions of Euromodernism, which freeze black and white, good and evil, sedentary and nomadic, sun people and ice people into an eternal antagonism. In contrast, the proponents of ethnophilosophy in Africa posit tribal religions, oral traditions, and drumology as the basis for identity formation and the rationalization of their Negritude.

Clearly, social agents can be pushed to retreat into the comfort zone of identity politics because they lack access to the tools that distribute universal ideas and objects; because there is no broad commercial dissemination of what they perceive as their culture; and because their images are still omitted from what is considered universal. But such resistance movements risk deviating from the very modernity that revealed itself to them during the Negritude poets' struggle for liberation.

In contemporary debates on universalism, it is easy to see that people who refute the existence of race on biological and cultural grounds are also those who deny the large majority of blacks access to the political, economic, and cultural means which will enable them to move beyond the simple determinism of color. It is becoming ever easier to point to the homophobia, sexism, and xenophobia of groups that espouse particularism, and ever harder for public intellectuals to provide such groups with access to the economic and political means that can lead white males to become less homophobic and sexist. Currently, white-male control over the definition of what is universal, beautiful, and rational also excludes particularists from discursive spaces. Writer and critic Ishmael Reed is right to refer to English departments as centers of white ethnic studies because, like departments of black and Chicano studies, English departments refuse to democratize the aesthetic criteria which admit other literatures to their lists of great books. We cannot continue to defend the claim for the universality of art, yet at the same time resist the universalization of access to the social and economic conditions that produce a taste for art.

On the last day of class, I again brought up Sartre's "Black Orpheus" and asked the students if they thought it had a place in a class on Pan-Africanism. The debate was as animated as it had been on the first day. Most students had not been swayed from their original positions, but this time they were more friendly. I was not surprised. As a teacher, I see my role as that of a facilitator; in other words, I wanted to provide them with enough arguments to defend whatever position they chose to occupy. There was one bright moment for me in all of this. One student confessed that she had taken the class because of the authentic sound of my African name. All the other courses on black people and Africa were taught by white professors. She did not trust them. She had wanted to study with a real African and see what it was like. "And?" I asked impatiently. "Oh!" she said. "Now I know that white people are not all the same, just as all black people are not the same. With more black professors like you around, I no longer feel mistrust of white professors and their knowledge of Africa. And I am glad that you made us read Sartre."

1

▲▼▲

In My Home

In January 1996, thirty-two years after my parents and I had been expelled from our home in Kankan, I returned to Guinea to begin research for a film documentary on the country's former president, Sékou Touré. I feel strongly that I have to write a book and produce a film about Sékou Touré, since my history is so closely tied to his. Walking down the streets of Greenwich Village, where I now live, I feel sometimes as if I do not exist, because I am a man whose past no one knows.

I belong to the independence generation in Africa, which has been forgotten or neglected in the debris of modern history because our leaders, such as Sékou Touré, Modibo Kéita, Kwame Nkrumah, Patrice Lumumba, and Mobutu Sese Seko, were assassinated, or were deposed by military coups d'état, or became paranoiac dictators. In Africa, the reigning military dictators forbid the telling and celebration of any history that is not their own. In the West, people are uncomfortable with the memory of African independence because it puts the West and the Cold War on trial. The only story that has so far been allowed to emerge about us concerns our leaders' love of tribalism; their failure to understand modernity, civil society, and governance; and our inability to feed ourselves and combat the diseases that afflict us. Sékou Touré, for example, is known as West Africa's most infamous dictator, an irrational man who revived tribalism, destroyed the educational system in Guinea, and sent his enemies to die in prison in the infamous Camp Boiro. Meanwhile the significance of independence and self-determination, the two pillars that make possible our modernization, is lost on us. We live only the existence that Western leaders and African dictators allow us. We cannot tell our histories in their full complexity.

I was also going to Guinea to see Sidimé Laye, whose memory had been haunting me recently like the ghost of Hamlet's father. I must confess that, living in American society, I often suffer from what I call "identity fatigue." Luckily for me, the cure is usually as simple as a phone call to a friend or relative who can assure me that I have another existence outside identity politics. But sometimes I must take a trip, get far away from it all, to verify an authentic existence for myself. In the early 1990s, every time I began to doubt my existence in the rush of New York life and the conundrum of identity politics at New York University, Sidimé Laye came to mind. I thought of him in the middle of faculty meetings, and during conferences that bored me. I thought of him whenever I wanted to verify for myself an identity that could not be touched by anyone else. Sidimé Laye became the cure I had to seek. The thought of finding Sidimé Laye in Guinea weighed on my mind as heavily as that of completing my film on Sékou Touré. After all, both men had modernized me—the latter by sending me to school, and the former by serving as my role model. Sidimé Laye stood out among all of my friends as the smartest and the noblest. He was, I surmised, the type of young African that Sékou Touré had wanted the Guinean revolution to fashion.

Sidimé Laye was a friend of mine. In 1958, when Sékou Touré had said no to de Gaulle and French colonial rule, Sidimé Laye and I had been too young to understand the full meaning of the country's independence, but had been old enough to participate in the euphoria of independence celebrations. In fact, in those days Sidimé Laye was already somebody. Unlike me, he was in school; he could speak fluent French, and could read and write. We used to play soccer together, and here—as in everything—Sidimé Laye was the best. I used to admire him in his khaki school uniform and blue tennis shoes, with his hair neatly cut and always combed. I can still remember him, like a black-and-white picture in a frame. He used to teach me French, and we did everything together: stealing mangoes from people's yards, swimming across the river in the hot months of March and April, sneaking into the movies, going through the initiation of manhood.

In 1960, when Sékou Touré decolonized the schools with a mass literacy project, I was already five or six years older than most of the kids in my class. I already knew the alphabet, as well as how to write my name and count to a hundred in French. I remember working very hard because I wanted to catch up with Sidimé Laye. But Sidimé Laye was not one to be caught off guard in a race; he had been a proud young man even before Sékou Touré had brought pride into Guinean culture. I learned to compete from my mother, who would always tell me that I was better than other Guineans because they were afraid of white people. When I discovered that Sidimé Laye's parents, too, despised the French, and the Guineans who lied and cheated for them, our friendship grew even stronger. Sidimé Laye seemed even smarter in the context of the new school curriculum, which emphasized the links between education and everyday life in Guinea. He was very proud of his family roots and traditions. Our friendly competition continued as the revolution progressed in Guinea and throughout the rest of Africa.

I remember the day Sidimé Laye and I were separated. It was in January 1964, in the middle of the school year. While my parents were packing, I sneaked out of the house to say farewell to all of my friends, who were playing soccer in a nearby field. I remember standing there and watching them play, feeling awkward about saying goodbye. Everything—the people, the place, the game—looked so familiar that I could not understand why I was leaving Guinea. But like all Africans who were not citizens of Guinea, my parents (who were citizens of Mali) had no choice but to leave. The Guineans had nationalized everything, so that it was impossible to conduct business or to earn any money without passing through the state and its police. White people, with whom my father used to work, had been the first to flee the country. Now it was the turn of Africans who were not from Guinea. My father, who hated Sékou Touré, believed that tribalism and selfishness were the logical outcome of the Guinean revolution. My father was a supporter of Félix Houphouët-Boigny of Côte d'Ivoire and Léopold Sédar Senghor of Senegal, who were allies of France and sworn enemies of Sékou Touré.

At that time in Guinea, foreigners like my father who were in charge of the distribution of goods and involved with the mining industries were considered thieves, smugglers, and enemies of the revolution. They were frequently put in jail as counterrevolutionaries, and even as spies for France. My friends used to participate in the jeering of businessmen, and supported the resolve of the revolution to defeat them the same way it had defeated colonialism and imperialism. So some of them must have thought that I, too, was a foe of their country, for they were glad to see me go. Even Sidimé Laye seemed indifferent to my departure. When I said goodbye to him, he quickly disappeared into the faceless crowd that now viewed me as an enemy. When Sékou Touré said in his speeches that young people were the future of Guinea and all of Africa, I had thought of myself as one of them. I always believed that I would be part of the youthful generation that would liberate the continent from colonialist, imperialist, and feudalist mentalities. But there I was, standing alone, unable to cry as I said goodbye to Sidimé Laye, my best friend, and to the revolution that had opened the door of modernity for me—the revolution that had invented me.

During my return flight in 1996, I imagined my reunion with Sidimé Laye several times. Would he remember more stories of our childhood than I? I would remind him about the time his father had asked me to lead the prayer and I had forgotten a verse in the middle. How funny! Young kids like us already playing at being Imams. Come to think of it, Sidimé Laye and I had always competed in memorizing verses of the Holy Koran. Since I could not catch up with him in school, I had wanted to beat him in the memorization of the Koran. I wondered what he thought of the stupid way we had said goodbye. Why hadn't we cried, or hugged each other?

What if Sidimé Laye, like me, had become a university professor? The two of us would hold court from dusk till dawn, and have a unique philosophical conversation on the future of Africa. We would meander down memory lane to our childhood, which had coincided with the greatest moment of modern African history, when young and old, men and women, had been proud of Sékou for saying no to de Gaulle and had been energized by the spirit of freedom. Sidimé Laye and I would speculate on the merits and crimes of Sékou Touré's legacy. If Sidimé Laye had become a politician in the current government, he would probably not be willing to have a frank discussion with me about Sékou Touré. But I wondered if our childhood ties and complicities would make a difference.

My strategy for finding Sidimé Laye was simple. A Guinean art dealer in New York, who had known him, had told me three years before that my friend had moved from Kankan (where we'd grown up) to Conakry, the capital of Guinea. I guessed that it was probably in order to take up a post in the government or as a professor at the university. So I would mention his name to the cabdriver at the airport. If he was a famous politician, the driver would recognize his name and take me to his house. Otherwise, I would simply begin by asking people at the hotel if they knew any Sidimé family in Conakry, or any people from Kankan. I love playing detective and looking for people; it gives me a good excuse to talk to people. I enjoy getting to know new places through them, while conveying a sense of mystery about myself.

Coming out of Gbessia International Airport, I was met by a crowd of cab drivers who quarreled over me and my bags. The winner was a bowlegged man dressed in a Hawaiian shirt, white denim shorts, and flip-flops. Even as he nonchalantly walked away with my bags, he cast a menacing glance at the other drivers, pursing his lips and hissing like a snake to show further contempt for them. Then he looked at me kindly as if I were a prized possession. He was dark-complected, with a bead-size pimple on the tip of his nose. I spoke to him in Mandinka, a language I had spoken as a child in Kankan with Sidimé Laye. He answered back. I was glad, because most people at the airport spoke in Susu. With a language bond established between us, I asked him, as soon as we were in the car, if he knew Sidimé Laye. He said that the name sounded familiar to him, but he could not yet put his finger on it. He kept repeating the name, glancing at me in the rear-view mirror, and finally said that he knew some people from Kankan who lived not too far from the airport. They might know Sidimé Laye. Did I want him to swing by there? I hesitated for a moment, knowing the reputation of Conakry as a high-crime city. Then I began reasoning to myself that I was not a foreigner in Guinea. I spoke Mandinka, like the driver; he could not therefore prey on me like a naive tourist.

Cémoko, the cabdriver, offered me his services for forty dollars a day while I was in Conakry. He said that it would be very easy for him to lead me to my friend, because in the neighborhood to which he had offered to take me (which was where his own home was) lived a very important man, a kind of chief for all the people from Kankan and Upper Guinea. That man was sure to know Sidimé Laye. As if to reassure me, Cémoko added that the man in question had lived in France for a long time before returning to Guinea. It was about ten P.M. —getting late. Cémoko said that the man played dominoes with his friends every night until one A.M. I was tempted, and Cémoko could feel it. He said that Sidimé Laye's name sounded very familiar to him, and that even though he could not remember where he had heard it, he was sure that the man would know him because everyone from Kankan came to him as a kind of elder citizen in Conakry. I was cautious, but this was the beginning of my adventure. I was feeling invulnerable, like the main character in a detective movie.

The first thing noticeable about Conakry at night was the absence of street and traffic lights. The whole city was immersed in a sea of darkness that was illuminated only in spots, and intermittently, by passing cars and motorbikes. Cémoko told me that the traffic and street lights had been out for more than a year, and that residences received only six hours of electricity per day. Most hotels, restaurants, and well-to-do homes had their own electric generators. I asked him why a capital city like Conakry was without light. He said because the government was involved in disputes with the World Bank and other international lenders over the terms of structural adjustment, and over the construction of a dam that would generate light for the whole country. The international lenders were accusing the regime of corruption, and the regime blamed them for interfering in national affairs. Meanwhile, he said, the country was sliding into the Dark Ages.

Cémoko appeared to be in his early thirties. I thought to myself that he was probably younger than thirty-two, the number of years that Sidimé Laye and I had been separated. But Cémoko, too, was doubtless thinking about me. He told me that, in the airport crowd, he had spotted me right away as "one of us." He had offered me the lowest fare because I was a "brother." By that he meant that I was a man from the interior of the country, which extended all the way to Mali. It also meant that I was not a Susu, a Fulani, a man from the rain forests of Africa, or a white tourist. Just the day before, he had taken a Togolese man from the airport to the hotel I was going to for double the price. He could charge Europeans even more than that. I asked how life was in Guinea. He replied that since Sékou Touré's death the Susu and the Fulani had taken over all the power and wealth of the country. In his opinion, Sékou Touré's one mistake was that he had not looked after his own when he was alive. He had given everything he possessed to Guinea. Now that he was dead, his family did not even have a home of their own in Conakry.

We veered from the main street onto a road filled with potholes and foul odors. The darkness was so thick that the car's lights were incapable of penetrating it for more than a few feet. Cémoko turned right—we seemed to be heading farther away from the airport road and perhaps from the city. At last we wound up on a road with some lighted spots here and there, at storefronts where people stood around smoking cigarettes. Cémoko said that we were not far from the man's house. He turned right, went over a tiny bridge, then headed left, to drive alongside an uncovered sewer canal. By then my head was aching from the foul odor which filled the car, and I was wishing that I had gone straight to my hotel. We took a right turn into a big yard, stepped out of the car, and walked toward the porch of a house where four men sat around a table playing dominoes. They were middle-aged, and dressed in the voluminous robes called *doloki-ba* in West Africa. Their *doloki-ba* made them look respectable, which was somewhat reassuring to me. We greeted them. Cémoko called to the side the man I assumed to be the proprietor of the compound and introduced me to him. I was by now a little embarrassed. It was very late, and I must have appeared ridiculous invading people's privacy on the flimsy pretext that I was trying to locate a childhood friend I had not seen for thirty-two years. I explained to the man the purpose of my late visit, trying to look as innocent as possible. He scratched his head, showing consternation. My mind went back to the early Seventies, when I had made a visit to Burkina Faso (called Upper Volta in those days). I had gotten off a train at eleven P.M. in Bobo Dioulasso and had asked a passer-by if he knew my friend Balima, who lived near the railroad station. The man had simply looked at me and said, "Bobo Dioulasso is a large city, you know!" I had just repeated the same mistake. Now the man in front of me was asking me to describe Sidimé Laye.

When I had last seen Sidimé Laye, thirty-two years before, he had been a good-looking boy with smooth black skin which would scintillate with beads of water after we'd been swimming in the river. He had been a little slimmer and taller than I. He must have grown into a perfectly handsome man. Diallo Telli, the tall and handsome number-two man in Guinea, had been his role model—Sidimé Laye had always wanted to look like him when he grew up. I, in contrast, had wanted to be like Sékou Touré, whose ancestor Samory Touré had come from Mali. I had recognized my own features in Sékou Touré's broad lips and nose, which made him look powerful and full of life. He was not afraid of white people. I identified with him in my childhood rivalry with Sidimé Laye over the leaders we liked the most. People had always said that Sékou Touré was jealous of Diallo Telli, who spoke better French than he did and had more secret admirers in Guinea. They said that Sékou Touré had gotten rid of Diallo Telli by sending him first to Addis Ababa as ambassador to the Organization of African Unity, and afterward to the United Nations in New York. Then, when he could no longer control his jealousy and suspicion of Diallo Telli, Sékou Touré had called him back home and sent him to die in the infamous Camp Boiro, among other political prisoners. Diallo Telli, a member of the Fulani ethnic group, had been so loyal to Sékou Touré and the Guinean revolution that he had ignored the warnings of people who told him not to go back to Guinea.

Now, in Conakry, I began describing Sidimé Laye the way I might have described Diallo Telli. I said that he must be taller than six feet and had Fulani features. He would no doubt be handsomely dressed, with a hat which he would tilt slightly to the right.

The man before me continued to scratch his head, repeating Sidimé Laye's name to himself. Then he yelled, "Sidimé Laye!" to the three men at the domino table, asking if they knew him. Luckily for me, one of them said he knew a Sidimé who owned a shop selling African masks and statues in the downtown area, near the new building that housed the Franco-Guinean Alliance. Cémoko said he knew the place. I thanked the man and apologized again for interrupting his domino game. Cémoko was elated as we bid them goodbye; with this first mission accomplished, he was sure I would use his services again. For my part, I was proud of having achieved so much in the first hours of my visit to Guinea. I told Cémoko to pick me up in the morning at eleven.

My hotel was called the Camayenne. It was very expensive—two hundred dollars a night—and was run by Sabena Airlines. In Dakar I had been told that the Camayenne was the only decent hotel in

Conakry; it had twenty-four-hour electricity, television (including access to the Cable News Network), and an international telephone line. I had been warned that the management accepted payment only in U.S. dollars or French francs. Cémoko offered to take me to a better hotel, which was managed by Guineans and cheaper. But I was too tired to embark on a new adventure. I also wanted to be able to call home as soon as I got into my room. I told Cémoko that perhaps I would change my hotel in a day or two.

With its dimly lit hallways, skinny bamboo armchairs, and rumpled cushions, the Camayenne seemed more like a no-star economy hotel than a three-star hotel charging two hundred dollars a night. The elevator squeaked and jerked at every stop; the corridor to my room was stuffy with the odor of a carpet that looked fried and wrinkled. I wondered why they had to put a carpet on the floor in such a humid climate. My room was small. There was barely enough space for a person to pass between the television and reading table on one side, and the bed and closet on the other. It was too dark outside to appreciate the view from the window. Only the bathroom, which was near the door, seemed all right; it had a large mirror, a bathtub, and a marble floor. I switched on the television, listened to the news on CNN, called my family in New York, and went to bed feeling connected to the world.

The next morning, Cémoko was on time to take me on my search for Sidimé Laye. My hotel was situated between the airport and downtown Conakry. The city extended into the Atlantic Ocean on a camel-shaped peninsula. My hotel was on the hump, and we had to drive over the long neck to get to the business district. Cémoko said that even though Conakry was a very long city, it was not wide enough—especially toward the neck, which was so narrow it could accommodate only two roads, one to and the other from downtown. At the end of the neck, before the road divided into several arteries that served the downtown area, we came to the Bridge of November 8, 1970, also known as the Hanging Bridge because some former ministers of Sékou Touré's government, including Ousmane Baldé, Moriba Magassouba, and Kara Dessoufiana Kéita, had been hanged there in the presence of a large and excited crowd.

Near the bridge was the Palais du Peuple (People's Palace), famous for being the site of Sékou Touré's long and eloquent speeches against colonialism and imperialism. It was also where he had read out the many names of people accused of treason and crimes against the state: people considered "enemies of the nation," members of "fifth columns," those branded as "nostalgic" (and hence against the revolution), and "collaborators." Sékou Touré had so passionately incited the population against such "traitors" that at the mere mention of a name the whole country boiled with anger and hostility against the person. Cémoko said that people were always afraid whenever Sékou Touré had entered the Palais du Peuple, because anybody could suddenly fall from grace to disgrace, from a ministerial residence to the cells of the infamous Camp Boiro.

We passed over the bridge toward the downtown area, also known as Conakry I, and Cémoko proposed to take me along the coast in order to show me the presidential palace. The road was being repaired, and the cars that sped past us raised clouds of brown dust which penetrated the cab, settling on our hair and faces. Cémoko had raised the windows of the old 404 Peugeot with an automatic button, but now it was getting hot inside and the air conditioner was broken. I told him to open the windows. We passed a colonial building with a long balcony and nice windows. Cémoko told me that it was the train station, which had been closed since Sékou Touré's death.

There was a port nearby for shipping aluminum. If there were no trains, I asked, how did goods circulate between Conakry and the rest of the country? By truck, said Cémoko; but with the poor condition of the roads, accidents and delays were frequent. When we reached the presidential palace, we had to make a detour: the road was barricaded, and guarded by soldiers with tanks. Cémoko said that this part of the road had been off limits since the army had taken over ten years before. We continued into the business district for a few blocks. The buildings were mostly two or three stories high and surrounded by walls; each had a guard out front, resting in the shade of the tall mango trees. Cémoko showed me the embassies of France, the United States, and Germany. We also passed by the Cathédrale, the main Catholic church of Conakry and one of the tallest buildings in the city. I saw vendors of newspapers, candies, and cigarettes sitting under the trees. There were children playing soccer in a schoolyard. I heard one of them yelling in French for the ball: "Passe! Passe!" He sounded just like my friends and me when we had been children in Kankan. I had captured the past for a moment, as if nothing had changed in thirty-two years. The sensation brought tears to my eyes, and it felt good.

We regained the coast road, and Cémoko showed me the Grand Hôtel de l'Indépendance (which had been closed for more than a year for renovations), the Palace of the Organization of African Unity (OAU), and the residences that Sékou Touré had built for the OAU ambassadors. Sékou Touré had wanted the OAU to move to Conakry because during the Ethiopian crisis it had been unable to function in Addis Ababa. Cémoko said the plan had been blocked by the collaborators of France in Africa—people such as Bernard Bongo of Gabon, Houphouët-Boigny of Côte d'Ivoire, Abdou Diouf of Senegal, and Paul Biya of Cameroon. Cémoko said that Sékou Touré's love for Africa was unlimited; he had dedicated his life to uniting the continent, but his efforts had been repeatedly sabotaged by France and its puppets. I gazed at the residences; there were more than fifty of them, all white, overlooking the ocean. Moroccan architects had designed them, which was the reason the roofs were shaped in an angular manner, spread out like the wings of a flying ostrich. They were beautiful villas—but I am not sure how I feel about the OAU.

To my mind, the reason the OAU had failed to focus on specific problems in the postcolonial period was that it had often silenced the differences between Africans. It was fashionable for Cold War–era theorists to emphasize unity among people who actually had quite diverse ethnic, cultural, and religious backgrounds. African scholars and politicians, like their counterparts in the West, conspired in the creation of a fiction—namely, that societies were homogeneous across the continent. Despite such theories, the only things that an Ethiopian and a Guinean had in common, besides the fact that they both lived on the same continent, were Western civilization and the religions and cultures emanating from the Middle East. It was also clear that during the Cold War and up to the present day, African nations had more in common with their American, Asian, and European allies than with other OAU members. Furthermore, African nations could not claim colonialism, imperialism, and oppression as markers of a specific identity; virtually all the countries in the world had those elements more or less in common. I felt that the OAU was ineffective because the ties that linked Africans were superficial in the first place. Unity should proceed from the bottom up—a concrete economic, cultural, and political emergence out of regional realities and imaginations—and not spread from the top down, as with the OAU.

I asked Cémoko who was occupying these villas now that Sékou Touré's plans had failed. He said that they were rented out to NGOs (nongovernmental organizations). The NGOs had taken the place of the likes of Sékou Touré as the new masters and mistresses of Africa, the purveyors of necessary modernity, civilization, and consumer products. They went under the aliases of international aid organizations and financial institutions, such as Doctors without Borders, the World Bank, and the Well Diggers. Nothing worked nowadays in Africa without them; and of all the witch doctors searching for a solution to Africa's ills, the NGO representatives who lived in these white villas had the strongest grip on people's lives. Everybody wanted to leave the government and work for these organizations because they offered better-paying jobs.

We had driven almost completely around Conakry I, when we entered a lively neighborhood called Boulbinet. Here the houses, shaded by tall trees, were considerably lower and had sheet metal roofs. Cémoko said that this was one of Conakry's oldest settlements inhabited by the Susu tribe. We drove through it quickly and turned onto the Boulevard de la République, where most of the banks and commercial stores were located. The traffic on the street was similar to that of most West African capitals: cars, bicycles, motorbikes, people pushing or pulling carts—all competing for the right of way. The only difference was that in Conakry there were no traffic lights, and policemen and -women had to direct the traffic from block to block. Their white gloves reminded me of the childhood days I had shared with Sidimé Laye, when soldiers clad in khaki uniforms and white gloves had marched around to the tune of brass bands. Now the sidewalks teemed with people: beggars, shoppers, pickpockets, and young women with trays of carrots, bananas, and peeled oranges on their heads mixed with loungers, *flâneurs,* European tourists, and businessmen carrying black briefcases. The traditional market was nearby.

We arrived at the shop which the man the previous night had said belonged to a Sidimé from Kankan. It was longer than it was wide, and quite dark; the contrast with the brightness outside momentarily blinded me. Then I saw that the space was cluttered with objects: on one side were African masks, statues, and ritual and antiquarian objects; on the other was a glass showcase displaying gold and silver jewelry, ivory carvings in human and animal shapes, and whole elephant tusks. When I walked toward the showcase, a man, mistaking me for a tourist, switched on additional lights to make the glass shine. "Come on, look, my friend! Nice authentic African objects!" He said in English. I cut to the chase, as they say in America, by greeting him properly in a down-home manner and following the prescribed ritual: I asked how he was doing at the moment, inquired after his family and neighbors, made sure he was experiencing no hardship, wished him good health, asked his last name, and indicated my respect for him and his genealogy. He in turn asked me my last name, where I had come from, how people were doing there, and whether everything was peaceful there. I said peace only, and thanked him. Other people joined us, and I performed the ritual with each man.

I told them that I was a professor in America, visiting Conakry for a research project, and that I wanted to see a childhood friend of mine named Sidimé Laye. At the mention of the name, the call-response ritual we had developed through the greetings died away. They were all avoiding my eyes, though I felt I was being silently scrutinized. Thirty-two years stood between these people and myself. I looked desperately for recognizable faces. I was hoping, too, that one of them would remember me from my childhood days. I told them about my father and mother, and what their life had been like in Kankan. I described, from vivid memory, the sights between my parents' house and the Sidimé compound in Kankan: the many mango trees; the Lebanese store where we had often bought candies, sardines, and tins of condensed milk; the field where we had played soccer or watched Toni, the Lebanese store owner, bet lots of money on bocce games. Toni had owned a mean German shepherd.

When I began to describe the compound of the Sidimé family, I remembered to mention the Z-shaped vestibule where Sidimé Laye's father had given us lessons in the Holy Koran. As kids, we had always been afraid to cross that vestibule at night, believing that it was inhabited by all the evil characters the Holy Koran warned us against. When I spoke of the yard, I explained that the compound of the Sidimé family had been very large—larger, in fact, than a whole city block—with three heads of families. Sidimé Laye's father had been the oldest; his two younger brothers had several wives. There had been three vestibules or entrances to the compound, one near each of the brothers' rooms. The youngest brother, a menacing fellow, had made the biggest impression on me. His house had been located near the Z-shaped vestibule. He had been a sculptor who carved effigies of antelopes, and of African women with beautiful traditional hairstyles, from ebony wood and elephant tusks. Children had been afraid of him because he never smiled. Moreover, my mother had always told me that it was evil to draw or carve human shapes; they could become alive and run out of control. This uncle of Sidimé Laye's had traveled to Conakry and other major cities in Africa and Europe. I described all the older women, who had their own rooms, and where the rooms had been situated with respect to each vestibule.

The man who had mistaken me earlier for an American tourist finally stopped me with a long "Wuuhh!" sound, which seemed to indicate a retrieved memory. He indeed noticed the resemblance between my father and me. So how were my parents? And how was my older brother, who had had a little kiosk across the street from the Lebanese store? And how was America? Was business alright? I cut to the chase again, sensing that I was not going to like this man. He looked to be in his mid-fifties. I had noticed that from time to time he would leave the small group that had gathered around me, to go to the back of the room or to speak with European and Asian tourists in different languages. He seemed to know everything, but I got the impression he really only cared about his business. I asked where I could find Sidimé Laye. He told me to leave the name of my hotel and he would give it to Burulaye (Laye's full name). I said that I had hired a cab; all he had to do was give me Burulaye's address and I would go there myself. He replied that Burulaye had just moved to the suburbs and had not yet given him his new address. Anyway, he said, Burulaye always came by the store in the evening after work, or in the morning on his way to work. Why couldn't I just leave the name of my hotel with him?

When I left the store, I was filled with the same lonely feeling I had had when I said goodbye to Sidimé Laye. It seemed as if the man in the store had erected a wall between Sidimé Laye and me. It was also the feeling I experienced in New York whenever I was tired of identity walls. Cémoko said that I should not worry about a thing. He was sure that Sidimé Laye would rush to my hotel as soon as he found out I was there. He said that people generally were cautious in Guinea. Ever since Sékou Touré's time, they had lived in a climate of suspicion and mistrust. It could be that the man in the store had not wanted to give me Sidimé Laye's address because he hadn't believed my story. Suppose Sidimé Laye owed me money? Or worse yet, suppose I were a spy for the government? Then the man would be responsible for getting him into trouble. Cémoko said that in Guinea you could not trust anybody, not even your own brother.

Cémoko kept talking to me about the Guineans' mentality. But I was no longer listening. I was thinking of what he had said about the man not believing my story. I was counting on the fact that I was an insider—that I was from the same culture, and that no one would shut the door in my face. But it is true that in West Africa we have lost a sense of trust. One of the prices we have paid for our modernization is that we would rather deal directly with white people than with one another.

I remember the time in Senegal when Kenyan writer Ngugi wa Thiong'o and I were making a film about Sembene Ousmane, the Senegalese writer and filmmaker. We had a crew of seven people, one of whom was white. The Senegalese people looked at him every time we had to pay a bill or deal with the authorities. It meant that we were invisible subjects of modernity—that our existence, though real, did not matter. The African who lives abroad, particularly in America, feels a sense of alienation when he returns to Africa, because he is accustomed to an equality that the civil rights movement has fostered between black and white people in America but that is lacking in Africa.

On the way back to my hotel, Cémoko and I passed a botanical garden, a cemetery, and a park. From a distance we could see Conakry's main mosque, which rivaled the Cathédrale in height. Cémoko said the cemetery contained a grave marked for Sékou Touré, but no one really believed he was buried there. I asked what this meant. Some people, he replied, said that Sékou Touré was buried in Morocco, in the family plot of King Hassan II. Some people even believed he was interred in Saudi Arabia, near the Prophet's tomb. The truth was, said Cémoko, that the president of Guinea and the king of Morocco had been very close friends. The king of Morocco had made his private jet available to Sékou Touré when the latter's bad health had forced him to seek emergency treatment in the United States. The same jet had returned his body to Guinea after he died in Cleveland, Ohio. Many foreign dignitaries had attended the funeral, including presidents from most of the African countries, Vice-President George Bush of the United States, and King Faisal of Saudi Arabia. Sékou Touré's body was supposed to have left Guinea with the Moroccan delegation in the same private plane. A life-size effigy had been wrapped in white sheets and placed in what is known today as his grave in the cemetery.

I was puzzled. Why all this mystery surrounding the corpse? Plenty of reasons, said Cémoko. First of all, many people believed that Sékou Touré would return to rule Guinea again. In other countries, when a leader died, the government invited the population to come and see their president for the last time; here, no one had been allowed to see the body after the funeral ceremony. The coffin that went to the cemetery had contained a dummy. People said that if he were actually placed in the tomb, his enemies could take revenge on him by desecrating the place, exhuming the body, and cutting it into pieces to prevent a possible reincarnation. But as long as the real Sékou Touré was not in that grave, then nothing could prevent his resurrection and his return to Guinea. In fact, the demand for such a return had been on the rise since Guinea had renewed diplomatic relations with France, considered for a long time the number-one enemy and saboteur of Sékou Touré's revolution.

The presence in Guinea of a great many French embassy personnel, professors, engineers, businessmen, and political advisers was a constant reminder not only of the Guineans' inability to take care of their own affairs, but also of their dependence on the very country that had hindered the first independence movement in Francophone Africa. The economic crisis, the widespread unemployment, and the high crime rate had also made some people nostalgic for the old days. Now Guineans were remembering what Sékou Touré had often said to them: that they would miss him someday—so much so that, like mad people, they would use flashlights in broad daylight to look for him. Cémoko said he had seen with his own eyes a Susu women with a flashlight in broad daylight, looking for Sékou Touré in the marketplace.

Cémoko gave another—equally breathtaking—explanation of why Sékou Touré was not interred in Guinea. He said that the president of Guinea had wanted to go to heaven, and for this reason he had not wished to be buried in his own country, where the prevalence of injustice, cruelty, and lies might have pushed the doors of heaven closed. He had wanted to put a distance between himself and all the evil in Guinea, and face God in a holier country, with his grave as near those of the other Muslim saints as possible. Muslims in West Africa believed that if you died in Saudi Arabia, the birthplace of the Prophet Muhammad, God would surely accept you into His heaven. It was also better to be buried among other saints who were descended from the Prophet, because they would all be going to heaven. I asked Cémoko if he thought the angels would mistake Sékou Touré for a saint. He said the idea was not to slip into heaven unseen—that was impossible. But the saints might intervene on behalf of someone they had known in this world. I said I got it: they had corruption there, too. Cémoko asked God to forgive him, for he thought I was being blasphemous.

We arrived at my hotel, and I told Cémoko to pick me up the next day at the same time. If Sidimé Laye had not shown up by then, we would go back to the shop. I would refrain from discussing my project on Sékou Touré with anyone else until I had seen my friend. For the time being, I was going to drink something, rest a while, and then take a stroll around the neighborhood.

Late that afternoon, enjoying the breeze as I walked down the street from my hotel, I wondered if the world of Sidimé Laye was as complicated by issues of identity as mine. I had the same feeling of numbness that I had often experienced in New York, a solitude which is akin to not existing. I was wondering if Sidimé Laye, too, had ever known this feeling—the loneliness of someone whose marks on history have disap-

Sékou Touré was my hero when I was young. He is shown here in New York on November 5, 1959, with Dag Hammarskjold, secretary general of the United Nations. (Photo courtesy of the United Nations.)

peared, been washed away by the reigns of terror, mutinies, conspiracies, and African-on-African violence. I have no history. Or, to put it another way, my history, like that of Sékou Touré, is a tragedy, and only its underside—the side of the defeated, the ugly side—is known. I am tired of the identity prison-house that Afro-pessimism has condemned me to endure.

My life began when the new nations of Africa were born, in the late 1950s. We had been full of hope then, determined to change Africa, to catch up quickly with the modern world, to show that black people could use their culture and civilization, as other people did, to lead them into modernity. We wanted to bring our message into the forum of world civilization. Some of us enrolled in school; some went to work in national factories, farms, and hospitals; some became civil servants. We modernized our music, our cuisine, our languages, and our philosophies. Our young people were like young people everywhere, concerned with emulating their national heroes, competing in international events, and being fiercely independent and proud.

Then came the Cold War, which divided us, isolated us from one another, created self-doubt in us, and forced us to put our priorities and dreams in the background. The way in which the Cold War related to Africa had little to do with our reality and dreams. The Cold War only obeyed the interest of the West against the Soviet bloc, and for the past thirty years our lives had been determined by the strategic perception of the Cold War by Moscow or Washington. It ruthlessly defended dictatorship and tribalism in one part of Africa, while ferociously combating them in another. Leaders such as Sékou Touré, Modibo Kéita, and Kwame Nkrumah, who were trying to uphold the sovereignty and equality of our nations and to resist the shaping of our identities by the Cold War, were opposed by other Africans who were on the payroll of France, Belgium, the United Kingdom, and their allies. The Soviet bloc, too, armed its men to the teeth and sent them out as its representatives on the African battlefield.

Thus, for the past thirty years, we had been involved in a battle that was not ours to fight, but that nonetheless had taken us out of history and brought us closer to the Dark Ages. Our leaders had become not only the victims of this drama, but also its unwitting villains. The line between fighting as an ally in the Cold War and fighting for independence had become blurred, and so had the roles of our leaders in the genocidal theater that was being played out in Africa. They were heroes one day, and monsters another. Tribalism was rearing its ugly head everywhere, and thousands of people were being maimed and killed in the name of their leaders and that of the revolution.

Now, in the late 1990s, when the Cold War is over and the West no longer considers African countries as allies or even as neocolonial outposts, we find our identities still mired in the narrative of the failed nation-states, the theaters of Afro-pessimism. Africa is known only as a continent that cannot feed itself, cloth itself, or teach itself. It is said that we are incapable of abstractions, that we find pleasure only in direct sensations of nature. My real history is buried somewhere in the stories of Sékou Touré, Kwame Nkrumah, and Modibo Kéita, whose histories of modernity have been banned forever.

In West Africa, the days are longer than they are in New York. People move parsimoniously, at the rhythm of the sun: the hotter it is, the slower they are. Modernity manifests itself only in a fragmented way, through the presence of cars, airplanes, telephones, and other electrical gadgets. But the people themselves are only incidently modern, because they have no regard for time in their nonchalant movements. Hotels can insulate the visitor from the misery, the traditional constraints, and the dirt of Africa. I like hotel living because it symbolizes the modernity that has eluded us in Africa. I say this because hotels, like the governments, are cut off from the African people. They serve only foreigners from the West. The majority of the clientele in hotels are white, and for this reason hotel employees treat African customers with suspicion, if not contempt. Government offices, too, prefer to deal with the various international organizations that supply them with financial and technical assistance; indigenous people, in contrast, seem always to *need* services from the government.

I once had a discussion with a World Bank officer while flying on an Air Afrique plane to Dakar. I was arguing that nation-states had become antiquated in West Africa because they divided tribes, restricted commerce and culture in the region, and forced people to depend on help from the West, instead of encouraging movement across frontiers, free enterprise, and competition. I thought I had him when I used the phrases "free enterprise" and "competition," which were the buzzwords then. But he simply dismissed my argument as unrealistic. Who could tell the Bêtés of Côte d'Ivoire to unite with the Wolof of Senegal, or with the Mandinkas of Guinea and Mali? Africa needed nation-states, according to him, for without them how could aid be distributed? To whom could the people turn for decisions regarding international affairs, and law and order? I told him I could see the governments' responsibility to the international community, but how about their commitments to their people? He said I was too impatient; things were changing gradually in Africa.

Yes, things have changed indeed. Instead of being organized by nationalist emotions, we are held captive by the nation-state so that we can be better exploited by others. Nations have seen their role inverted: they have gone from builders of modern institutions which emancipate the population, to neocolonial outposts serving the interests of international organizations; from revolutionary states to tribalist enclaves; from nation builders to beggar nations. As in the time before independence, the symbolic capital—whiteness—has enlarged its scope in Africa: everybody wants to deal directly with the white man. Africans exist only through serving whites, making love to them, bribing them, and being seen with them.

As I strolled away from my hotel, I heard drums beating in the distance and decided to walk in that direction. The crashing of the sea against the rocks ate away parts of the drumbeats. Women came out of their compounds carrying big tubs filled with dirty dishwater, which they dumped into the ocean. Wood smoke from cooking fires rose above the walls of the compounds, along with the distinct aroma of chicken and fish in groundnut sauce, before dispersing into the air. I came upon a woman frying plantains under a tree, and bought twenty cents' worth, which she placed on a banana leaf with some hot sauce. I walked by peddlers of oranges and cigarettes, and groups of men standing in front of houses and watching women moving in the direction of the drums. For a moment I felt like everyone else, a West African eating my plantains in the street and admiring beautiful Guinean women. The drumbeats were now clearer, and were accompanied by the sounds of clapping and stamping. It was a circumcision ceremony. The soon-to-be initiated had been gathered from several compounds, to become witnesses to the manliest of dances.

I saw one man perform the dance of the blacksmiths' clan, one of the most dangerous displays of masculinity ever devised. The dancer handled a razor-sharp ax with all the delicacy and finesse of a man performing a pas de deux with a beautiful woman. First he set the rhythm for the drummers with the ax, which he swung up and down to mimic the cutting into pieces of different objects. He threw the ax back and forth between his legs and up into the air, catching it with the blade toward his head. The drummers beat faster as he increased the pace of the dance, and stopped abruptly when he did.

Then there was the dancer of the hunter clan, who wore a mask ornamented with ram horns; a mud-brown cotton gown that was hung all over with fringes, antelope horns, and little mirrors; and pants that were baggy in the rear and tight at the knees. He danced a step called the Simbon, gesticulating with a rifle which he fired from time to time. The other dancers were women masquerading in traditionally masculine roles. The boys themselves seemed too young to perform serious dance steps. I assumed that the women were dancing for their children because there were no men to accomplish the ritual for them. The presence of the women, the general absence of men in the ceremony, and the early age at which boys were being circumcised were all signs of the weakening of tradition.

I remembered my own initiation with Sidimé Laye in Kankan. Mandinka men had performed all the masculine dances that were now being staged by women. In the old days, women and children had been afraid to attend some of the performances, precisely because these were demonstrations of masculinity and therefore dangerous. The purpose of the initiation dance was to declare the boys men—to tell them that they were not women and that they could no longer exhibit signs of weakness or emotion in public. I now believed that this ritual had also been used to brand homosexuality as taboo. I still remember my own embarrassment when my mother had danced for me, instead of my father or some other man from our clan. My friends had made fun of me for a whole year, with the taunt that I was not a real man because a woman had performed the ritual for me. I also remember to this day my mother's song, which had been sung in my language and which had praised me above all other Mandinka boys. My father's clan and his religion (Islam) had been against dancing and singing in public.

That afternoon in Conakry, as I walked away from the drums and the celebration, I felt the power of ethnic difference over racial and national unity in West Africa. Race and nationality are still modern concepts for us. We know ourselves more as members of blacksmith clans, warrior clans, religious or shamanist clans than as black people. We have not been interested in inventing enemies far away from us, or in mobilizing ourselves as a group in the name of a race or nation against a common demon who is plotting to exclude us from modernity, the way African Americans, Jews, and other minority groups have mobilized in America. We are often united by ethnicities that extend beyond national boundaries, and we do not hesitate to deploy ethnic loyalties against the nation-state, as was the case in Guinea when the Susu and the Fulani resisted Sékou Touré, or in Senegal when the Lébu of Casamance rebelled against the ruling Wolof.

Further down the street I heard people shouting and clapping at a soccer game. I wanted to see the game, but there was a long wall topped with broken glass standing between me and the field. I walked for about half a mile looking for an entrance. Then I found a breach in the wall which children used as a shortcut to the ocean. Children of about five to seven years old were playing on a mound of garbage; others, a bit older, were throwing rocks at the fruit growing on a giant mango tree. The odor of rotten mangoes, mixed with that of dead rats and cats coming from the garbage pile, filled the air, and chased away the fishy smell of the ocean. The children on the garbage mound were looking for plastic bags and other things to recycle. They were barefoot and naked; their noses were running; they were surrounded by flies. The children under the mango tree were now fighting over the fruit as if they had no conscience. All this, too, had been part of my childhood with Sidimé Laye.

I decided to take advantage of the break in the wall, even though it was not an entrance. The children paid no attention to me. I walked through a grove of giant mango trees and reached a group of huts where women were cooking supper in front of their doors. No one looked up or said a word to me as I passed. I turned right, still looking for the way to the soccer field. I noticed then that it had been a good while since I had heard the cheering and clapping of the game. I was lost. I had to make a decision: go back where I had come from, or continue walking to my right. I was sure that the soccer field was in that direction. I saw more huts about hundred feet ahead of me. There were more mango trees blocking my view. If I went past those huts, perhaps I would reach the soccer field.

Suddenly, on my right, I saw barracks with metal doors, and on my left a guardhouse with a watchtower. Before me was an entrance flanked by uniformed soldiers, two cannons facing the street and the city, and a pole displaying the Guinean flag. It was getting dark; my whole body was traversed by a quick chill. I was in a police station or a military camp. I noticed other civilians, like myself, who were casually walking around, or carrying out normal transactions with a street vendor nearby. I instinctively walked toward them, bought a pack of Hollywood chewing gum, and asked the vendor how to get to the soccer field "over there." I didn't point in any particular direction, since I was trying not to give myself away. He said, "Il faut sortir du Camp Boiro par là!" ("You have to exit Camp Boiro that way!"), and indicated the direction I had come from.

So I was in Sékou Touré's infamous prison, from which no one had ever come out alive. Kaman Diaby, Kéita Fodéba, Barry Alpha Oumar, Ansoumane Traoré, Diallo Telli, and countless others had been killed here. It was said that people had been thrown in prison here and left to die of hunger. It was said that people had been tortured in vau' given electric shocks to their testicles until they confessed to crimes they had not committed. It was said that the guards had been demonic and perverted, happy to torture men whose wealth and position they envied. The guards of Camp Boiro had hated to see beauty and intelligence flourish; they had been trained to keep a man on his knees, to debase every human dignity in him.

I was afraid that one of the soldiers would call me over, ask what I was doing here, take my passport away, accuse me falsely of treason. I began to sweat, and was humiliated by my own fear. I also felt cowardly for not wanting to confront this place, for lacking the courage or desire to at least look around. I pretended to go in the direction that the vendor had pointed to, and retraced my steps toward the breach in the wall. I was so terrified by what I had heard and read about Camp Boiro that I couldn't bring myself to even glance at it. I did not look back until I was back on the street again.

Today I am angry at myself because I feel that we Africans have naturalized Afro-pessimism as a way of life. Afro-pessimism is a condition of life in which the evil part of human beings dominates their good side. The result in Africa has been a continued reign of misery, African-on-African violence, and oppression of women. The guards at Camp Boiro were not the only incarnation of this evil. It exists in some of our traditions that have survived slavery and colonialism. What could be more evil today than female genital mutilation? The tribalism and genocide in Rwanda? The way in which military regimes cynically oppose democracy in the name of tradition? We are driven by evil whenever we close our eyes to our neighbors' suffering; and we have been overtaken by it when we in turn become jailers and captives of the Camp Boiros. I am angry at the whole world—blacks, whites, Africans, and Europeans—for marketing our suffering for profit.

2

▲▼▲

Williams Sassine on Afro-Pessimism

Two days passed and I still had not seen Sidimé Laye. I went by the shop a couple of times, only to have my patience tested by the man there, who said exasperating things like: "He hasn't called you yet? Don't worry, he will!" Faced with the difficulty of reuniting with Sidimé Laye and of finding the Guinea of my childhood, I decided to put off that search momentarily and turn to my documentary project on Sékou Touré. I was going to face up to the real Guinea on my own, to look for Sékou Touré's legacy and the scars it had left on the lives of Guineans. I wanted to learn about the people's daily struggles under the military leaders who had replaced Sékou Touré. Finally, I was curious to see how Afro-pessimism, a fatalistic attitude toward economic and social crisis, was affecting Guineans' everyday choices.

I opened my address book for the names of important people to visit while in Guinea: Williams Sassine, writer; Djibril Tamsir Niane, writer, historian, and owner of a bookstore; Tiemoko Diakité, filmmaker, and director of the National Film Center; and Gislain Meurat, French expatriate, and director of the Franco-Guinean Alliance. Some of these people, like Sassine and Niane, had lived in exile while Sékou Touré was alive. They were part of the Guinean diaspora that had constituted not only an opposition to Sékou Touré's government, but also an economic and brain drain from the country. They had now returned home en masse to rebuild Guinea. I knew that their points of view would be crucial to my documentary.

Williams Sassine is a novelist with more than five books under his belt. His novels describe the loneliness and ineptitude of people in the face of the crushing force of Afro-pessimism. His style is characterized by wordplay that draws on Mandinka idioms to bend the meaning of French expressions. Sassine's dark sense of humor, his laughter at the miseries of his characters, is justified in the novels as a way of coping with the unrelenting pressures of Afro-pessimism. The fatalistic *Weltanschauung* of Sassine's characters and their capacity to endure pain make them kin to comic book characters, which are often mentioned as role models in the novels. In fact, Afro-pessimism is naturalized in Sassine's work as expressed through popular songs, traditional folktales, and poetry, which are all intertwined in the novels.

I was particularly interested in his novel entitled *Le Zéhéros n'est pas n'importe qui,* set in 1985, just after the death of Sékou Touré, and based on the return of Guinean exiles. The word *zéhéros,* which combines *zéro* and *héros,* denotes the unstable position of the main character's identity, which changes from nameless shopkeeper in exile to resistance hero, during his trip home after Sékou Touré's death. The *zéhéros,* named Camara, is set up by his white boss, who spreads rumors that Camara has been secretly leading a resistance movement against Sékou Touré. Camara suddenly finds himself surrounded by prominent French journalists, who ask him what he plans to do after returning to a Guinea without Sékou Touré. At first, he considers the whole thing a harmless game in which he has to play his part. Then he gradually changes his way of relating to people, becoming more assertive and more demanding. In short, Camara acquires the identity of a postcolonial hero—that is, one who approaches reality as if it were magic, as if everything were possible and nothing real.

Le Zéhéros deals with a common strand of Afro-pessimism. It presents Camara as a symbol of the many Guineans who rushed to take on heroic identities after Sékou Touré's death, and returned home.

They believed that Guineans at home would celebrate their return—would name them as ambassadors and ministers, or put them in charge of large enterprises. But they soon found that the soldiers who now held power did not intend to share it with anybody. To make matters worse, the returnees suffered rejection by the Guineans who had stayed home during Sékou Touré's reign. The return of Guineans from exile also coincided with an influx of French diplomats, businessmen, and professionals, who took the jobs of those Guineans who were deemed loyal to Sékou Touré and therefore incompetent. Guineans at home thus considered the returnees no better than the foreigners and imposters whose only desire was to exploit the country. Moreover, the newcomers were seen as nouveaux riches or brainwashed intellectuals who sided with the capitalist devil first, before caring about Guinea. In the novel, Camara is berated by an acquaintance who accuses him of loving white people more than his own brothers and of scorning the things that Guineans accomplished during Sékou Touré's time. For Williams Sassine, the soldiers and returnees were as incompetent to run the country as the Guineans who had been trained by Sékou Touré.

Sassine's depiction of the clash between the diaspora and the Guineans at home made me think of my own voluntary departure from Africa. Often I would wake up in the middle of the night, when I was eighteen, and implore the gods (including my deceased mother) to take me out of Africa. I used to envy French youths my age who had unlimited access to freedom. They ate well, were properly dressed, and could have all the sports equipment and music records they desired. I also wanted to be like the Jackson Five, Jimi Hendrix, Wilson Pickett, Angela Davis, Muhammad Ali, George Jackson, and those black Americans who had brought the world to its knees with their music, athletic ability, and defiance of white power. I wanted to get out of this place where children had no chance, where the life expectancy was less than forty-five, and where tradition conspired with poverty and religion to oppress people. I used to promise the gods that if only I got out, I would do anything in return—even forfeit going to heaven. I just wanted to be happy for a few years, able to determine my own life, and invulnerable to the fatalistic blows of Afro-pessimism.

Le Zéhéros argued that the returnees had sold their souls to white people. I wondered if that was true of me, too. One always feels a sense of guilt when leaving one's community for better chances, for an opportunity to become modernized. One also tends to feel that success in life depends on working with the same devil which thrives on racial superiority and which excludes the majority of one's brothers and sisters from participating in history. On the other hand, staying in place makes one more vulnerable to Afro-pessimism, exploitation, and the negative effects of tradition. Exile transforms a person forever, and it makes one wish that everyone in Africa could taste the pleasure of one's own alienation—an alienation which entails loyalty neither to captive traditions nor to a racialist categorization of the world.

I had met Williams Sassine at the offices of *Présence Africaine* in Paris a long time before. When I rang him up, he remembered me right away and asked me to come over—and not to forget to bring some alcohol with me. I took my tape recorder and went out of the hotel, feeling a sense of progress for the first time since arriving in Guinea. I gave the address to Cémoko, who informed me that Sassine's house was thirty minutes away from the hotel, past the airport and near a small suburban market. We found the place without any problem. It was a small, weathered villa surrounded by a wall and a garage door, near a gravel-covered soccer field. When I knocked on the large metal door, Sassine opened it saying: "I always keep my door locked because Guineans don't believe in the concept of private property." He burst out laughing at his own joke. He was a small man in his mid-fifties, with a light-brown complexion like a Syrian's, and a mustache. In the yard were a sheep, a dog, and a duck. We walked past them and sat under a mango tree. The house reminded me of Camara's compound in *Le Zéhéros*.

When Sassine had finished opening the bottle of liquor, I told him that I had come to do research on Sékou Touré for a documentary.

"Sékou Touré is an unknown man known well to us, and famous to the world in a manner unknown to us. Do you know what famous person used to say that?" he asked, laughing.

"Sékou Touré," he answered, looking suddenly serious. "He used to say that man is an unknown known and a known unknown.

"Sékou Touré left Guineans in a state of confusion about his origins and his ending. Did you know that he was not originally from Guinea and that he was not buried here when he died? This makes him twice unknown in Guinea. Do you see what kind of leader the Guinean people had for a quarter of a century? A man they never really knew." He laughed again and refilled his glass.

"Is this one of the theories of Afro-pessimism you developed in *Le Zéhéros*?" I asked. "It seems to me you were a bit too cynical about heroism in that novel." I wanted to address right away the two issues important to me: Sékou Touré and Afro-pessimism in African writing.

"I wrote *Le Zéhéros* to describe a problem faced by every Guinean, every African, who believes that things will change after a coup d'état," he said. "Africans believe they can achieve victory against adverse situations without doing anything. Sometimes they're following a religious belief; sometimes they trust someone else to do it for them. This is why I say that the hero here is a zero. Look at the soldiers—they all raise their fingers in a victory sign after a coup d'état. And the people raise their fingers with them. They are zeros that take themselves for heroes. The soldiers are not to be encouraged; they have not achieved anything for the people. They are as avid of power as the civilians."

"Why," I asked, "is power a disadvantage for development and modernization in Africa, when it has been used as a motor for discipline and progress elsewhere?"

"In Africa," he said, "underdevelopment is rooted in the culture, not in economic poverty. We have lost the meaning of myth in Africa. I don't mean superstitions and legends, but something larger, bigger than life, something of epic dimensions."

"That is not true," I retorted. "We had epic heroes, like Sundiata and Samory. And more recently we've had Kwame Nkrumah, Modibo Kéita, and Sékou Touré, who had grandiose visions for the region."

"That's not what I am talking about," he said, frowning and chasing a fly off his face with a scornful gesture. "I mean religion, I mean culture, you know? I mean something to connect us in our movement toward greatness. The problem in Africa is that our history has been disconnected in its continuity. It has been deformed too often, to the point that it is unrecognizable today. We have changed gods and religions too many times."

"But Sassine, don't you think that, as Richard Wright said in *Black Power,* religion—whether it is African polytheism, Islam, or Christianity—is what has kept us from a truly democratic society, from our total freedom? That is, freedom from god, tribal chiefs, priests, white racists, and oppressors of women. Religions are against modernity."

"Nonsense! Every modernity is founded on religion and culture. The same white people who destroyed our gods gave us their religion in order to colonize us. Both Muslims and Christians have a god in their own image, and they represent evil as black. So even those of them who no longer believe in their gods use their culture to perceive blackness and Africa as evil, dangerous, and hopeless. I'm telling you, we need a god that can help us to educate our children and respect ourselves, and that most of all can serve as the foundation and continuation of our culture."

"The problem, Sassine, is that religion only helps us to survive. What we actually need, as Richard Wright said, is to compete and win in the global market, to become uncolonizable and unexploitable by white people. What Africa needs most today are democratic systems which allow people more mobility, more communication among themselves, and more freedom from oppressive traditions and religions."

"You forget something," said Sassine, laughing as he paused to refill his glass and light a cigarette. "There is no equivalent for the word 'democracy' in any of our languages in Guinea, Mali, or Senegal." Again, he erupted in laughter. He must have felt that he had me, because he refilled my glass with the alacrity and generosity of a winner.

"But Sassine, listen," I said. "That does not mean anything, because the French, German, and English had no such word either. They borrowed it along with many other concepts from Latin, Greek, and Arabic, and they are better off for it. The trouble with us is that we cannot borrow anything without someone saying, 'That's not our African way.'" I was deliberately hitting Sassine hard with my words, because I sensed an attempt on his part to treat me like his fictional characters who return to Guinea.

"I'm telling you, Diawara, don't come to us with that business of democracy," he said. "Democracy is a foreign concept here, an imported idea in our cultures. My concept of democracy is that my children vote the way I do on election day. I don't want them to vote for my enemy. Since I am the head of the family, the eldest, everyone should come to me and ask whom to vote for. You see, if my enemy wins, my family will be the first to pay. So democracy is a difficult notion to define in Africa. The head of the family is always right; then the mother; then the oldest son. You cannot say, 'I am against this party, but my son can vote for it.'"

"But Sassine, what about the individual? What about women voting for the party that promises more freedom for them? What about someone who wants to vote against polygamy but whose father is for it?"

I knew the conversation now hinged on the binary opposition between tradition and alienation. Between Africans who stayed and those who participated in the diaspora. Between Sassine and me. He was, I told him, beginning to remind me of Sembene Ousmane, a respected elder figure in African writing and filmmaking who likes to pigeonhole me as the Diawara who left.

"Thank you very much," he said. "But from what I already know about the development of individualism in Africa, I prefer our traditions. We used to do everything collectively. Listen to our myths of creation and our morality tales told by the fireside. We used to bring in the harvest together and celebrate together. We were stronger. Now the individual has appeared, thanks to the massive proliferation of video cassettes and books. You read a book by yourself, you watch a video by yourself. We have become fragmented. We go home to our videos and our books; we no longer know or care about our neighbors. That's the individual."

"Yes, that's the individual. But individuality is something more. It also has to do with the creativity of the individual genius against the stagnation of the group. It has to do with being a person against the anonymity that collective identity imposes on us. Fundamentally, it has to do with freedom and rights which ultimately outweigh all the advantages you mentioned about collective living. What Africa needs is more democracy, more rights, more freedom, more individuals than the ones we see in the streets today."

"Such slogans," he countered, "only create more sadness in Africa. We have already seen this happen with the independence movement. We wanted to be free, and we only became sadder for it. All the revolutions in the name of autonomy did nothing but produce an autonomous sadness."

Sassine was becoming livelier. His small eyes were shining. The phrase he actually used (which I have rendered as "autonomous sadness") was *indépendant triste,* a play on words characteristic of Afro-pessimist writers such as himself, Henri Lopes, Amadou Kourouma, and Sony Labou Tansi. Those writers liked to "deform" the meaning of French words by playing on their pronunciations (for example, *indépendantiste* and *indépendant triste*), by literally translating African imagery into French, or by connecting specific words to local events like coups d'état and economic crises. I could see that Sassine was enjoying our conversation from the way he took a sip from his glass and blew a cloud of smoke into the air.

"It was," he resumed, "Sékou Touré who brought slogans like 'Work,' 'Justice,' 'Equality,' and 'Solidarity' into currency here. Unfortunately these words were misused right away, and divested of their meaning. So that even for religious leaders they stopped meaning what they had denoted. In Sékou Touré's time, truth was unitary—it was the truth of the leader. African revolutions were also sad because we soon realized that behind every black master, there was a white leader who was present everywhere."

Sassine's last sentence reminded me of *Xala,* a film by Sembene Ousmane in which a white man with a briefcase follows the black president of a chamber of commerce everywhere he goes. But surely there had been no white man behind Sékou Touré. In fact, that was one of the reasons he had been admired all over Africa. That was what had made him unique. He had not taken his cues from France, as Félix Houphouët-Boigny and Léopold Sédar Senghor had.

"Don't tell me that Sékou Touré was independent," Sassine protested. "He said no to de Gaulle and turned around to say yes to Mitterrand. It was not François Mitterrand who came here; it was Sékou Touré who went to France. It was he who sought out Mitterrand, not the other way around. What I mean is that Sékou Touré went to the Left in order to reach the Right." Sassine was laughing at his own joke again. He laughed and laughed until he started coughing.

"But," I said, "didn't it take at least three regimes in France before Sékou Touré reconciled with them? De Gaulle, Pompidou, and Giscard d'Estaing—they all led covert and open warfare against Sékou Touré. There were also the neighboring countries like Côte d'Ivoire and Senegal, and the Guinean opposition based in those countries."

"De Gaulle had his pride, just as Sékou Touré had his. They were two people difficult to reconcile. But Sékou Touré was a man who wanted only power, so he took power. He loved it, and he was married to it. He kept it jealously, as if it were a woman. It made him crazy, and he thought that everyone around him was a spy for France." Sassine was now uttering every word with emphasis, as teachers do.

"I still think Sékou Touré was one of Africa's great men," I objected. "And if it hadn't been for the Cold War and abuses of power by some in his government, he would have been an even greater man today."

"That's the problem with people like you," he said, frowning. "You speak in superlatives. In reality, Sékou Touré lived between the two opposing objects of his hatred: French power and American power. One saw him when he was born—meaning he came into the world under French colonialism; and the other saw him dying, by which I mean that he died in an American hospital."

"But Sassine," I interrupted, "are you blaming him for trying to free his country—for hating people who colonized him, exploited him, and punished him for speaking out? Or are you blaming him for seeking a cure for his sickness in America? Fanon, too, died in America, you know."

"Come, Diawara, don't give me those tired slogans. Sékou Touré always lived in ideological confusion; for this, we in Guinea loved him or hated him. He had his partisans and opponents. Most of the partisans were following him out of fear. I personally did not like him, because he made me miss some years in my education by sending me into exile. What I can't stand is that some of the same people who did his dirty job for him are now his biggest critics. There are lots of them in the present government. Before this country can be truly healed, they must pay for the crimes they committed."

"But seriously, Sassine. Can't Guineans be reconciled and build on Sékou Touré's legacy? He made all of us proud to be Africans, you know. And that is no small feat."

"Sékou Touré killed too many people for every minor achievement he made. He lived between two extremes—love and hate. He was never temperate; he was boiling on one side and icy on the other. The icy side produced the infamous Camp Boiro. I've examined documents at Camp Boiro and found only two pages written by prisoners, in a cryptic script. All the real documents are held by people in the present regime—and those people would not release them, for fear of being implicated in Camp Boiro. What was Sékou Touré's direct role in it? The griots are not reliable, because they say what you pay them to say. Today's griots know only how to say, 'It's good! Everything is good!'

and they do it for the money. As for Sékou Touré's legacy, you have to look at the state the country is in today. Japan, for example, gives millions of dollars to the present regime so that it can buy rice from Thailand. We have accepted the terms of the agreement, although the farmers of Upper Guinea, where I am from, grow plenty of rice at a cheaper price. But they cannot bring their rice to Conakry, because the trains are not working. People in Guinea do not know where Thailand is, how far it is from here, but we have accepted Japanese money to buy Thai rice to the detriment of our own farmers. That's the sad independence I was talking about. Our situation is tragic and comical at the same time. Sékou Touré is not an easy man to study."

Sassine looked at me in defiance. I knew that his last sentence was directed at my project on Sékou Touré. I decided to change the subject.

"Let us turn now to your work, Sassine. *Le Zéhéros* is so negative. Camara, your main character, does not even know how to work an electric light switch. Do you think that Africans are incapable of handling the basic accessories of modernity? Are you a pessimist like Axel Kabou, who wrote *Et si l'Afrique refusait le développement?*"

"I am a positive-pessimist. It is like mathematics, where there are positive zeros. I consider myself a writer-in-vain. You have to break the French word for writer into two: *écri-vain*. I am a writer-in-vain because I am not read in my own country. In Guinea, I am better-known as an editorial writer for the journal *Le Lynx*. People don't know my books. I am better-known outside. I am read outside my own country. It is my positive-pessimism which enables me to keep believing that one day I will be read in Guinea. I know that a lot of change would have to take place before that could happen."

And how did Sassine deal with Afro-pessimism in his work? "Afro-pessimism is black by political coloration. And as you know, everything bad is black in Western and Arab cultures. So Afro-pessimism is a style which resists the tendency to use pessimism and blackness as a way of putting down black people. It's like Afro hairdos or Afrocentricity, you know. Black people are not pessimistic by nature. On the contrary, they accept reality as it is, thinking that there will always be a way out. White people are threatened by black people's positive outlook toward more babies, more leisure, and more pleasure. White people say to them, 'Do not have too many babies—it's bad.' But black people continue to make babies. For them, it's a question of survival in a land of high mortality rates. The way white people see it, the more babies blacks make, the more they will be tempted to emigrate and invade the space of whites. So you see, black people are practicing positive-pessimism.

"Let me give you an example. Liberia has the world's largest rubber plantation, in a place called Firestone. The Americans use the rubber to make condoms and tires. They send the condoms and cars to Africa. They pose problems for the positive outlook Africans have on life. The condoms control the birthrate, and the cars kill because the roads are bad. So who's to blame? The Africans who are fighting one another in Liberia and disrupting the rubber business? Or the Americans who are taking away the raw materials and sending back products that kill us and our culture?"

"Don't you think your kind of literature is a false resistance to modernization?" I asked. "I believe that the only way to fight modernity is to become modern, and to develop a politics of interest that can harness technology for different purposes. That's why we have to resume the independence and modernization project."

"Clichés!" he responded. "So far in Guinea, Sékou Touré's revolution has created three types of mutants: the flatterers, the floaters, and the deflated. The flatterers say anything the president wants to hear— that's why they become the ministers, general managers, and ambassadors in every regime. The floaters barely survive between governments. The deflated, on the other hand, constitute a race unto themselves. I don't mean the unemployed; a flatterer and a floater can both become unemployed. A deflated person is someone beyond good and evil, beyond feeling the blues of unemployment. He has reached a point where he says to himself, 'They don't need me because I don't know how to do anything. They don't know me. They don't see me.' African dictatorships are producing this kind of man every day. He knows that no matter what he does, he will not get anywhere. The statistics are against him: he will die young. He sits down and looks to see if people see him. He sees from the others' gazes that he is transparent. He does not know how to do anything, and he does not want to do anything."

Sassine noticed that the liquor bottle was empty. It was getting late. He went into the house and brought out a quarter-gallon of cheap wine in a carton. He served himself and tried to pour some into my glass. I told him no. I told him that if he did not stop, that stuff would kill him. He said that it kept him from killing people he couldn't stand—all those hypocrites in the present government who had always flattered Sékou Touré. "In Guinea, you have to drink yourself to death to keep from killing the bastards."

"Look at Nigeria," Sassine said, resuming his comfortable position in the reclining chair. "The soldiers killed Ken Saro Wiwa. To think that Nigeria is a member of ECOWAS [Economic Committee of West African States], and no one in West Africa raised a finger to try to stop the Nigerians from killing that man. All the protest came from the West and from South Africa. African leaders remained silent because they were friends and accomplices of the Nigerian leaders. They could not defend Ken Saro Wiwa, because they were living in glass houses themselves. They could not say, 'Don't kill him, because he has the right to speak out against the exploitation of his people by Shell Oil.' Not one among them said, 'Do not hang this man.' I find this to be a common tragic flaw in Africa. We say, 'We are pals, we are friends, we shall not condemn one another.'"

Sassine had grown somber, and it was getting late. I felt sorry for him because I understood him. Luckily, we were distracted for a moment by a helicopter that flew over the house.

"There he goes! It's the president of the republic—he is on his way to get more alcohol from the private reserve on his farm. It's no secret. The whole of Conakry knows about it."

51
▼

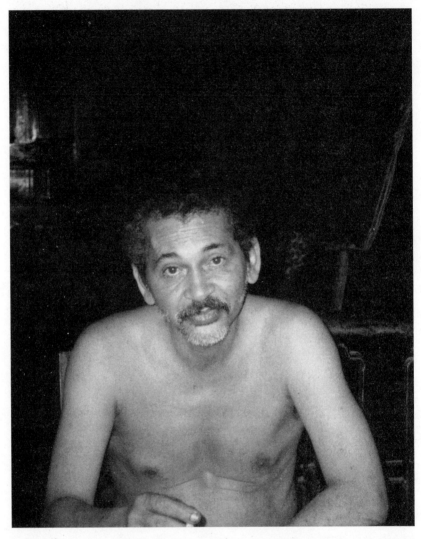

Williams Sassine, shown here in 1995, was an older brother to all of us. He symbolized the tragic flaws of African dictatorships. (Photo by Manthia Diawara.)

I was amazed. Sassine was laughing and chuckling like a child again. I remembered a character in *Le Zéhéros*—Taram, a survivor of Camp Boiro—who does an electric dance called the Robot to entertain people. The grotesque part is that Taram is tortured with electric wires in prison.

"You know, Sassine," I began, "the humor in your work is grotesque. Take Taram, for example: he believes in magic, begs Camara to bring him magic from overseas, and thinks that everybody more powerful than he is has magic. He's a grown man who thinks like a child. And he is not the only one."

"We must laugh," he said, "in order to transcend certain misfortunes. We live in a state of extraordinary misery. Our death rate is high. We have wars. We have everything. If we do not learn to laugh, we will die—we will commit suicide."

"I noticed also that there is a lot of violence in *Le Zéhéros*."

"I'm telling you the whole of Africa is waiting to erupt. When a man has nothing to lose, you have to be afraid of him. Look at Liberia, Somalia, Rwanda, and Burundi. Children with guns. A thousand people were killed in the northern part of Ghana in a dispute over a wild goose. All of these are signs of what is going to happen on the continent. We will witness a fundamental shakeup of frontiers; few heads of states will survive the upheaval. If people are killing each other for a wild goose, what won't they do for more important things?"

I asked Sassine what the solution was. "The only solution is violence. You must break everything. As they say, 'You cannot make an omelette without breaking eggs.' Things will just continue if you don't destroy them. They will transmit their power to their children. And on it will go. You cannot create anything new without breaking the old things. We need an apocalypse to clean everything."

The helicopter was hovering over our heads again. Sassine said that the president was on his way back. He tossed away a cigarette butt, which glowed in the darkness left behind by the setting sun. The duck rushed over and swallowed it. Sassine burst out laughing.

All the way back to the hotel, I thought about my conversation with Sassine. Could it be true that Africa was bound to violence—that our independence would produce only sadness and that our modernization project, just like the attempt to make a hero of Sékou Touré, was not worth the loss of our traditions and the number of innocent people killed? I knew that Sassine was not alone in advocating violence as a cleansing device in Africa today. Sembene Ousmane had once told me in a film interview that we had to begin from zero, by cutting off all the branches and rotten fruit from the tree. He had said that the older generation was corrupt beyond redemption and must be destroyed before it contaminated the younger one. Everywhere in Africa today, people are embarrassed by their leaders' irresponsibility, their greed, their inefficiency and decadence, and their lack of love for the continent, which they have sold to foreigners.

But I disagreed with Sassine on many of his conclusions. For one thing, the desire for violence as a cleansing tool is too easy a solution, which Afro-pessimists share with other extremists. It is based on a belief that peace, reconciliation, and love are impossible between the perceived winners and losers in Africa. Just as blood enemies are condemned to eternal hatred of one another, modern ideologies of the nation-state forever set the Sassines in opposition to the Sékou Tourés. They cannot govern together; they cannot live together. Each thinks that the world would be a better place without the other.

The will to violence is also animated by the desire for pure and simple vengeance. I noticed that Sassine was angry at the present regime for several reasons, including its failure to purge itself of all those who had collaborated with Sékou Touré. It seems to me that such a purge would be unrealistic: if the government got rid of all those who had worked under Sékou Touré, it would be composed only of formerly exiled Guineans, or of soldiers arrogant enough to assume they needn't be competent. No wonder, then, that there has been no progress in Africa since independence. There has been no attempt to build on the structures left behind by previous governments, or to establish permanent values that can resist ideological difference. Each new government breaks up everything that has been built, and then surrounds itself with family members and foreign advisers.

Another problem with Sassine's theory of violence as a solution lies in its psychological implications. I think that Afro-pessimists, like Afrocentrists and ethnophilosophers, are faced with a contemporary image of Africa that they must deny. The Afrocentrists proceed by investing in the past as the only site for identity formation and for the continent's renaissance into a scientific, political, and economic empire. The motivation behind this return to the past may be found in their unwillingness to concede African peoples' backward attitude toward modernity, which, if not challenged by an assumption of blacks' anterior superiority, they think will be interpreted as inferiority to white people. Afro-pessimists displace their denial and self-hatred onto African leaders and African culture, turning these feelings into blame and vengefulness. They think that violence is inevitable, but the fact of the matter is that there cannot be any revolution in violence, except to incite the families of the victims to seek retribution.

Sassine's condemnation of African modernity also appears premature to me. First, the notion that independence and modernization have transformed Africans into unhappy mutants seems to contradict the Afro-pessimists' thesis that we need to begin modernization from a clean slate. Afro-pessimists seem to assume both that Africans have corrupted modernity with their traditions, and that modernity is to blame for disrupting African traditions and thereby their ability to survive in this world. I think that movements toward independence and modernization have been necessary and worthwhile in Africa. Like Richard Wright in *Black Power,* I believe that the salvation of Africa lies in modernization, the creation of secular public spheres, and the freedom of individuals. I am therefore more interested in the first part of Sassine's argument, which concerns the corruption of modernity by Africans, than in his defense of tradition against modernization. That Africans are incapable of playing the game of modernity, which they pervert with certain aspects of their cultures, is a theory not only supported by Afro-pessimists but also driven by white supremacists, who find comfort in black people's position on the lowest rung of the socioeconomic ladder.

I believe that, in West Africa, if tradition helped us to resist the various brainwashings of colonialism, independence jump-started our true modernization. The mass education of young Africans, the valorization of African cultures and the rights of individuals, and movements for equality (between men and women, between nobles and casted people) have been made possible by independence, and could not have been achieved under colonialism. Thus, independence counteracted colonialism in Africa in the same way that U.S. civil rights laws counteracted segregation and Jim Crowism: by endowing oppressed people with the consciousness of a truly modern subjecthood, including the right to freedom, self-determination, and equality under the law.

There is no doubt that in Africa several contradictory forces are delaying the fulfillment of these promises. First, there are the traditions which were engaged in the fight against colonialism over African identity. These traditions are still trapped in resistance mode, opposing, as did our colonizers, the birth of the individual, education for all children, and women's emancipation. Tradition, with its encumbering rituals, chauvinism, and tribal identity, presents the same threat to African modernization that it posed to colonialism. I often wonder why we have not put our traditions in museums and folklore centers, as have other nations. Traveling to Europe, America, and Asia, I have had occasion to observe that other peoples once had some of the same rituals, masquerades, and belief systems that we Africans consider unique to our traditions today. The difference is that they have put the relics of their traditions in museums, preferring to come to their rendezvous with modernity with as little baggage as possible, whereas we always come to the table burdened with our traditions—approaching things as Africans, not as individuals.

Second, it is clear that our modernization rides against certain interests of the developed countries and white supremacists. Africa, like every other continent, constitutes a market in which every little change influences the global economy. From the Atlantic slave trade to the industrial exploitation of raw materials from the continent, Africa has not only been utterly scarred by Europe and America, but it has also served in the consolidation of the economies of these continents. Any modernization scheme will therefore stumble into the affairs of developed countries, and will have to be negotiated with their strategic interests in mind. Add to that the desire of white supremacists to maintain Africa as its ideological opposite in modernity, and you will have a sense of the magnitude of the obstacles that lie before us.

Finally, there is the implacable speed of modernity. Until the latter half of the twentieth century, Africa was kept largely at a medieval stage of development. The independence movements brought it back into history, and devised various structural strategies for catching up with the industrialized countries. But all of this has been taking place in a global competitive market in which no one is sleeping and waiting to be caught up with. Our fight to become modern, to make things new in our own image, began only recently with our independence movements, more than 150 years after the French Revolution. We need to redouble our efforts, to fight twice as hard, and to be eclectic in our strategies of development in order to compete with the rest of the world.

But I do not think that the above problems have succeeded in positioning Africa as the antipode of modernity. We are modern in the way in which we keep fighting for our independence, defying certain traditional taboos judged archaic by our new standards, and in our perpetual attempts to redefine our nation-states. Afro-pessimists will remain unable to perceive the extent of our modernity as long as they persist in comparing our styles and material accomplishments with those of the West. A true measure of our modernity lies in our desire for freedom and better lives. The independence revolution which was spearheaded by Sékou Touré and others made clear the need to seize time away from both the colonizer and atavistic tradition. We are now engaged in a history of which we are the protagonists, and we will win at the end because the future belongs to us. The very failure of Sékou Touré constitutes a lesson about democracy and about the obstacles that lie ahead in this historical narrative. Sékou Touré, like a tragic hero, jumped ahead of the fire of French imperialism, and in so doing rendered visible what we desired most and had to struggle for. Sékou Touré is the beginning of our history; that is why he is so important to us, and why we cannot leave him buried in the dustbin of history.

Our desire to be modernized has been awakened, and it cannot be denied. Women want liberation from traditional oppression; we all want access to education and material wealth; and we are tired of being ignored by the world. We know that the modern world is full of new and exciting things, and we want them for ourselves. Like all men and women, we want to be happy.

SITUATION II

▲▼▲

RICHARD WRIGHT
AND MODERN AFRICA

In an essay entitled "Alas, Poor Richard," a memoir of Richard Wright, James Baldwin made an extraordinary revelation about what he considered the structure of feeling of African Americans toward Africans. Baldwin opened this intriguing and off-limits subject by reporting what one African had told him about Richard Wright in Paris: "I believe he thinks he's white." For Baldwin, this sounded like more than an indictment of Wright alone. It brought into question the African American identity, shaped outside Africa, and the loss of community ties that both Wright and Baldwin had suffered in exile. For Baldwin confesses—with the seeming vulnerability which was the trademark of his essayistic style—that

> I had always been considered very dark; both Negroes and whites had despised me for it, and I had despised myself. But the Africans were much darker than I. I was a paleface among them, and so was Richard. And the disturbance thus created caused all of my extreme ambivalence about color to come floating to the surface of my mind. The Africans seemed at once simpler and more devious, more directly erotic and at the same time more subtle, and they were proud. If they had ever despised themselves for their color, it did not show, as far as I could tell. I envied them and feared them—feared that they had good reason to despise me. What did Richard feel? (Baldwin, 1985: 281)

What sounds strange to me today in these lines is Baldwin's seeming unawareness of the heterogeneity of African populations, who display more hues than you could easily count. But to Baldwin's credit, the essay raises important questions about the relation between Africans and African Americans, and, more crucially for us here, about the place that Wright occupied among black artists and writers in Paris at the time of his untimely death.

In an even more surprising declaration, Baldwin said that Wright had been able, "at last, to live in Paris exactly as he would have lived, had he been a white man, here, in America." This implies first of all that Wright was freed from racism in Paris, and that, with this freedom, he ceased to be black. For Baldwin, there was a price paid for Wright's acceptance in Paris, just as there was one for the general acceptance of African Americans in the West: such integration came at the cost of a profound sense of self-hatred. This is why, according to Baldwin, "when [an African American] faces an African, he is facing the unspeakably dark, guilty, erotic past which the Protestant fathers made him bury—for their peace of mind, and for their power—but which lives in his personality and haunts the universe yet."

Again, it is important to bear in mind that by today's standards of travel, information access, globalization, and pride in black culture, some of Baldwin's reading of blackness as a repressed essence may seem like a strange notion, or even a simplistic Freudian interpretation. But remember that Baldwin was discussing Wright, whose imagination was at that time filled with Africa. Baldwin raised one last enigmatic point in the essay—a point that I will merely mention now, and consider more fully later. He said: "What an African facing an American Negro sees, I really do not know; and it is too early to tell with what scars and complexes the African has come up from the fire."

The Paris Congress of 1956, held at the Sorbonne's Descartes Amphitheater, put Africans in a face-off with African Americans and Caribbeans. The conference was organized by Alioune Diop and the *Présence Africaine* group, which included Senghor, Césaire, Jacques Rabemananjara, and Wright. It was the first conference organized in Paris by black writers and artists. They came together to make an inventory of all the cultures of African origin, and to define them for a positive representation of black people in the modern world. In order to ensure that the conference participants would be able to define their own agenda, only people of African descent were invited to address the audience.

The Paris Congress was controversial for more than one reason. Some people felt that the emphasis on blackness as a criterion for inclusion was unfortunate, because at the end of the day racial solidarity could not be distinguished from racism. Others felt that the only thing people in the conference hall had in common was that they were all victims of white racism—a factor that provided no guarantee of a common culture. The CIA and the KGB were also said to be in the mix, looking after their interests and counting their enemies. W. E. B. Du Bois sent a telegram stating that the U.S. government had taken away his passport, so that he could not attend the conference. His message, which was read aloud, cast doubt on the integrity and commitment of the African Americans who were able to travel and be at the conference. As Baldwin said, the telegram "very neatly compromised whatever effectiveness the five-man American delegation then sitting in the hall might have hoped to have. It was less Du Bois's extremely ill-considered communication which did this than the incontestable fact that he had not been allowed to leave his country" (Baldwin, 1985: 44).

These tensions and controversies were but the first signs of the debates that would emerge over the definition of black culture. In the face-off that the conference produced between Africans, Caribbeans, and African Americans, the discussion of unity had to first pass through the messy history of black cultures—cultures which maintained some people in privileged positions, while sending others into slavery; and which opened doors for the modernization and emancipation of some, while branding others as savages. There was a disparity in social mentalities, such that the gap between the people in the Descartes Amphitheater was as marked as the racial bond that united them. Thus, there was no guarantee that some people at the conference would accept the blackness and culture of others.

The Paris conference found it extremely difficult to achieve an open dialogue and relationship between Africans, African Americans, and Caribbeans. I see two reasons for this. First, the people living in Africa, or born there, tended to link the definition of black cultures to notions of continuity and authenticity, to empire, ethnicity, clan, and family. They felt threatened whenever the identity of a black person from the diaspora deviated from their own. They always wanted to see themselves in the cultures of other blacks. The diasporic black, on the other hand, was afraid of the African, simply because he represented Africa—the unknown, in the imagination of the West, and the symbol of darkness, fear, and ignorance. The diasporic black wanted to hide this Africa, and present a more fantastic one to the modern world.

The tone of the conference was set by Léopold Sédar Senghor's speech,

"L'esprit de la civilisation, ou les lois de la culture négro-africaine," which is one of the founding texts of Afrocentric philosophy and art criticism. The first part deals with what Senghor calls a "physiopsychology" of the Negro, or an existential ontology of the black subject. He describes the mode of being in the black world as intuitive, prone to an unmediated identification with the object of desire, and driven by a vital force whose essence is obtained from the ancestors and other totemic and mystical sources. Senghor places emphasis on intuition as the black person's primary way of knowing the world; he asserts that knowledge in Europe is analytical and discursive, whereas the African apprehends his world through intuitive participation in it.

Senghor masterfully arranges his theory of existential ontology in Africa by arguing that this ontology governs the social, artistic, and metaphysical reality of blackness. The ancestors are the purveyors of the essential vital force, which enables them to put the human world in a position of dependency, instability, and weakness, and finally obliges humans to strive for ancestral blessing and favor in their daily life. Senghor describes the dominance of metaphysical forces over economic and political forces in Africa as the result of a hierarchized and concentrically shaped reality in which the ancestor-gods are on top, followed by kings, tribal chiefs, heads of clans, heads of families, and leaders of sororal and fraternal groups. Thus, the existential ontology explains the harmony of black societies held together by authentic religions, cults that brought the vital forces to earth through sacrifices, art, and literature.

In the second half of his essay, Senghor sees art and literature in Africa as by-products of social and religious activities; this view accounts for his belief that African art is functional, collective, and committed. Art and literature become rituals of identity formation that mobilize the vital force through performance and connect the ontological self to the totemic and legendary ancestors, weaving a relationship between the individual and the collective and putting human beings in tune with the animal and vegetable world. For Senghor, art and literature, like the religion they serve, permeate every aspect of African life, from work songs and funeral dances to rituals of harvesting, planting, birth, initiation, and marriage.

Senghor surprised and delighted the audience with his description of African artforms as polyvalent, interconnected, and performative. He declared that the African mask is fully complete as a work of art only when it is accompanied by song, dance, and the recitation of a poem. He then proceeded to show that the masked dancer identifies with the ancestor he represents, and whose power flows into the dancer and the community. For Senghor, art is a magical means through which the essence of the vital force from the ancestors is called up and made to empower the performers and the spectators. Art in Africa is not an imitation or a representation of the world; it is a new beginning, a reenactment, a rebirth of the world through ritual. Senghor illustrated his vision of interrelated artforms by drawing on a now-famous example from Camara Laye's *L'enfant noir*—a scene in which the father of the young narrator is crafting a piece of gold jewelry. As Senghor puts it, "The prayer or rather the poem that Laye's father recites, the praise song that the griot sings to encourage him while he is working on the gold jewelry, the dance of the blacksmith at the end of the work: it is all of this—the poetry, the song, and the dance—that accomplishes the master-piece, beyond the technical movements of the artisan" (Senghor, 1956: 56).

It is important to bear in mind that Léopold Sédar Senghor and Cheikh Anta Diop were cultural retentionists who believed that the European Renaissance took off from the ruins of African civilization. What is important about this is that they both also believed that the Paris conference was a point of departure for an African cultural Renaissance. For Senghor, black people can find in the arts and oral literature of Africa the classics of their Renaissance, just as the Europeans of the sixteenth century turned to Virgil and his contemporaries for their cultural rebirth. Furthermore, Senghor believed that African culture already existed for African Americans and Caribbeans at the unconscious level, and that this could be apparent in their willingness to study the classics from Africa. Senghor cited Richard Wright's *Black Boy* as an example of an African American narrative which bore the influence of African culture.

Richard Wright delivered his own paper on the third day of the conference, when it seemed that the cultural retentionists had already won the sympathies of the audience. At any rate, Wright's task was a difficult one: he wanted to clear a third space, which was to be identified with neither the theorists of cultural survival nor the sociologists of culture operating under the influence of communism. Wright was no longer interested in describing the mental and moral disposition of the racialized subject, as he had done so well in *Native Son*. He now turned to Africa, and to the role of Africans and other colonized subjects in decolonization and enlightenment.

The title of Wright's essay, "Tradition and Industrialization," resituates the conference debate on the track of modernity itself, away from the conflict between the transhistorical culturalism of Senghor and Diop, and the sociological discourses on race and culture in colonial, semicolonial, and paracolonial situations (as Césaire and Fanon put it). Using modernity as his subject and object, Wright wanted to create an economy of time over culture, of industrialization at the expense of tradition, of secular spheres against religious spaces. The essay's dramatic opening phrase—"The hour is late and I am pressed for time"—was not simply intended to underscore Wright's awareness of the general fatigue of a patient audience; it was also intended as a rhetorical move, to create a historical awareness and make the people in the Descartes Amphitheater conscious of their place in that history. The essay's originality comes through in this beginning, which demonstrates Wright's belief that the world was quickly becoming one, and that the role of the black elites at the conference was to extend the promise of enlightenment to their people.

Wright's presentation had two main components: a polemic against religions, and a call for enlightenment and individual freedom. He told the audience that two types of religious fundamentalism, Christian beliefs and indigenous traditions, were competing for the loyalty of Africans and blocking their entry into the secular modern and industrialized world. Here Wright stated one of the discomforting truths about the African and diasporic elites who were listening to him. He had no doubt already alienated this audience when he had responded to Senghor's talk in the following manner: "I have the feeling, uneasy, almost bordering upon dread, that there was a fateful historic complement between a militant white Christian Europe and an ancestral cult religion in Africa. They complemented each other, and this morally foul relationship remained for more than five hundred years" (Wright, 1956: 68). But even though Wright had realized by now how conservative his audience was, he did not back down. He simply pointed out the irony of the situation in the room: "I wrote this paper up in the country, projecting an ideal room filled with secular-minded Africans more or less like myself in outlook." Wright continued to shock the weary audience (it was half past eleven in the evening) by saying that European colonialism had proffered a boon wrapped in its gift of brutality—that because colonialism had been a carrier of the promise of enlightenment, it had enabled the development of science and industry in Africa, "negated the past notions of social structures, negated norms of nobility, of tradition, . . . and fostered new social classes, new occupations, new structures of government, new pleasures, hungers, dreams."

It may seem naive of Wright to have so easily dismissed religion and culture, the two most important fundamentalisms that have called people to action and violence since the end of the Cold War. But it is also important to remember that he was responding to the Negritude school, mainly to the retentionist branch represented by Senghor and Diop. One must also remember, as Michel Fabre put it, that to Wright, "the question of how much African culture an African retains when transplanted to a new environment is only a cultural problem."

By 1956 Wright was the most important black public intellectual, if not in the world, then certainly at the conference. By resigning from the Communist Party and leaving the United States to take up residence in France, he increased his cultural capital beyond the borders of any one nation and assumed the stature of a world authority. By 1956 Wright had visited Latin America, traveled to Ghana to collect the material for his book *Black Power,* and participated in the historic conference on developing nations held in Bandung, Indonesia, in 1955. As a result, he was a reluctant nationalist; he believed that "nationalism is one of the necessary and transitional forms of an expanding industrial system, and there was no reason why nationalism and industrialization could not, for a time, coexist, mutually enriching each other" (1995a: 61). Wright's historical awareness of Africa thus demands that we reassess his notion of a "third point of view" first in relation to his own American works.

Although Wright had earned his reputation as the most important American writer of protest literature and exponent of black rage with such books as *Uncle Tom's Children, Black Boy,* and *Native Son,* he moved away from this genre after his self-exile to France. The exile also marked the moment he broke away from the Communist Party, which he added to his list of the demons of racism, next to the church, colonialism, and imperialism. Wright's internationalism made him aware of the colonial situation and the threats that the Cold War posed to African progress toward enlightenment. For Wright, travel narrative was a better genre than the novel for describing his newfound energy and drive. He believed that a new form of enlightenment, one that was devoid of racism, could emerge out of Africa and Asia. If the new leaders of Africa and Asia were able to stop religion from competing with the state for the people's emotions, the wretched of the earth could rise to the occasion as the modern heroes of this grand narrative. Wright's American readers, who were used to his protest novels and their pathological protagonists, were unprepared for this new spirit of optimism. His readers in Europe and Africa, where his reputation had preceded him, did not fully understand *Black Power* either. But before we turn to that book, we must first look at James Baldwin's classic review of the Paris conference.

Baldwin's essay, entitled "Princes and Powers," deals with the conference from the point of view of a participant who was skeptical about a monolithic definition of black culture. The essay raises the question whether the history and psychology that had molded the African Americans at the conference were commensurate with those of the other people in the room. For Baldwin, African Americans were different from Africans because of the unique experience that had shaped them: African Americans "had been born in a society which, in a way quite inconceivable for Africans, and no longer real for Europeans, was open, and, in a sense which had nothing to do with justice or injustice, was free. It was a society, in short, in which nothing was fixed, and we had therefore been born to a greater number of possibilities, wretched as these possibilities seemed at the instant of birth" (Baldwin, 1985: 45).

What is interesting to me in this essay is the manner in which Baldwin links the meaning of blackness in America to freedom and permanent movement, and, at the same time, elevates this revolutionary way of constructing black identity in the modern world beyond the reach of Africans. Instead of problematizing the definitions of culture at the conference, Baldwin himself ends up constructing and maintaining a binary opposition between Africans and African Americans. It seems that Baldwin's African has a fixed identity, whereas the African American is black not only because he or she is the object of American racism but also by choice, by virtue of a depth of involvement and experience in black American culture. The African lives in a cohesive society, a "healthy" culture which has a much lower tolerance for individualism. The African American, like all Western people, is an individual who is caught in an "awful and brutal isolation . . . to flower or to perish." Baldwin's African is by implication a primitive, while his African American is modern. In retrospect, this too seems strange, given that the conference was taking place in Paris in a room named for Descartes. At that time, French people, including Francophone Africans and Caribbeans, believed that only France was cultured and that the Americans and the British, including blacks, were savages when it came to *savoir faire*.

Baldwin's praise for Senghor's presentation at the conference is firmly grounded in the received ideas and stereotypes which set up a dichotomy between Africans and Europeans. Senghor's Africa was itself firmly grounded in those same received Western discourses on the "primitive" mind. Baldwin defends Senghor's talk on aesthetic grounds because it argues that, for Africans, "the artistic image is not intended to represent the thing itself, but, rather, the reality or the force the thing contains. Thus, the moon is fecundity, the elephant is force." Baldwin goes on, I must say naively, to add that "the distortions used by African artists to create a work of art are not at all the same distortions which have become one of the principal aims of almost every artist in the West today. They are not the same distortions even when they have been copied from Africa." One might ask if "the West" here includes African American artists. For Baldwin, "the only thing in western life which seemed even faintly to approximate Senghor's intense sketch of the creative interdependence, the active, actual, joyful intercourse obtaining among African artists and what only a westerner would call their public, was the atmosphere sometimes created among jazz musicians and their fans during, say, a jam session" (Baldwin, 1985: 48).

Baldwin is more critical when he turns to Wright's presentation. He takes issue with Wright's notion that colonialism might be a good thing for Africa in the long run if it could enlighten Africans and rid them of their old traditions and gods. To his mind, Wright misunderstood blacks in America if he thought they were free from the church and therefore secular. Finally, Baldwin is less optimistic than Wright about the spirit of Bandung and the authoritarian manner in which the emerging Third World leaders were running their states in the name of modernization.

After reading Baldwin's essay on the conference, I went back to Wright's *Black Power* and read it again. I must confess that what struck me most was its similarities with Fanon's *The Wretched of the Earth*. Both books condemn tradition and ethnicity as obstacles to the formation of national identity; both aim a stinging critique at the local elite, educated in Europe and ferociously set against revolution; and both extol peasants and market women as the authentic heroes of modernity. What saved Fanon's classic book from the criticism reserved for Wright's *Black Power* in Africa and black America was, I believe, its heavy reliance on theory and abstraction. Wright's travel narrative, in contrast, relied on ethnography and a scholarly analysis of the way in which Ashanti tradition and religion competed for the emotions of the people against the West African state that Kwame Nkrumah was attempting to build.

Wright's ethnographic eye was harsh and at times justifiably discomforting to Africans and African Americans, who felt that he might be participating in what Baldwin has called "a deep [racial] self-hatred," or seeking revenge against African elites for their ancestors' role in slavery. Wright's materialist criticism, like that of Fanon, has led people to believe that he did not allow any space in his book for the appreciation of indigenous African cultures. Finally, his injunction to Kwame Nkrumah to "militarize" people's daily lives in the Gold Coast is read literally and considered a fascist statement. Fanon's call for a new man and a new woman, on the other hand, is interpreted positively by the theorists of postcoloniality.

Wright wrote *Black Power* out of concern that the world was rapidly becoming more interconnected, and that modernity was shaping people's reality and focusing their desires on the need to travel and communicate quickly, to have access to unlimited consumer goods, and to preserve their democratic and individual rights. He used freedom as the overarching metaphor in the book. For him, it was not enough that the Africans of the Gold Coast, led by Kwame Nkrumah, were seizing their freedom from the British colonizers. For Nkrumah to realize his dream of independence, these West Africans would also have to be freed from themselves, from tribal religions which formed a psychological barrier between them and the modern world, and from the chiefs who had usurped a godlike position: "Their huge umbrellas are foolishly gaudy, their never-ending retinue of human slaves is ridiculous, their claim about their ability to appease the dead is a fraud, their many wives are a seductive farce, the vast lands they hold in the name of the dead are a waste of property, their justice is barbaric, their interpretations of life are contrary to common sense" (Wright, 1995a: 344).

In an effort to help Africans prepare themselves to play a role in the modern world, Wright ends *Black Power* with a now infamous letter to Nkrumah, advising him that "there is but one honorable course that assumes and answers the ideological, traditional, organizational, emotional, political, and productive needs of Africa at this time: AFRICAN LIFE MUST BE MILITARIZED."

Every time I read *Black Power,* which to me is one of the most penetrating books about Africa and the psychological relation between African Americans and Africans, I am unsettled by this passage. For it brings to mind the devastating effects of the militarization of Nazi Germany, fascist Italy, and the communist states of the Cold War. *Black Power* was greeted with silence and was little discussed, because many people felt that Wright wanted the same kind of militaristic fascism for Africa. Or, at least, it was seen as a book full of hatred for Africa. It came at a time when people were beginning to celebrate African traditions and identities. Essentially, the passage raises as many questions about Wright himself as it does about Africa. Was he still a communist, or was he taking revenge on Africans for selling his ancestors into slavery? The passage has always been unsettling to me because I feel that siding with Wright would mean I was opting for a simplistic solution which did not take human suffering into account.

Yet Wright was prescient about the unprepared state of Africans to face modernity or globalization. Even today, they are victims not only of exploitation and racism by white people, but also of tribalism, disorganization, and superstition. Wright was hungering for Africans' participation in the modern world: "I yearned for them to break away from this and master machines, dig the minerals out of the earth, organize themselves, grow strong, sovereign . . . And why? So that the British would not exploit them, so that they could stand equal with others and not be ashamed to face the world" (163).

I have recently encountered Africans and African Americans who are willing to discuss *Black Power* openly, and without being too self-conscious about it. The end of the Cold War has provided an opportunity for us to discuss the advantages to Africans of discipline, punctuality, the inner organization of the personality, solidarity, focus, perseverance, and stalwartness, which are the meanings intended by Wright's statement, "African life must be militarized."

For example, I had a fascinating conversation with Dr. Abdoulaye Ly, a retired history professor and former minister in Senghor's government in Senegal. When I told him that I had some problems with Wright's use of the term to "militarize," Professor Ly, who is a veteran of the Second World War, explained to me how commonly the word was used in the Forties and Fifties—not only in the communist sense of creating a proletarian army, but also in the sense of educating the African people, creating fraternal bonds beyond tribal groups, and forming disciplined militants for the Pan-African cause of decolonization and modernization of Africa. He reminded me that in French the words *militaire* and *militant* had the same root, the Latin *militis,* which means disciplined and committed to an ideal, ready to fight for a cause.

Then Professor Ly offered me his own extraordinary experience as an example of how one can quickly be militarized. When he was nineteen years old, he had been drafted into the French Resistance army, taught to drive a tank in one month, and sent to fight the Nazis. In this sense, he and millions of others, Americans and Russians included, had been militarized to liberate France from fascism, to defend the liberties of individuals, and to ignite the flame of decolonization and equality in Africa and other oppressed parts of the world. In Africa, men like Mobutu, Idi Amin, Moussa Traoré, and many others had given militarization a bad name by linking it to disorder, dictatorship, and oppression. Ly said that in the Forties and Fifties the term had been intended to signify "equalization," getting rid of tribal chiefs, eliminating corruption in the army, and treating African soldiers the same way French soldiers were treated. In other words, militarization in Africa signified nationalism, with the masses as the basis of political power. To militarize meant to make every African a soldier of Pan-Africanism. Finally, for Ly, militarization was tied to citizenship. In this sense, to militarize means to make new citizens for the nation. (Even in America, the image of militarization can represent the discipline and mass mobilization needed for nation building. Franklin Roosevelt used the metaphor in his inaugural address of 1933.)

Wright, too, felt that militarization was the fastest way to draft Africans into the modern world and to liberate them from their dead ancestors and living tribal chiefs. In *Black Power,* Wright's anger is directed at the British for the manner in which they exploited Africans and deprived them of modern technology and the spirit of freedom: "Was it possible that Great Britain had ruled here for 104 years? Three generations had passed and things were like this?" (163). Even the British clergy was blind to the problem of freedom for Africans: "So intertwined was Christianity and this getting of gold and diamonds that it was not until now that any real crime had been felt" (168). Wright interpreted this as a betrayal of the Western sense of justice. For him, although the West had instilled a sense of justice and freedom in the hearts of Africans, this did not negate the fact that it had voluntarily surrendered this sense—its strongest moral weapon—to marginalized and oppressed cultures in favor of its weakest weapons of greed and racism (xxxvii).

But Wright reserved much of his energy and written argument for the liberation of Africans from systems of thought that erected barriers between them and the modern world. Today, after the end of the Cold War, most people see religious fundamentalism in Israel, Iran, Palestine, and

North America as the biggest threat to democracy, individual freedom, and the market economy. In the Fifties, Wright had already identified tribal belief systems, and the oral traditions which provided a permanent support for them through everyday practice, as the biggest enemy of modernity in Africa. For Wright, the whole of African life is pitched on a sacred plane: "In matters of politics, death, childbirth, . . . it's the teachings and beliefs of the tribe that people—even those who are literate—turn to, give support to and trust" (255). Wright could not see a place for a romantic hero in such a system. He found in tribal belief systems the same forces of repression as in the colonial and missionary systems, which oppose secular democratic institutions, the liberation of women, and the rise of the individual. For him, the complicity between tribal religion and Christianity was the deadliest weapon against secular rule and government by the masses. Wright knew that religious institutions were "jealous by their very nature and felt an understandable panic at the emergence of sweeping nationalism that was bent on creating not only new institutions for the people, but also new emotional attitudes, values, and definitions" (61).

Wright was shocked, therefore, to find out that Nkrumah himself was using tribal religious practices to win votes for his Convention People's Party. Nkrumah decreed that every head of family had to take a blood oath to be a card-carrying member of the party. In so doing, the party acquired the votes of the entire family: "When a head of the family joins the Convention People's Party, the entire family joins . . . The clan and the family form the basis for his [Nkrumah's] drive for power. His aim is to replace the chiefs entirely, and eventually the British too" (233).

Clearly, Wright was even more disappointed with Nkrumah and other emerging Third World leaders than with colonial forces for surrendering the weapon of individual freedom to religious and political power. For Wright, driving the British out was meant to create a space of equality between people, a third space where the individual was neither a captive of tribal gods and chiefs nor a victim of racial prejudice. But it seemed that politicians like Nkrumah were driving out the British only to take their place. They were replacing white dictatorial rule with an African one, preparing the ground for an even more oppressive and archaic system of rule based on magic and superstition, instead of science and objectivity.

Wright had reason to be concerned and even disturbed, for he had seen in the emerging Ghana of Nkrumah the limits of his theories. In other words, he had to question whether Africa could be the new place of hope, given that Europe and America had betrayed the traditional hopes of Westerners—the sense of justice, of freedom. Could Africa ever be the place of freedom untainted by racism and sexism, the place where the masses might form the basis of political power in the modern world? Wright had thought this was possible through education, which enabled people to forgo old values and create new ones according to their growing needs: "Only when men break loose from that rot and death and plunge creatively into the future do they become something to respect. Life then becomes a supremely spiritual task of molding and shaping the world according to the needs of the human heart" (225).

With Nkrumah, Wright found that neither Europeans nor Africans would easily let go of their past. And this revelation left him feeling terribly lonely and pressed for time. Why couldn't the European men and women forsake racism when all modern scientific evidence showed that they should? And why did the African, once he had found the tools of his liberation in modernity, have to revive his traditions, which oppressed African women, and oppose the creation of secular and democratic institutions? Why did the African make modernity itself his enemy, by appropriating it into tribal religions and Negritude philosophies? These unsettling questions are what makes *Black Power* a classic for me. Wright was for Africa, and he gave Africans the most precious weapon he had to offer: his theory of modernity. He was well aware of the price to be paid, which included alienation, loneliness, and despair. But for Wright, the price was well worth it if it enabled the African "to control his own destiny, with that romantic sense of self-redemption," so that "the British could not continue to suck his blood and wax fat" (261).

Black Power also addresses the question of culture, which often leads people to resist change and even reject modernization. Cultural retention as a theme is treated throughout the book not only with reference to Africans but also with regard to African Americans, who still retain aspects of African culture in their modern lives. In fact, Wright had two goals in writing his book. The first and most obvious was to be an eyewitness to the Ghanaian independence movement, and to assist Nkrumah in the liberation of his people from the British. The second and more personal objective of the book concerned the myth of returning home, of the African American identification with Africa. From the time Wright set foot in Africa to the time he left, he was besieged by two contradictory emotions toward the people: identification and estrangement, love and hate.

James Baldwin, in his review of the Paris congress, alluded to some of the psychological reasons that push African Americans to distance themselves from Africa. He interprets the resurgence of Africanism among African Americans as the return of the repressed. It can be blamed for the persistence of white racism toward blacks; it explains why people are denied jobs or access to certain places; and why people do not find themselves beautiful, or adequate for certain positions. In *Black Power,* Wright agrees with this basic psychological analysis. "The American Negro's passionate identification with America stemmed from two considerations: first, it was a natural part of his assimilation of Americanism; second, so long had Africa been described as something shameful, barbaric, a land in which one went about naked, or a land in which his ancestors had sold their kith and kin as slaves—so long had he heard all of this that he wanted to disassociate himself in his mind from all such realities" (72). We have seen how Baldwin referred to himself as a Western man, in contrast to Senghor the African. Wright, too, draws a distinction between himself and Africans by claiming his Western identity. The real qualitative difference between Wright and Baldwin is that the latter considered Westernness unavailable even to men like Senghor, whereas the former equated Westernness with modernity and therefore thought it readily accessible to all.

Perhaps it was this difference in approaching the question "What is Africa to an African American?" that compelled Wright to go to Africa to find an answer, while Baldwin was content to keep his distance and his difference. Wright wanted to find out for himself what Africa is. And when he reached the Gold Coast, he was determined not to identify with the people on a racial basis: "I'd long contended that the American Negro, because of what he had undergone in the United States, had been basically altered, that his consciousness had been filled with a new content, that 'racial' qualities were but myths of prejudiced minds" (62).

It is therefore possible to read *Black Power* not so much as Wright's protest against Africa, but as an expression of his anger both at America for maintaining a binary opposition between black and white as racial categories and at himself for not being able to get rid of them. Wright sees in Africa cultural practices that not only remind him of African American culture, but that he knows are used in America as marks for racial identification. For example, he recognizes as his own the "snakelike veering and weaving of the body," the "laughter that bent the knee and turned the head (as if in embarrassment)," and the powerful improvisational dances of African women: "Was it possible that I was looking at myself laughing, dancing, singing, gliding with my hips to express my joy?" (63).

Wright describes his journey to Africa as a homecoming full of anxieties and disturbances, which are caused by uncanny events and images that are "strange but familiar" (72). Africa is for him a mirror in which he sees historical memories and the present melt together. He wants to shatter the mirror into pieces, or will the images to disappear. In one scene in the book, he witnesses an Ashanti funeral ceremony unfolding in the middle of an Accra street. Men and women are dancing under the hot sun with a coffin atop their heads. A German tourist in Wright's hotel invites him to come and take pictures of this extraordinary scene. Wright is so shocked by the events in front of him that he is incapable of photographing it: "I took the camera from my eyes, too astonished to act; passing me were about fifty women, young and old, nude to the waist, their elongated breasts flopping loosely and grotesquely in the sun" (143). Wright is frozen and unable to distance himself from the event, whereas his German companion continues to take pictures. The German tourist sees the "other," the savage whom he wishes to photograph and show to the people back home. Wright, in contrast, sees himself in the scene, and he cannot handle it. This is the dilemma of the African American: he cannot take Africa out of himself and behave just like an ordinary Western man. It is useful here to turn to psychoanalysis, in order to understand how Wright sees himself in the mirror constituted by the bodies of those women. The African American identifies with Africans in a way that he cannot identify with other oppressed people, such as Asians and Europeans. Africa represents for him that which he must repress in certain circumstances and celebrate in others. It is therefore through a psychoanalytic reading that we comprehend Wright's vulnerability in this magnificent book. "I had understood nothing, nothing," Wright says. "Why were they rushing so quickly and seemingly at random with that brass coffin? . . . My mind reeled at the newness and strangeness of it. Had my ancestors acted like this? and why?" (144).

Wright insists that his protest is not against Africa and Africans. It is directed against the British, the Americans, the French, and the Germans, who built and maintain racial categories to entertain themselves and solve their problems at the expense of Africans. Wright also feels guilty for being part of the West, which is responsible for such crimes against Africans. He believes that every single person in the Western world is guilty every time a Western government or business maintains people in the Dark Ages in order to exploit them, or kills them for attempting to become free.

As a modernist, Wright was a purist, and that was the source of many of his difficulties with both Africans and African Americans (not to mention the white people he blamed for racism). He trusted scientific enlightenment to solve people's problems. He relied on the objective knowledge of the world to rid people of racism and to foster democratic institutions. He was against theories which used the presence of Africanism in the new world to posit binary oppositions between black and white people and which made these oppositions a basis for racial categorization. For him, "the question of how much culture an African retains when transplanted to a new environment is not a racial, but a cultural problem. (He remains black and becomes American, English, or French.)" (295).

If we are dealing with culture, we might as well raise the problem of access. For Wright, African Americans kept to their old African ways, not to mention "primal attitudes," either because no other way of life was available to them or because they were intimidated in their attempt to grasp those new ways to which white people had access. Thus, to the degree that the African American "fails to adjust, to absorb the new environment (and this will be mainly for racial and economic reasons!), he to that degree, and of necessity, will retain much of his primal outlook upon life, his basically poetic apprehension of existence" (295–296).

With *Black Power,* Wright went where few people had dared to go before, and he initiated a frank conversation between Africans and African Americans. He proposed a new ground of identification, which is not racial but ignited by the desire to win freedom for oppressed people all over the world. He believed that his freedom as a black Westerner was tied to the freedom of African people, not because of racial kinship but because of the racism which lumped all black people together and prevented them from forging their own individual identities. He said that he was ashamed of being a Westerner, because the West had surrendered its most important weapon—the pursuit of justice for all. He believed that culture was not a fixed entity: its movements and changes were tied to the group's access to modernity. *Black Power* may unsettle many readers, but one thing is certain: Wright was for Africa.

Looking at the African continent today, I cannot help saying that Wright was right in his assessment of ethnicity, tradition, and religion. The

African elites have not only entered into complicity with the agents of the Cold War to block the road to nation building in Africa, but have also maintained women and casted clans in their subjugated positions. Today, Africa is badly in need of some of the secularism that Wright talked about in *Black Power*. He wanted West Africans to become modernized and industrialized because, if for no other reason, modernity and industrialization are the best antidotes to white supremacy. He wanted the people of the Gold Coast to break away from their traditions because the alienated man is not only the man who hates the West, but also the one who wants to be like the West, free like Western man to be an individual, to control his own destiny. Wright was hoping that Nkrumah would create a West African *Weltanschauung* so the British would not exploit his people, so they could stand equal with others and not be ashamed to face the world. *Black Power* is perhaps a hard pill to swallow, but one of the most important books ever written on Africa. Nowadays, with Afro-pessimism becoming *de rigueur*, Wright takes a well-deserved place as one of the first prophets to have warned us against the pitfalls of nationalism, ethnicity, and religious fundamentalism.

So much, then, for the way in which African Americans saw their encounter with Africans at the Paris conference. I want to return now to Baldwin's question: What does an African facing an African American see? Surely the world has evolved and many structures of feeling have changed since 1956. Largely because of the success of black writers and artists, the world knows Africa better; and Africans, African Americans, and Caribbeans have grown closer together in many ways. The capital of the black world has also changed, from Paris to New York. Harlem now is the destination of many blacks from Jamaica, Haiti, Senegal, and Nigeria. How do blacks from these diverse cultural backgrounds perceive one another?

3

▲▼▲

Cémoko's Sékou Touré

The next day in Conakry, I awoke thinking about Baldwin's question. What does a contemporary African—like me—feel when he sees an African American? First of all, I feel my humanity finally accepted by the world. Whenever I see a black person from the diaspora, I see Toni Cade Bambara, I see Kamau Brathwaite, I see James Baldwin, I see Bob Marley, I see James Brown, I see C. L. R. James, I see Muhammad Ali, I see Paule Marshall, I see Malcolm X, I see Edwidge Danticat, I see Walter Mosley, I see Maryse Condé, I see myself. I am free to see a human being, a person, an individual. Wright's dream of the romantic African self-redemptive hero is within reach; for if we consider that W. E. B. Du Bois captured the imagination of the world by positing color as the main riddle of the twentieth century, Wright's work on freedom outside the United States in the Fifties lay the groundwork for getting us out of this racial conundrum.

That day, I prepared myself to meet historian Djibril Tamsir Niane, author of the classic book *Soundjata: L'épopée Mandingue* (translated as *Sundiata: An Epic of Old Mali*). Based on the oral traditions of the griots, this work recounts the legend of Sundiata, founder of the Empire of Mali, who lived in the thirteenth century. I had first met Niane in 1985, at Sembene Ousmane's house in Dakar. He'd been a consultant to a project on Samory Touré that Sembene had been working on. He was a quiet man, who spoke softly but always with authority. I remember being intimidated by him because of the precise way he selected his words in French. He had been exiled from Guinea, like most Fulani intellectuals, and was working in Senegal at a research institute, the Institut Français de l'Afrique Noire (IFAN), where he barely earned a living.

I remember asking Sembene why a brilliant historian like Niane was not employed as a professor at the university. He had replied that it was because Senegal, like most African countries, was not truly independent—that it was an appendage of France, capable only of making decisions that had been approved by the *la métropole* (meaning Paris). French scholars had tried to discredit Niane for reworking the text of *Sundiata* into a narrative form similar to Western epics and novels. They accused him of falsifying history by adapting the griots' tale, and of attempting to manipulate public opinion by presenting *Sundiata* as an epic similar to the *Odyssey* and the *Chanson de Roland*. In other words, Western scholars had tried to bury Niane in the dustbin of history—just as they had tried to bury Cheikh Anta Diop, who claimed that Egypt had been inhabited by black Africans at the time it laid the foundations of modern civilization.

Cémoko picked me up around eleven A.M. for a visit to Tamsir's bookstore. I wanted to surprise Tamsir, so I had not made an appointment. Cémoko's dark hue was absorbing the late morning sun like an indigo dye. As he exchanged the traditional morning greeting with me, I noticed that his teeth were black with cigarette smoke and cola stains. Once again, Cémoko knew where he was going. He said that Niane's bookstore was past the airport, behind the market of Medina on the main road to Kankan. When we arrived at the market of Medina, I was struck by the upholstery and carpentry of the wares displayed along the street. There were couches, sofas, beds, chairs, tables, and dressers, all homemade. The Guinean currency, which is virtually worthless in neighboring countries, forces people to produce and consume locally.

Traffic was clogged with shoppers trying to get from one side of the street to the other. I like markets, so I did not mind the delay. Markets are an indication of how well a country is doing; one can see who the shoppers and vendors are, and what products are being sold. Markets reflect the colors and vibrancy of the country. But since Cémoko seemed impatient with the crowd, I was reluctant to ask him to stop so I could fully enjoy the feel of the market by walking around.

Sékou Touré's legacy of self-determination was more evident at the market than at my hotel, where the management had been handed over to Europeans and the customers were virtually all white. The hotel accepted only American dollars or French francs. At the market, people were producing primarily for local consumption. The market—like the airport, where the health officials, customs agents, and gendarmes were mostly women dressed in pants—embodies the new Guinea, which started with Sékou Touré. Here the body was free and modern.

But Afro-pessimism has inverted the meaning of these revolutionary signs. In reality, with his corrupt revolution Sékou Touré shut Guineans out of modernity and at the same time alienated them from their traditions. His dream of a nation sleeping in Guinean-made beds, eating at Guinean-made tables, and wearing cloth made by Guinean weavers has been devalued—like the Guinean currency, which has become a symbol of worthlessness in West Africa. The saying "Don't take me for a Guinean franc!" means "Don't disrespect me!" Since Sékou Touré's death, local products and culture have lost their worth and the respect of the people. The frontiers have been opened, flooding Guinea with foreign consumer products. The French have come back en masse to redress thirty years of retarded economic development, miseducation, and isolation from the civilized world. Guineans have revived their preindependence envy of Frenchness. Afro-pessimism is a good alibi for the recolonization of Africa through consumerism.

But I wonder if the average Guinean views Sékou Touré the same way. I wonder if people believe that Côte d'Ivoire and Senegal, which have had close ties with France for the past thirty years, are more modernized than Guinea. It is important here not to limit the meaning of modernity to a preponderance of tall buildings, electricity, highways, hotels, and shops—in other words, to consumerism and glamor. There are other ways in which Sékou Touré's Guinea ranks in the forefront of African nations. For example, it was one of the first to institute a national currency, without which there can be no real economic independence; it has accorded women great freedom and included them in the modern workforce; and its popular culture (sports, music, the arts) successfully blends tradition and modernity. In fact, from the time of my arrival I had been struck by the way in which the body is free and modern in Guinea, unlike in Mali or Senegal, where tradition still has a strong influence on people's appearance and movement. Whether women are wearing army fatigues, the lab coats of doctors and nurses, or the traditional printed wraparounds, they wear them with a distinctive style that defines their individualism and modernity. They do not hide their bodies, nor do they let their attire become an obstacle to their mobility in the public sphere. Each woman moves like a heroine in Africa's theater of modernization.

As we drove through the market, I wondered about Sékou Touré's legacy. The traffic was so heavy that at times we were forced to stop for more than ten minutes. Cémoko seemed nervous, commenting often on the competence of the other drivers. The air was polluted with smoke. Every time a driver hesitated, pedestrians took advantage of the opportunity to cross the road. Cémoko said that the traffic lights had ceased working soon after Sékou Touré died, and the new government had never bothered to repair them. They had been that way for ten years.

I asked Cémoko what he thought of Sékou Touré. He replied that no other African leader had loved his country and Africa more than Sékou Touré had. Everything Sékou Touré had done, he had done in the interest of his country. He had never put any money in Swiss banks or bought mansions in foreign countries. His family had not even inherited a home after his death: everything of his had belonged to Guinea.

I could see that Cémoko, a Mandinka, was the opposite of Williams

Sassine. Cémoko embraced without criticism everything Sékou Touré had done, even to the point of blaming the victims of the regime's repression. He said that the Susu and the Fulani had been bitter foes even before Sékou Touré came to power. But Sékou Touré had tried his best to stop tribalism and to unite all the Guineans. Sékou Touré had neglected his family and his ethnicity for the unity of all Guinea. But look at how he had been repaid: the Susu had amassed all of the power for themselves, the Fulani could hardly wait for their turn, and the Mandinka had been left with nothing. It was no secret that since Sékou Touré's death, everybody wanted to keep the Mandinka from power. Cémoko's only regret was that Sékou Touré had left nothing for his own people to inherit. There was a Mandinka saying that a man's success is measured by his investment in his fatherland. According to Cémoko, Sékou Touré had failed in that sense: his success had only benefited other ethic groups.

I asked Cémoko what kind of man he thought Sékou Touré had been. He responded that Sékou Touré had been a great man, a great speaker, and a great leader. He had not been an ordinary man, and he had not been small-minded like other African leaders. He had thought big—he had been bigger than Guinea and bigger than Africa. He had been a world leader who could not be ignored by his enemies. He was considered a hero not only in Guinea but all over Africa, because he had not been afraid of white people. He had made black people count in history again, as had Samory Touré and Sundiata Kéita before him.

Cémoko said that Sékou Touré's power had been protected by magic. He had been no ordinary leader—in contrast to the soldiers, who had come to power with guns as their only protection and their only way of speaking to the people. Sékou Touré had been capable of speaking for nine hours nonstop without losing his audience. He had been able to see, from miles away, plots being fomented against him. Sometimes he had transformed himself into a fly that would alight on the wall in order to listen to the conversations of his enemies. Sometimes he had made himself invisible. Sometimes he would appear in places where he was not expected. He had known everything, because he could see where ordinary people could not see and he could read people's minds.

Sékou Touré had derived his magic from his father, Alifa Touré, who had been a great sorcerer. Alifa Touré had come from Mali, and had moved to Guinea because he knew that a great son would be born to him there. Alifa Touré had known that he would have to make a big sacrifice to the gods to prepare for the arrival of the child, who was predestined to be a great ruler. The elders of the cult of hunters in Mali, who were masters at predicting the future and seeing beyond space and time, had recommended the sacrifice of sixty black bulls, after declaring that Farana was to be the birthplace of the future ruler, who would be greater than Samory Touré. Alifa Touré had been a poor man and could not afford to sacrifice sixty bulls. But as if possessed by uncontrollable forces, he had left Mali on foot, and, after walking many miles through several cities and villages, had settled in Farana, where he had become a butcher. Every time he had slaughtered a black bull, he had given away the left hind thigh to the oldest lady in Farana. He had stashed away a bundle of sixty sticks, and every time he had sacrificed the left hind thigh of a black bull, he had pulled out one stick, until there had been none left. Then he had married Aminata Fadiga, Sékou Touré's mother.

People did not realize, said Cémoko, that Sékou Touré had come to power in 1958, exactly sixty years after the death of Samory Touré, who had fought against French colonialism for eighteen years. Sékou Touré himself had died at age sixty.

I asked Cémoko what he thought this meant. Would we have to wait for the sixtieth anniversary of Sékou Touré's death to witness the emergence of another hero? Cémoko said he did not know, but it showed that Sékou Touré had not been an ordinary man. Like Sundiata and Samory, he had been able to awaken the whole of Africa to the idea of the preciousness of freedom, and now that he was gone the region had gone back to sleep for a long time. Another puzzle remained, however. Cémoko said that Sékou Touré was not in his grave in Guinea. And Samory Touré had not been buried in West Africa either—the French army had taken his body all the way to Gabon. This is why we had to see Sékou Touré as the reincarnation—as the return—of Samory Touré. Cémoko said that the profane could never read our mysteries correctly, let alone recognize Samory in Sékou Touré.

The fact was, said Cémoko, that Guinea—like most African countries—had been difficult to unite after colonialism. The Susus and Fulanis had been competing for the attention of French colonial administrators. When Sékou Touré arrived, his attempt to unite the country against France had been perceived by the Fulanis, who in those days held many important offices with the colonial administration, as an assault on their ethnic group. Ever since, the Fulanis had plotted coups d'état against Sékou Touré. Guineans, Cémoko said, were false through and through. Sékou Touré had helped many of them, and had even trusted them with important positions. But they had not been satisfied until they had attempted a coup d'état against him. Even Lassana Conte, the current leader of the country, had been shaped by Sékou Touré: he had been a presidential guard and a protégé of Sékou Touré. Who would have thought that Conte would put Sékou Touré's family in jail, and mobilize the whole country into a conspiracy against the Mandinka people?

Cémoko said that Sékou Touré had never used one tribe against another for political gain. In fact, that was the reason the Mandinka thought he had not behaved like a legitimate son of his tribe. For only an illegitimate son would ignore his own tribe and family to help others. The horrible things that had taken place at Camp Boiro had been the fault of Sékou Touré's half-brothers, Issiaka and Soumaila Touré. Sékou Touré had been very much under the influence of his uncles in Farana, which is 150 kilometers from Conakry. All important decisions had been made by the family there. And since Sékou Touré had had an uncle who was older than he, Sékou Touré had found it necessary to submit to the will of that uncle. He had been unable to contradict his uncle, even though he was the president of Guinea. That was the African way. So his half-bothers, Issiaka and Soumaila, had sowed terror in Guinea, and Sékou Touré had been powerless to do anything about it.

Sékou Touré, said Cémoko, had warned Guineans that one day he would not be around—and they would wish that he were, so that he could protect them against France's recolonization of the land and the humiliation of not being masters in their own country. Now French people were back in control in Guinea, the economic crises were worse than they had ever been, and tribalism and corruption had reared their ugly heads. Everything had to be obtained through bribes. To get a driver's license, Cémoko said, he had had to drive across the frontier to Mali to take a test. He couldn't have gotten one in Guinea without a beautiful sister or a lot of money to use as a bribe.

Yes indeed—Sékou Touré had warned the Guineans. He had often stood at the Palais du Peuple and said: You'll miss me one day, when my sun is no more. When my sun goes down, it will be like the sun of Sundiata and the sun of Samory. You'll wish I had never left, for your enemies will use Guinea as their playground with no regard for your dignity and your welfare. People of Guinea, you are now taking your freedom for granted, but one day you will miss me and your freedom and your pride.

As Cémoko fondly reminisced about Sékou Touré, I was beginning to understand what Sassine meant by Africa's yearning for great myths. Cémoko's Sékou Touré had taken himself for Sundiata, the great emperor of Mali, who in turn had aspired to surpass the glory of Alexander the Great, as mentioned several times in Niane's version of the epic of old Mali. Cémoko was correct in his description of Sékou Touré as a world leader who represented Africa's position on global political, cultural, and economic issues—unlike other African presidents, who merely received their marching orders from France and other countries in the West. But Sassine's analysis of the blind side of such ambition is also on the mark. Many Guineans had been sense-lessly tortured and killed, thereby putting the merits of Sékou Touré's revolution in doubt. The problem with great myths, as we know, is that wherever they have existed, they have been accompanied by usually untold stories of massacres and genocide. A major difference between Sékou Touré and his predecessors Sundiata and Samory is that the hand that molds great myths is today watched by modern information systems such as radio, newspapers, and television, and by the moral authority of international human rights groups. It was the philosophy of this new humanism that enabled Sassine to condemn Sékou Touré's revolution for its cruelty to his political opponents.

4

▲▼▲

Return Narratives

Niane's *Sundiata:* The Power of the Griot

We arrived at Djibril Tamsir Niane's bookstore. Workers were busy fixing the road with jackhammers and rollers. The air was thick with brown dust and earsplitting noise. The store was closed because of the construction work, but I could see the sign, "Librairie du Niger," covered with dust atop a blue metallic door, and a few crumbling books and school supplies in the window. Cémoko said that we should park the car and knock on the door adjacent to the bookstore. It was Niane's house. A watchman at the door told us to wait while he went to call the host. He came back with a woman in her fifties. She was wearing a blue gown called a *bassan doloki,* and a long white scarf covering her head and neck like a veil; only her face was visible. She was chewing on a stick which is used in West Africa as a toothbrush. Her attire suggested that she might have accomplished her pilgrimage to Mecca, and deserved to be addressed with the honorific title "Hadja."

She was Mrs. Niane. She informed us that her husband was out of the country and that the bookstore was closed until the road construction was completed. I introduced myself as an old friend of her husband's, and asked if I could look around the bookstore. She invited us into the store and offered us some water as a sign of welcome. Many of the books were in boxes, and the shelves were coated with the reddish-brown dust. I asked her if there were any books on Sékou Touré or the history of Guinea. She said that there weren't any. The store specialized in school supplies and contemporary bestsellers and thrillers from France. I took my leave, somewhat disappointed in the bookstore. She was quite a nice woman, who spoke a very clear French that reminded me of my elementary school teachers. She looked dignified in a traditional way, more like a mother figure than the businesswoman I would have expected.

My brief encounter with Mrs. Niane left an unforgettable impression on me. Her face looked so peaceful and confident that it seemed immune to the impact of the previous fifty years of vicissitudes. Revolutions have come and gone, but she was like a rock that had been shaped during Sundiata's empire, or during that of El Hadji Oumar or Samory. She had made the French words hers to such an extent that they did not stand in the way of her Muslim faith and her Fulani and Mande culture. She reminded me of La Grande Royale in Cheikh Hamidou Kane's *Ambiguous Adventure,* and of many respectable women from my own childhood, even though she was not much older than people of my own generation.

I began to wonder whether Mrs. Niane and other women and men like her did not constitute Sékou Touré's Achilles heel. They were a breed apart—people who refused to embrace modernity fully, who still valued the best in clans, tribes, and family names. They refused to participate in the catch-up race that modernization had condemned Africans to, and they persistently regarded the past, particularly the Sundiata empire, as their glorious future. In this sense, it was modernity that had to catch up with them, not the other way around. As Cémoko's portrait of Sékou Touré suggests, the Guinean revolution had always had to suppress caste and ethnic divisions. But Sékou Touré himself had from the outset been trapped by tradition: he had been forced to defer to his uncle in Farana when making important decisions, and to use his half-brothers as his right-hand men in his ostensibly modern and revolutionary government. The snare of tradition was also apparent in the Sundiata-like legend that surrounded Sékou Touré's birth and in his reputed knowledge of magic. The mystery concerning the whereabouts of his body reminded me of the legend of Soumaoro Kante, the evil king of Susu, whose body could not be found after he had been defeated by Sundiata in battle.

In fact, the continuing influence of Sundiata and his thirteenth-century empire is greater than that of modern institutions, largely because the former produced a caste of people called "griots" who still control the definition of identity in the region. In Niane's book, the griot who recounts the tale of Sundiata states that whoever knows the history of a country can read its future. In West Africa, griots "are the depositories of oaths which the ancestors swore." They therefore control the imposition of taboos, the meanings of heroism, and the boundaries between clans and tribes. Griots "know the history of kings and kingdoms, and that is why they are the best counselors of kings. Every king wants to have a singer to perpetuate his memory" (Niane, 1965: 40).

Even today in West Africa, everybody wants the griot to sing his or her praises, for there is no recognition without a griot who can immortalize the deeds through his art. Lack of recognition by the griots is tantamount to failure in society. It is in this sense that rich and poor, modern intellectuals and peasants, men and women alike seek the favors of griots. No one is important enough or respectable enough until he or she attracts the attention of griots. As the narrator in *Sundiata* puts it, "I am the word and you are the deed; now your destiny begins" (58).

Indeed, the griots have enormous influence over the destinies of the Mande, or Mandinka, people, descendants of the thirteenth-century Empire of Mali. (Mande-speaking groups are found in Gambia, Guinea-Conakry, Guinea-Bissau, Liberia, Sierra Leone, Senegal, Mali, Burkina Faso, Mauritania, and Côte d'Ivoire.) Some people are pushed into exceptionalism and selfishness to get the griots' attention; others, after studying at the most prestigious universities, renounce modernity to engage in still-celebrated medieval performances that originated in Sundiata's empire. Presidents have their own griots, who compare their leaders to Sundiata or to kings and generals who made names for themselves as Mande heroes. Thus, in Mande culture, heroism is a function of the griots' songs.

For this reason, I thought about exploring further the role of griots in the epic *Sundiata* and in present-day Mande West Africa. Not only have griots fixed for eternity the meaning of the hero, the leader, and identity in Mande societies; their narratives have also constituted an insurmountable obstacle toward modernity for men like Sékou Touré. There are at least three songs in *Sundiata* which correspond to the key transitional moments in the life of the hero, and which still serve to define Mande character in the twentieth century. These songs—"Simbon" (also known as "Hymn to the Bow"), "Duga" (also known as "Janjon" or "Song of the Vulture"), and "Sundiata" (also known as "Niama" or "The Glory of Mali")—were composed by Bala Faseke Kouyate, Sundiata's griot. Today they constitute the deep structure of the popular music of such stars as Salif Kéita, Mory Kante, Toumani Diabaté, Oumou Sangaré, and Bambu Suso, who are singers and composers from Mali, Guinea, and Gambia. The independence generation of the Sixties also scored the songs for electric guitar and piano, and translated them into French, in order to define the identities of the new nations. In their many transformations and adaptations, these songs served on the one hand to maintain the authenticity of Mande culture in the region, and on the other hand to consolidate the practice of certain archaic customs such as polygamy, magic, witchcraft, caste structure, and clan allegiance as necessary elements of the environment of the Mande hero.

The first song, "Simbon," corresponds to a revelation—a sign of one's manhood, of great things to come, of departure from the status quo. It sings of the day Sundiata, the seven-year-old crippled son of Sogolon Kolonkan, puts his weight on an iron staff so that he can stand up. The staff bends into the shape of a bow, which Sundiata uses to hunt buffalo and elephants. On the day he first walks, Sundiata also singlehandedly uproots a baobab tree, which he plants in front of his mother's house in order to spare her the shame of having to beg other women for baobab leaves. The song is thus for Sundiata and Sogolon Kolonkan, his indefatigable mother, who for seven years has endured the humiliation and pain of having a crippled son. In Mande culture, children are good because their mothers suffered during the process of raising them. That is why there is a saying, "Each is his mother's child." In other words, the mother's suffering is reflected in the heroism or lack of heroism of her child.

"Simbon" commemorates the deeds of the best Mande hunters, among whom Sundiata has no equal. It heralds the arrival of the incomparable hunter, the one whose totem is the lion, the one who is king among kings, the sorcerer who sees beyond the naked eye and the night and who knows all the secrets of the wilderness. "Simbon" also praises the characteristics of someone who, like Sundiata, restores the honor of deprived and oppressed people. The song calls for people to come out and see "how wonderful is the day Sundiata walked; God has not made a day like this one." It is a song that marks with a vengeance the beginning of a new era.

When modern-day Mali acquired its independence in 1960, it used several excerpts from the melody of "Simbon" in its national anthem. The fact that the first president of the republic, Modibo Kéita, had the same last name as Sundiata filled people with hope for the future, and there were predictions that the new leader would perform heroic feats. "Simbon" is sung today in nightclubs and at concerts by superstars like Salif Kéita and Mory Kante, who exhort Mande audiences to new forms of heroism which, like Sundiata's uprooting of the baobab tree, will avenge the people for all their suffering and humiliation.

"Duga," or "Song of the Vulture," is also about heroism. Bala Faseke Kouyate composed it on the eve of the decisive battle between Sundiata and his archenemy, Soumaoro Kante. It is a song of war in which the griot asks the heroes to remove every vestige of fear from their hearts. "Men of Mande, tomorrow let me sing you the song of vultures, for I want to see your enemies' blood run like a river." The vulture eats its prey with its beak, while scratching the ground with its claws. For Mande people, these gestures symbolize destruction and creation at the same time. Bala Faseke Kouyate's song asks Sundiata and the brave warriors to dance on the battlefield like a vulture, destroying one life in order to plant another. "Duga" is also a song about reincarnation—about the way in which men can appear on the battlefield in the shape of terrible animals, or in the guise of the most fearless warriors their lineage has ever known.

"Duga" is primarily a military song which valorizes brutal power, fearlessness, and cunning battle strategies. One explanation for the song's survival from the thirteenth century to the present is the continual involvement of the region in armed conflicts: the Mali Empire's conquests of smaller kingdoms in Senegal and Gambia; wars of resistance against Muslim crusades, the European slave trade, and colonialism; the two world wars; and the postindependence military coups. The griots have immortalized several war heroes with "Song of the Vulture," putting their names next to Sundiata's and comparing their battlefields to Krina, where the first emperor of Mali defeated the Susu army. The military leaders whose praise songs awaken structures of feeling similar to those of "Duga" in Mande culture include Tira Maghan, who fought in Sundiata's army; Bakari Jan, a nineteenth-century king of Segou; and Jajuru, a Bambara warrior of the early twentieth century who "fought like a whole army." Now that there are no wars, the griots sing "Duga" for the military men who took power away from civilians. The philosophy behind "Song of the Vulture" is that "strength makes a law of its own and power allows no division" (62).

It is clear from the persistence of "Duga" through the ages that the Mande people reserve their esteem and admiration for a leader who, like Sundiata, carries authority in his voice, has arms like iron, and is "the husband of power" (47). In Souleymane Cissé's film *Finye* (1982),

the military governor puts it plainly to the students who are demonstrating for more democracy: "Our power is a manly power; no one
can take it away from us. If you do not cooperate, we will kill all of
you." The resistance to democracy in the region also has to do with the
fear of losing one's masculinity, which is celebrated in "Duga."

Another reason for the song's survival into the present is the manner
in which the concept of the hero has been appropriated for such
postempire occupations as farming, trade, politics, and overseas work.
The griots now praise as a hero anyone who distinguishes himself by
emigrating to France as a worker and returning with savings which he
distributes among them. The Mande men who smuggle precious stones
out of Zaire, Zambia, and Liberia are also called heroes when they
return home with their fortunes. "Janjon," a song that belongs to the
"Duga" genre and that was formerly used to praise brave warriors and
deride the fainthearted who fled during battle, has now been appropriated to describe the fearlessness of Mande traders who smuggle diamonds across national frontiers. Despite the colonial and neocolonial
domination of Mande West Africa by the West, and the religious
influence of Islam, it seems that the actions of the hero still belong to the
"Duga" genre, which the griots feel free to extend to new social themes
and events. In other words, "Duga" leaves room for modern heroes
who desire to emulate those of the past.

"Simbon" and "Duga" emphasize heroism, magic, fearlessness,
masculinity, and danger in Mande culture. "Simbon" reveals the hero
in unexpected places, signifying that the outer trappings of heroism
count less than fearlessness and manhood. "Simbon" is a song for
hunters. "Duga," in contrast, is a warrior song, a song for empire
builders. "Duga" is therefore more inclusive than "Simbon," which
addresses itself more strictly to the hunter clans of the Bambara,
Mandinka, and Senufo.

The third Mande song with a lasting influence on the character of
people today is "Sundiata," also known as "Niama." "Sundiata" is
about leadership, unity, and peace. It commemorates the return of the

hero from the battlefield and the lasting peace and joy he brings to the people: "He has come and happiness has come; Sundiata is here and happiness is here" (79). "Sundiata" is a song of celebration, greatness, mythmaking, and the consecration of a king: "Niama, Niama, Niama: You, you serve as a shelter for all. All come to seek refuge under you. And as for you, Niama, nothing serves you for shelter; God alone protects you." The song comments on the generosity of the leader, his unlimited wealth, his love, power, and impartiality. It asks the children of Mande to love one another the way the king loves them. It says that Mande is the best nation in the world, that the sons of Mande have everything.

"Sundiata" is a long narrative song about the triumph of the king of Mande. Depending on the type of celebration, marriage, initiation, harvest, or political rally, the griots who sing it emphasize different episodes in the life of Sundiata. Their aim is always to establish continuity between the event being celebrated and the shining moment of the Mande Empire, which Sundiata symbolizes. Young boys dream of greatness by listening to the story of Sundiata, who grew from a hunter of the category of Simbon into a Duga-like warrior and a great leader. When griots sing the song in honor of present-day officeholders, it awakens in its hearers feelings of vindication and victory; the song restores people to their thirteenth-century greatness. Let us not forget that Sundiata, through the griots' songs, gave to the people in the region what no one else could bestow on them: he defeated an oppressor and transformed his father's village and clan into an empire. Today, there is no one to fill Sundiata's shoes, to wash away the shame of European neocolonialism and the oppression by African dictators. Sundiata's story is the proof of every Mande man's heroism and greatness. Once a crippled porter, he became a world leader whom the griots compare to Alexander the Great.

The griots place this mirror of Sundiata's greatness in front of contemporary leaders and the people. The songs constantly exhort the population to step into Sundiata's shoes, to overthrow foreign domination, and to return to the glory of old Mali. So far, the griots' songs have prevailed over philosophies of modernity, which might have persuaded the people that there are advantages to emancipating women, dissolving caste systems, and sharing power. Sékou Touré's dependence on a Sundiata-like heroism reflects both the limitations of his kind of modern African socialism, and his popularity in West Africa.

Salif Kéita's "Mandjou"

In a recent song by Salif Kéita entitled "Mandjou," Sékou Touré is great because of the characteristics of his leadership, which remind us of the Sundiata Kéita, Mansa Moussa, and Samory Touré of the griots' songs. "Mandjou" celebrates Sékou Touré first by tracing his nobility through the bloodline of Samory Touré, a great resistance leader who fought against the spread of French influence in the region at the end of the nineteenth century. As the genre dictates in "Sundiata" and other Mande songs of celebration, Salif Kéita uses the opening of "Mandjou" to cite the names of all Sékou Touré's relatives: "Do not cry, Touré, the grandson of Almamy Touré, the son of Alifa Touré and Aminata Fadiga, the brother of Aramata Touré, Kukumba and Issiaka Touré. Do not cry; there is only cause for celebration."

In Mande, the last name is proof of legitimacy and nobility, and the further back the last name goes (possibly all the way to the beginning of the Empire of Mali), the bigger the first name becomes. In Mande, you are your mother's child and her good behavior may elevate you. But it is your last name, the one you receive from your father, which removes doubts about your nobility, authenticity, capacity for heroism, and commitment to your word. This is why Salif Kéita cites all the Touré heroes who bring honor to Sékou Touré.

"Mandjou" then proceeds to commemorate Sékou Touré's greatness in the same way the song "Sundiata" consecrates the leadership of the king of Mali. Sékou Touré is "Mandjou, owner of the truth of eloquence, faith, peace, unity, love, and wealth." Salif Kéita praises

Sékou Touré for vindicating Guineans and bringing them honor, for securing independence for them, and for providing enough food for all. He says, "Mandjou, do not cry—for there is no one like you, and no one has done what you did for your people."

With this song, Salif Kéita captured the imagination of Mande West Africa. The refrain, "Mandjou, do not cry," elevates Sékou Touré to the rank of Sundiata Kéita and Samory Touré. It implies that the Guinean leader, like his predecessors, was guided by a divine force to free and defend his people, that Sékou Touré had achieved perfection in his leadership, and hence that there is nothing to regret or to weep about. The refrain also summons the listener to participate in the glory of a true Mande leader—one whose lifetime echoes the great moments in Mande history. The listener identifies with Sékou Touré as a hero who is misunderstood, or who has been maligned. "Mandjou, do not cry," means that history will vindicate him and that his enemies will be proved wrong. "Mandjou, do not cry," positions Sékou Touré—like Sundiata in "Simbon"—as a victim whose time will come. It says that the Mande hero is right, even if the world refuses to recognize him.

Ten years after Sékou Touré's death, Salif Kéita reissued "Mandjou" on an album entitled *Folon.* Interestingly, the title song, "Folon," evokes the past, the time of the ancestors, when people lived by their words, were fearless, and avoided acts and things that would dishonor them. The version of "Mandjou" on this album displays more emotion on the part of the singer, and awakens more feelings of nostalgia in the listener. When people asked Salif Kéita, on tour in the United States, why he reissued a song which immortalizes Sékou Touré, he answered that he himself loved the song: "'Mandjou' is the truth."

"Mandjou" is an infectious song that fills the listener with the sensation of the victory of the old ways over the present, of the omnipresence and omnipotence of Mande culture. To surrender to "Mandjou" is to accept Sékou Touré unconditionally; it is also to give in to the griots' version of the history of Guinea. As an African intellectual, I have looked at the griots' version of history with some doubt, knowing that they are prone to flattery and to stroking the egos of their listeners. Salif Kéita, who is not a griot, has succeeded with "Mandjou," a griotic tour de force. Despite my resistance to embracing what I consider archaic aspects of tradition, he brings back to life within me an unquestioned identification with Mande structures of feeling.

Salif Kéita, like Sékou Touré, is therefore an ambiguous modern hero for me. Both defy white colonial supremacy through authentic voices that they derive from Mande culture. But ironically, the pull of tradition has prevented each of them from reaching his goal: in Sékou Touré's case, African unity; and in Salif Kéita's case, international appeal beyond the ghetto of ethnic and folk music.

On the surface, Salif Kéita is modern because he defies the dictates of clan and caste, which are the backbone of Mande tradition, to become a "modern griot." A son of the Kéita clan, Salif Kéita is noble by birth and therefore exempt from the limited future imposed on the casted clans, who are condemned to such lowly occupations as blacksmith, leatherworker, slave, and griot. In traditional Mande, it is beneath noble men to be dancers, singers, or public speakers. The Mande believe that words are for griots and other people of caste: "But words are nothing but words; power lies in deeds. Be a man of action; do not answer me any more with your mouth, but tomorrow, on the plain of Krina, show me what you would have me recount to coming generations" (Niane, 1965: 63). When a noble man dances, sings, or talks "too much," he has become a griot, which is equivalent to not being a man of his word. A griot is a man of several words, and therefore a liar. To talk "too much" in Mande is also a sign of femininity in a noble man. In Mande, griots, women, and slaves are judged by their words and the indecent display of their bodies through dance and other performances. But a noble man can lose his dignity through similar conduct.

Salif Kéita is a product of the 1960s independence movement, which declared people of caste and women equal to noble men in Mande West Africa. Salif Kéita's modernization began when he left his village and settled in the city of Bamako, capital of Mali. Like many young men and women of the Sixties, he came to the city in search of the modernity portrayed in "B" movies; Saturday night parties filled with Cuban cha-chas, American rhythm-and-blues, and French melodies; boulevards lined with shops selling the latest fashions from France. He was more at ease in the city, where his albino coloring made him less of an outcast. In Mande culture, albinos are considered bad luck. Kings used to sacrifice them to prevent calamities from befalling their kingdoms.

Having endured the status of an outcast in his village, Salif Kéita found refuge in the city among the new *Lumpenproletariat*. He played guitar and sang in back-alley bars, meat-grilling joints called *dibi* that were gathering-places for the least fortunate, who could not afford the nightclubs at the Grand Hotel, the Lido, and the Trois Caimans. In addition to being an outcast among the Kéita clan because of his musical career and his albinism, Salif Kéita is set apart by his high-pitched voice, which places him in a category with female griots. In Mande, male griots usually play instruments and recite verses in praise of noble heroes, leaving to women the songs that require higher voices. Salif Kéita is among the few Mande male singers who can compete with griot women—that is, who sing the classic Sundiata songs with comparable emotion, operatic force, and vocal versatility. In 1969, when the Rail Band was looking for a lead singer in an effort to change its image from a band playing Latin music to one oriented toward authenticity, it hired Salif Kéita. Along with Mory Kante, he contributed to the modern revival of Mande songs performed to the accompaniment of such instruments as electric guitar, piano, bass, and drums, as well as the traditional Mande balafon, ngoni, and kora.

Salif Kéita is thus a modern hero because he has made Mande music, Sundiata's praise songs, an important part of the world-music genre. He is also a hero because he represents on the stage the outcast, the albino, and the female—all symbolized by his own persona and voice as the image of Mali's modernity. The world today comes to know

Mande West Africa not through the historical accounts of heroes like Sundiata or Samory, or the deeds of contemporary politicians and soldiers, but through the music of artists like Salif Kéita, the modern griots.

But to my mind, Salif Kéita's music, like Sékou Touré's politics, has not subverted Mande culture enough. Both of them stop short of totally liberating the Mande character from the Sundiata-like heroism that still works to maintain the clan—the symbolic capital of the last name—and therefore the superiority of noble families over people of caste, and of men over women. The great achievement of songs like "Mandjou" is that they distribute the role of the hero to all people in Mande West Africa. Salif Kéita's songs induce the audience to identify with the dreams of poor people and outcasts—with their desire to become heroes, rich and powerful. They thus rethematize the major tenets of Mande masculinity.

In my view, the real challenge posed by Sundiata, not only to Sékou Touré and Salif Kéita but to all of us who hail from the region, is to avoid the griot's snare in our attempt to build our modernity on the ruins of the Mande Empire. Sundiata transformed his father's village into an empire by changing "Simbon" hunters into fearsome "Duga" warriors. He built institutions which were based on the autonomy of clans, the undivided authority of the king, and the superiority of men over women. These institutions, far from collapsing under the influence of several centuries of Islam, colonization by Western powers, and recent trends toward globalization, have in some areas been strengthened by them. During the independence era, the Cold War became the most intimate partner of ethnic groups and clans in West Africa, as the French government began to support them against Sékou Touré's regime. The question in my mind is, how can we further modernity by transforming Sundiata's empire into a clanless and democratic united Mande state? How can we transfigure farmers and factory workers, engineers and schoolteachers, men and women into heroes of our modernity—into people who put their lives on the line to build railroads, hospitals, and dams? To judge from Niane's classic book, the task will not be easy: "Maghan Sundiata was unique. In his own time no one equaled him, and after him no one had the ambition to surpass him. He left his mark on Mali for all time, and his taboos still guide men to their conduct" (83).

Afro-Kitsch and Woodstock in Bamako

I came back to the hotel with my head full of *Sundiata,* the impact of the griots on our lives, and the serene face of Mrs. Niane. I turned on the television to catch up with the O. J. Simpson saga. CNN has the power to connect me to America (which I now consider my second home) as a child is connected to its mother's breast. The news felt reassuring, and for the moment I forgot that I was not in the United States. Snow was falling in New York and Philadelphia; airports in the Northeast were shut down because of the weather, which put a damper on the Republican primaries in New Hampshire; in Los Angeles, women were going in busloads to see the movie version of Terry McMillan's *Waiting to Exhale;* O. J. Simpson had been spotted in a fancy restaurant in Beverly Hills; the L.A. chapter of the National Organization for Women was venting its anger over his acquittal. But soon CNN began to repeat itself, and my mind turned to the griots.

I have been fascinated with griots and the power of song since I was young. When I was in high school in Mali (where my family moved after leaving Guinea), I had a friend named Seydou Ly. We used to call him Sly, because of his Afro hairdo (which he still wears) and because of his love for the blues. When we were in high school, our group, which was called the Rockers, often met at his house for tea, grilled meat, and music. Some members of the group played guitar, and there was a turntable with piles of rock and R&B records: James Brown, Wilson Pickett, Otis Redding, Jimi Hendrix, Howlin' Wolf, Aretha Franklin, Nina Simone, Ike and Tina Turner, Sly and the Family Stone, B. B. King, Buddy Miles, and Albert King, as well as white musicians such as the Rolling Stones, Bob Dylan, Paul Simon, Carole King, Joni Mitchell, the Who, the Cream, Faces, the Grateful Dead, Joe Cocker, the Doors, Led Zeppelin, Grand Funk Railroad, Steppenwolf, and Crosby, Stills, Nash, and Young. We wore shirts with peace signs and flowers on them; we smoked marijuana; we were against the war in Vietnam and apartheid in South Africa; we supported Black Power, the Black Panthers, and the Black Muslims in America.

Seydou Ly (Sly) and I, along with a few others in the group, thought that our Afros had power enough to set us apart from our peers in Bamako and to transform us into black Americans, whom we admired so much. The imagination of the youth in Africa at the time was captured by the defiant images of George Jackson, Angela Davis, Muhammad Ali, Eldridge Cleaver, Malcolm X, and James Brown. We used to spend hours washing our hair with special shampoos and combing it. We dressed to resemble our black American heroes. We walked tall in packs and pretended we couldn't speak French. We called one another by our American nicknames, and slowly we became aware of race in our daily relations with French people. We began to see racism where others before us would have seen colonialism and class exploitation.

We felt that we were immersed in world youth culture and far ahead of our peers, who did not listen to Jimi Hendrix or even know about Woodstock. We decided to organize our own Woodstock in Bamako, to educate people. Sly and I knew the music of all the musicians who had played at Woodstock, and we wanted to make sure that our Woodstock-in-Bamako would present the real thing, not imitations from France or African musicians stuck in Cuban jazz. We especially did not want any Johnny Hallyday records—we considered him too French to be a genuine rock-and-roller. Aside from musical authenticity, we also wanted our Woodstock-in-Bamako to include a competition for best outfit, a teach-in on freedom, and enough marijuana for everybody.

We rented for the event a place in the center of Bamako called the

Maison des Anciens Combattants, a veterans' building, which had space for theatrical performances and a bar. There was a man in Bamako called Addy Sow who had just come from Switzerland with plenty of new albums that we could use, in addition to our own collection. Addy Sow was a member of a group called the Beatles of Bamako, who were older than we were. So we designated him the leader of our Woodstock. We made huge posters displaying a drawing of Jimi Hendrix with the slogan "Woodstock-à-Bamako," and we invited all the youth groups in the city to attend. These groups—which consisted mostly of young men, but did include some women—bore names like the Rolling Stones, the Sofa ("knights"), the Tonjon ("foot soldiers"), the Kings, and the Stars. Our biggest rivals were called the Soul Brothers.

On the day of the event, Sly and I prepared together to go to the Maison des Anciens Combattants. We spent the entire afternoon "doing" our Afros. Then Sly put on a mud-cloth (traditional cotton) vest with a V-sign drawn on the back and "SLY" written underneath. He also had "SLY" written vertically on the vest's front, on both the left and the right. He wore juju necklaces and bracelets. He had on Levi jeans ornamented with holes and fringes. He really looked like Sly of Sly and the Family Stone. I wore a red cotton-and-polyester short-sleeved shirt with "Keep on Truckin'" written on the back of it. Over the shirt I put on my embroidered blue-satin jacket, combining these with my blue bell-bottom trousers and my red clogs from Denmark. When I had added my Venetian-glass necklace, my cowrie-shell juju bracelets, and my dark glasses, not only did I look like Jimi Hendrix—I felt like his reincarnation.

People admired us on our way to Woodstock-in-Bamako. We felt good about that. When we arrived, the amplifiers were blaring "With a Little Help from My Friends," by Joe Cocker. There were many people who had copied our style—that is, they were dressed like Jimi Hendrix, George Harrison, Richie Havens, Buddy Miles, Sly Stone, Frank Zappa, Alice Cooper, and James Brown. But there were some who had donned traditional hunter suits: tight-fitting trousers and mud-cloth blouses oversewn with cowrie shells and mirrors. Some of them wore hunters' elongated hats, which covered their ears and cheeks all the way to their chins. They had bows and arrows, and they looked like Simbon initiates. Needless to add, many of these people belonged to our rival group, the Soul Brothers. There was smoke in the air, and Sly and I really felt good about ourselves.

Soon Jimi Hendrix's "Voodoo Child" filled the air, and by then we were on top of the world. The songs we played that night, the marijuana joints, and the Afros helped to cement my friendship with Sly and other members of the Rockers. I remember taking the podium at the teach-in and talking about peace, with quotes from Bob Dylan's "The Times They Are A'Changin'," Marvin Gaye's "What's Going On?," Jimi Hendrix's "The Wind Cries Mary," and Grand Funk Railroad's "I Am Your Captain." Sly said that I'd done well, because I had mentioned the songs he dug the most.

I do not remember who won the prize for best outfit, or how many people fell asleep on the premises, stoned. But Woodstock-in-Bamako opened the door for the creation of Afro-rock bands in Bamako, and it was one of the important highlights of my friendship with Seydou Ly, a.k.a. Sly.

We were kitsch, and we were living on the cutting edge. In 1965, I remember, Radio Mali advertised a concert by Junior Wells and his All Stars at the Omnisport in Bamako. They were described as a Chicago-based group that was going to electrify the audience with tunes made famous by such artists as Otis Redding, Wilson Pickett, and James Brown. I was very excited, because I had records by Junior Walker, and in those days, when my English was limited, Junior Wells and Junior Walker were one and the same to me. It was a little disappointing that we could not have James Brown in person. I had heard that Anglophone countries (Ghana, Liberia, Nigeria) were luckier. They could see James Brown on television, and they even had live concerts by Tyrone Davis, Aretha Franklin, and Wilson Pickett.

Sure enough, the concert was electrifying. Junior Wells and his All Stars played "My Girl," "I've Been Loving You Too Long," "It's a Man's World," "There Was a Time," "I Can't Stand Myself," "Papa's Got a Brand-New Bag," "Respect," "Midnight Hour," and "Say It Loud—I'm Black and I'm Proud."

During the break, some of us were allowed to talk with the musicians and ask for autographs. A white guy from the United States Information Agency was the translator between us. I remember distinguishing myself by bypassing the translator and directly asking one of the musicians in English, "What is your name?" His eyes lit up as he told me his name and asked for mine. I said, "My name is Manthia, but my friends call me J.B." He said something about James Brown, and I said something further. By this time, everybody was quiet and looking at us. My total experience with English consisted of two years of classes in junior high school and three month-long summer vacations in Liberia. I'd gotten the J.B. from James Brown's songs.

The next day, the news traveled all over Bamako that I spoke English like an American. This was tremendous in a Francophone country, where one acquired subjecthood through *Francité*—that is, thinking via French grammar and logic. Our master thinker in those days was Jean-Paul Sartre. We were also living in awe, a form of silence, at the thought that to be Francophone subjects we had to be as adept at *Francité* as Senghor, who spoke French better than the French. By being considered as one who spoke English like an American and was able to converse fluently with star musicians, I was acquiring a new and equal type of subjecthood that put me perhaps above my comrades, who knew Sartre's "Chemin de la Liberté" by heart. I was in the vanguard. I was on the front line of the revolution. You see, for me and for many of my friends, to be liberated was to be exposed to more R&B songs and to be up on the latest news about Muhammad Ali, George Jackson, Angela Davis, Malcolm X, and Martin Luther King Jr., all of whom were becoming an alternative source of cultural capital for African youth and were creating within us new structures of feeling,

which enabled us to subvert the hegemony of *Francité* after independence.

Sly dropped out of school in the ninth grade and eventually became a successful businessman. Today he and I are both in our forties, and our friendship is still going strong. We have increased our repertory of music to include jazz and African music. Every time I visit Sly, I bring him the latest jazz and blues from America. In other areas, he has become more conservative. He is wealthy, and attracts many griots at his business during the day and at his home in the evening. They sing his praises, and he gives them money.

Two very cool young men, photographed in 1963 (left) and 1964. (Photos by Malick Sidibé. Copyright © Sidibé, C.A.A.C., The Pigozzi Collection, Geneva.)

One day, as we were taking a stroll at his ranch some years ago, Sly confided to me that he sometimes felt like giving a lot of money to one of the top griots, so that he could have a song written just for him. He said that in Mali, no matter what you did or gave away, you were nobody unless there was a griot who could set you apart with a song. As an example, he cited Babani Touré, a *nouveau riche* who had come to Bamako and given away millions to griots. Salif Kéita had written a song for him.

An admirer of James Brown with one of his albums, 1970. (Photo by Malick Sidibé. Copyright © Sidibé, C.A.A.C., The Pigozzi Collection, Geneva.)

One of our Rockers' parties, early 1970s. Seydou Ly (a.k.a. Sly) is standing at the far right. (Collection of Manthia Diawara.)

The president of the Rockers, Seydou Coulibaly (a.k.a. Joe Cuba), early 1970s. He's the one on the right. (Collection of Manthia Diawara.)

My cousin Yaya Diawara (a.k.a. Alvin Lee), Bamako, 1973. (Photo by Malick Sidibé; collection of Manthia Diawara.)

I said that I was firmly opposed to giving a lot of money to a griot so he would sing my praises. In fact, I was opposed to handing out money to griots, period. I believed that a person created history by building something which engaged and benefited others. Sly was already doing this with his paint factory, where he employed more than fifty people. He also supported his extended family in Bamako and in his father's village. I told him that if he had some extra money to give away, he should invest it in a cultural center where young people could come and listen to music, watch movies, read books, and produce their own artworks. He would be thus immortalized as the benefactor of the young generation of Malian artists. That would be ten times better than entrusting to griots the task of making his name. History and the people should be the judges of our reputation—not griots, nor even ourselves.

Toumani Diabaté: A Kora Master

But I myself once succumbed to the flattery of a griot. In 1995, when I was visiting Sly in Bamako, I asked him to come with me to a live performance of kora music by Toumani Diabaté. I had fallen in love with kora music in Dakar, at a jazz club called L'Atelier. A friend had taken me there to see Soriba Kouyate perform. L'Atelier was a hole in the wall with hardly enough room for twenty-five people. Its clientele was usually limited to French expatriates who came to hear old songs by Charles Aznavour, Georges Brassens, and Edith Piaf. When Soriba played, on Thursday nights, there was scarcely room to stand. Soriba was a big black man, about six feet tall and two hundred pounds. He played electric kora in the dimly lit, smoke-filled room. Sometimes he would play sitting down and sometimes he would stand, swinging his kora around the way a hunter swings his rifle as he dances to the tune of "Simbon." The kora is a tall instrument with twenty-one strings; its base consists of an oval calabash covered with cowhide, and its neck is a long pole attached to the calabash. The musician plays it by holding it upright like a bass viol and plucking the strings. Soriba's repertoire ranged from "Duga" and "Yarabi," classic kora songs, to music borrowed from Jimi Hendrix, Michael Jackson, Miles Davis, and John Coltrane. When standing up, jabbing at the kora strings, and moving his big body left and right with the instrument, Soriba could remind one of Simbon hunters, Charlie Parker, and Jimi Hendrix all at the same time.

The fusion of African American and Mande music in Soriba's performance had blown me away. I had said to myself that, at last, African music was not afraid of becoming modern. Soriba knew the kora well enough to create improvisations that transported the listener through great jazz and blues, yet always returning to the Mande by maintaining the presence of the "Duga" or "Yarabi" tune in the rhythm section. It was as if Soriba's kora would suddenly tell us that Charlie Parker and Jimi Hendrix were in the Mande, and vice versa. I had stayed until the end of his performance, so that I could speak with Soriba about the kora. He had told me to visit Toumani Diabaté when I was in Mali. Soriba had called Toumani the best kora player of his generation. I had been impressed by that.

Sly and I went to see Toumani Diabaté perform in Bamako in a place called Fast Food. It was literally a fast-food place, specializing in meat-and-onion sandwiches and cold drinks. The room was small, with a kitchenette, a counter where the orders were placed, and fewer than five tables. Outside, there were two or three additional tables, with umbrellas to block the sun. Fast Food was located in the heart of downtown, and during the daytime it was hardly noticeable amid the crush of pedestrians, the slow traffic, the vendors pushing their carts filled with lemonade and Coca-Cola, and the women with trays of oranges and bananas on their heads. At night, the street was empty and quiet except for the music drifting out of Fast Food and the activity around Black and White, the nightclub at the end of the block; patrons would circle the area looking for parking spaces, and a crowd of cigarette vendors would hawk their wares in front of the club. I suspect that the owner of Fast Food had opened it in this vicinity to catch some of the nightclub's customers on their way home or during breaks.

When Sly and I arrived, the chairs inside were already taken, and the standing room outside did not provide us with a good view of the performance. There were people outside who had obviously dressed up to go to the nightclub, not to listen to Mande blues and jazz at Fast Food. The sandwiches and drinks were selling very fast. I was impressed by the entrepreneurial drive I was seeing in Bamako during this visit. Luckily for us, the owner noticed Sly and came to welcome us and thank us for coming. He gave us two chairs inside, making us the envy of many of his customers. Toumani Diabaté was sitting behind his kora.

According to Toumani Diabaté, the original kora had twenty-two strings. It was invented in Gambia by a griot, an ancestor of the Diabaté clan. The griot had been running after his fiancée, who had suddenly disappeared into a cave. He had followed her; but when he'd emerged from the cave, he'd been holding a kora instead of the woman. His fiancée had vanished. The griot ancestor played the twenty-two-string kora in memory of her until his death, after which one string was removed from the instrument in his honor. Since then, the real masters of the kora have played it with twenty-one strings. A good kora player can use it to fulfill three functions at once: it can serve as the bass, the accompaniment (guitar or balafon), and the solo instrument. That night, Toumani Diabaté was performing with two other artists, one playing a ngoni (a four-string, guitar-like instrument) and the other a balafon. The kora, the ngoni, and the balafon are the three traditional instruments of Mande culture.

When they found out we were in the audience, the musicians played "Duga." Toumani first allowed the ngoni player to improvise and show his virtuosity. This musician made the ngoni sing Sundiata's praises and added his own riffs and syncopations. The crowd loved it. I let myself be transported by the ambience, stamping my feet and snapping my fingers. Then Toumani himself came on. He took the familiar beats of

Toumani Diabaté (right) playing the kora at Fast Food in Bamako, 1995. (Photo by
Manthia Diawara.)

"Duga," but kept climbing higher and higher with them until our
foot-stamping and finger-snapping could no longer keep up.

Suddenly, a griot woman rose and burst into a "Duga" song. She
first praised Toumani for his virtuosity, declaring that he was the son
of Sidiki Diabaté, another great kora player, and that there was no one
equal to him. Then she turned to me and called me a hero like my
great-great-grandfather Daman Guile Diawara. It was breathtaking,
but I pretended not to understand what she was talking about. After
all, I was a modern man and I had to resist the temptation of giving
money to griots.

But then Sly reached into his pocket and pulled out a bundle of
francs, which he handed to the griot woman. I tried to kick him under
the table, but it was too late. I was anxious and nervous over several
things at once. Toumani's music had created an atmosphere of heroism
and well-being that had taken away my self-control. I was upset with

Sly for paying for me and thus depriving me of my right to belong to this culture, to understand it, and to respond to it in a proper manner. His gift had made an outsider of me, but it also registered as a debt that would have to be paid off. How could I show my friendship to him in Mande terms? The only choice I had was to repeat his gesture. This would not only consolidate our friendship through the reciprocity of gift-giving, but would also vindicate me in the eyes of the audience by showing that I understood Toumani's music and that I could pay for my own praise-song.

The musicians did not keep me waiting for long. They played "Yarabi," a tune about love. "Yarabi" is one of the few modern songs from the Mande repertoire. Relative to "Duga," "Simbon," and "Sundiata," it is new; it was created in the Fifties in Guinea to provide young people with a song that was easy to dance to, like the modern Cuban rumba and cha-cha, which were all the rage in dance halls from Dakar and Abidjan to Conakry and Bamako. Songs like "Yarabi," "Alalake," "Kaira," and "Cebendo" inaugurated a style of street party called Goumbé or Bals Poussières, which became extremely popular among the boys and girls of Mande West Africa. The parties brought together in the streets young people who considered themselves urbanized and "civilized," but who were not rich enough to afford the cover charge at nightclubs. The Goumbé had the reputation of bringing together elegant young men, or *zazou*, and beautiful young ladies who were sophisticated enough to dance arm-in-arm with their men. The young people who organized Goumbé in the cities were usually migrant workers from villages and neighboring countries. The Goumbé brought them together regardless of clan and traditional gender divisions. People put on their best Europeanized outfits to come to these street parties. If they did not have trousers of alpaca or Tergal (a shiny, wrinkle-free imported fabric) for the occasion, they borrowed them from their friends. In the Sixties, when we were turned on to rock music, we looked down on Goumbé as primitive and started the tradition of house parties.

"Yarabi" and other Goumbé songs were also modern because they were about women as objects of desire, and about the Mande hero. They had lyrics like, "My lover is innocent. Let me teach you how to smile, let me teach you how to dance." In "Yarabi," the singer says, "My love never offends anybody. Let me give you a scarf; let me take you for a ride on the back of my scooter, because you're the one I love." The current wave of Mande jazz and blues performances by such artists as Oumou Sangaré, Morfinla Kante, Zani Diabaté, Ali Farka Touré, and Toumani Diabaté is indebted to the Goumbé songs, which introduced love lyrics into the Mande repertory. Songs like "Yarabi" also marked the beginning of secular entertainment in Mande West Africa. Unlike "Simbon," "Duga," and "Sundiata," they were not associated with any traditional rituals. They merely provided entertainment for young people in the city.

When Toumani began his solo improvisation with "Yarabi," he was simply unstoppable. He brought to mind the comment Miles Davis once made about the style of Charlie Parker: don't try to rival him—just let him do his own thing, and wait until he is finished. Toumani plays the same way; that is, no one can keep up with him, yet all his notes feel good. Again, the griot woman jumped in at the moment Toumani had everyone hooked. She praised him, and then turned to Sly as the subject of her "Yarabi," her love. She said that he was the handsomest man in Bamako, the hope of the poor and the rich alike. She went on and on. And before anybody could move or do anything, I put my hand in my pocket and handed her a hundred-dollar bill. (Generosity toward griots is *de rigueur* in Mande culture—it is a sign of heroism. Some people even give them houses and cars.)

I cannot remember Sly and I having so much fun together since Woodstock-in-Bamako. We felt victorious, as if we owned the world. Sly still had his Afro; only mine was missing. But when he dropped me off at the end of the evening, I was beside myself. How could I have given money to a griot?

Lying in bed that night, after Toumani's concert, I thought about the griots' power to keep West Africans in a retrograde position, to make us respond to feelings that have not changed in seven hundred years. Despite our attempts to catch up with the modern world, they have trapped us in a narrative of return, a permanent identification with Sundiata, Mansa Musa, Samory Touré, and the other heroes of "Duga" and "Simbon." They keep telling us to return to Mande, for there is no place like it. No other people know us as well as the people in Mande; no other place welcomes us as fully as Mande. We are kings in Mande, even if we wash dishes or clean toilets in other lands. People abroad may not recognize who we are or know what clan we belong to, but in Mande we are well-known and acknowledged. In Mande it is often said that we are like disenfranchised clans when we travel overseas; foreigners have no idea of how noble we are, or how much history we have. We say that no matter how well we do abroad, we belong in Mande: our homeland is Mande; we have to return to build our homeland; we have to return to claim our inheritance. No matter how long a log stays in the water, it will never be transformed into a crocodile. We can never be anyone else's children. We are our mother's children; we are the children of Mande.

A year later, in my hotel room in Conakry after my visit to Niane's bookshop, I likewise pondered these injunctions of the griots. They bar the door to cosmopolitanism and any serious mixing of cultures. *Sundiata: An Epic of Old Mali* is carefully crafted to include the hero's departure or exile from Mande, and his triumphant return or restoration to the culture. Because the role of the hero is often rarefied and beyond the reach of the poor and the handicapped, exile is often necessary for the individual to transform himself into a new type of hero. Sundiata had to leave Mande for Wagadu, the capital of old Ghana, because his half-brother Dankaran Touma was unwilling to share power with him. His exile was also necessary because it enabled him to train himself in war and to become a war leader. Since hunting was the only occupation available to him in Mande, he needed to exile himself to know the world, to learn from other cultures, and to return with enough resources to transform Mande from a collection of hunter clans and smith clans into an empire of warriors.

Sundiata warns us about the difficulties of exile: "Their feet ploughed up the dust of the roads. They suffered the insults which those who leave their country know of. Doors were shut against them and kings chased them from their courts. But all that was part of the great destiny of Sundiata" (28). This wisdom still sustains the new Mande heroes who sweep the terrace of the Eiffel Tower and the streets of Paris, or peddle African objects to tourists on 125th Street in Harlem. They are not looking for recognition or belonging in these places, for recognition and belonging are sweetest only when it comes from Mande.

Once, in a seminar in Paris, I tried to explain black American culture to a room full of Sub-Saharan, Algerian, and French students. I proposed that the black American civil rights struggle was the most advanced form of black modernity, because it successfully deployed race to change laws on the subject of belonging, citizenship, and national identity. Blacks in Europe are modern only via Marxism or religion or a Eurocentric version of humanism and universalism, while Africans and Arabs form resistance cultures to modernity in the name of religion (Islam) or ethnic identity. Only black Americans have an authentic modernity, which serves as a culture to conquer America and the world. I pointed to Martin Luther King Jr. and the black church, Malcolm X and the Black Muslims, jazz and other forms of black music, and African American literature and theater as concrete examples of a unique form of black modernity.

At this point an African student raised his hand and stated that black Americans have lost their African identity, that they were therefore lost, and that he would not call their alienation a culture. As for him, he had been born in Paris twenty-three years before. He had lived here all his life, but he would never consider himself French. He was from Senegal and proud of it. He was prepared to return home to Africa as soon as he finished his studies. He would work anywhere in Africa before considering work in Europe. In fact, he hated France.

I responded by stating what the black American experience had taught me on these matters. Where would he be returning to? He sounded more French than Senegalese. His defiant attitude itself was more a product of French culture, which advocates individual freedom, than of West African culture, in which his voice would have been suppressed by the elders, the clan, and the social divisions governing discourse. But more important, he was contributing to his own exclusion from the French society that he had helped to build and shape. He was denying himself the right to belong and to become a full citizen of France.

But as I think about the issue now, I realize how much I underestimated the power of the narrative of return that permeates the everyday decisions of migrant workers and their children. Like Sundiata, they live for the moment of the heroic return. When Toumani Diabaté played "Duga" and the griot woman praised me via the song, I was momentarily the envy of everyone. Sly's money and my money, which we gave to the griot woman, were a token acknowledgment of the incomparable supremacy of that moment of return. It makes people forget all the pain and humiliation they went through in exile; the only thing which counts is that moment. In Mande, the time of exile is but a season, no matter how long it lasts. It is the return that is eternal.

So far, our modernity, the modernity of Sékou Touré and Salif Kéita, has not succeeded in subverting the aesthetic contract put in place by the return narrative. Modernity, and even capitalism and Islam, have had very little effect on the structuring power of return narratives throughout Mande West Africa and its diaspora. Just as the persistence of clans constitutes a barrier against the creation of democratic societies in Mande, the tendency to resort to an immutable identity—as did my student in Paris—constitutes an obstacle to progress and cosmopolitanism.

My giving money to the griot woman represented my participation in the consolidation of the discourse of Mande heroism which, together with the subordination of women through the practice of polygamy and the repression of casted people, hold the clan structure in place. I had felt guilty for succumbing to the flatteries of the griot woman. Was it possible that culture was more powerful than rationality? Was I witnessing in Conakry the vengeance of culture over Sékou Touré's revolution? As I looked in my mind's eye at the broken and stagnating system, and saw the debris that filled the city of Conakry, I felt like Sundiata returning from war and exile to the ruins of his native Niani: "From the top of the hill Djata gazed upon Niani, which looked like a dead city. He saw the plain of Sounkarani, and he also saw the site of the young baobab tree. The survivors of the catastrophe were standing in rows on the Mali road. The children were waving branches and a few young women were singing, but the adults were mute" (Niane, 1965: 80).

How could the griot woman's song make me rejoice in the midst of such a catastrophe? Only modern rationality can help us to rebuild the ruined cities of Mande West Africa. Why are we once again leaving to white people the task of our modernization?

SITUATION III

▲▼▲

MALCOLM X: CONVERSIONISTS VERSUS CULTURALISTS

Culture, defined as a whole way of life, is that which the traveler both brings to a destination and carries back home, in altered form, from the place visited. In other words, cultures and their attendant modes of dress, names, customs, and ideologies are always influenced by commercial, religious, and political relations between inside and outside. This broader definition of culture, which animates the best works in contemporary cultural studies, is eclipsed in black studies by a narrower, purist definition which sees culture as a people's nostalgic relation to images of themselves, or as the best achievements and thoughts of a people. Furthermore, black intellectuals, be they apostles of Afrocentricity, black conservatism, Islam, or liberation theology, tend to discredit and categorize as pathological certain cultural practices that challenge their ideal of blackness. I shall provisionally call "culturalists" those practitioners who work with the broader definition of culture, and "conversionists" those who regard culture as an elitist and exclusionary domain.

Here we will look at black conversionist and culturalist discourses, and their relation to life issues, politics, and economics as depicted in *The Autobiography of Malcolm X*, by Malcolm X and Alex Haley. Conversionists and culturalists have long been fighting a custody battle over the first part of the book, which includes such pivotal chapters as "Homeboy," "Harlemite," "Detroit Red," and "Hustler." Despite the conversionist discourse in the second half of the book, which warns the reader against embracing the early chapters, these constitute the appeal of the book today, giving significance to inner-city youths' identification with

Malcolm X as a "homeboy," and making "Detroit Red" the archetype of rap songs and black male films of the 1980s and 1990s. A culturalist reading, which resists the second half's definition of the first part of the book as black pathology, is better able to account for the popularity of Malcolm X among today's youth, who see their own lives mirrored in the experience of Detroit Red, Malcolm X's young self.

What fascinates readers in the *Autobiography* is its detailed description of black life in Harlem, particularly the nightlife. Malcolm X presents Harlem in the 1940s in a cultural, political, and economic setting. Harlem's nightlife attracts not only blacks but also World War II soldiers, whites from midtown, and tourists. The fact that audiences form around the black good-life institutions (clubs, bars, theaters, dance halls) and entertainers in Harlem evokes concern for the stability of traditional black-white relations during a climate of war. In the text, Harlem's culture defies the ban on interracial relations and subverts the code of morality imposed on black and white soldiers during World War II.

Crucially, Detroit Red's relation to and fascination with this black culture of Harlem, the way in which he views and takes pleasure in its institutions and entertainers, enable the reader to identify with him and the text in ways that are not convincingly deconstructed in the latter part of the *Autobiography*.

The Conversionists

How ridiculous I was! Stupid enough to stand there simply lost in admiration of my hair now looking "white," reflected in the mirror in Shorty's room.

—*The Autobiography of Malcolm X*

Conversionist discourses deploy narratives about the worst sinners to justify the need for transformation. At the end of the chapter entitled "Caught," Malcolm X confesses: "I have never previously told anyone my sordid past in detail. I haven't done it now to sound as though I might be proud of how bad, how evil, I was" (Malcolm X and Haley, 1992: 150). Malcolm X tells the story of his depravities, which lead to his discovery of Allah and the religion of Islam. He presents the narrative as proof that he has been there, so to speak, down with the rest of the people, and that they, too, can join him on the other side. He states that, once motivated, "no one can change more completely than the man who has been at the bottom. I call myself the best example of that" (261). The difficulty of conversion is not emphasized here; Malcolm X stresses only the superiority of his new world over the old one. Conversionist discourses, whether motivated by religion, science, or politics, always underestimate culture or liken it to pathology. Conversionists, whether politicians or religious leaders, build their audiences by blaming the culture of the people they are trying to convert. They always expect people to achieve a revolutionary conscious-ness or a spiritual awakening and walk out of their culture, shedding it like a shell or a cracked skin, in order to change the world.

The rhetoric of the second half of the *Autobiography* seems to move too rapidly to its conclusion, condemning black culture with the demise of Detroit Red. Malcolm X uses alienation as an analytic tool for disparaging the Harlem culture which he describes so well in the first part of the book. He shows Detroit Red's transformation from observer of culture to par-ticipant, presenting black people's consumerism and their relation to style as major manifestations of estrangement. Malcolm X's charge that "conked" (straightened) hair is an expression of black people's unnatural desire to look "white" (54) is consistent with other conversionists' views on the subject, and it informs the decision by many black youths to abandon conked hair for "natural" styles such as the Afro.

Malcolm X also detects symptoms of alienation in the way in which black people buy products: "I was really a clown, but my ignorance made me think I was 'sharp.' My knob-toed, orange-colored 'kick-up' shoes were nothing but Florsheims, the ghetto's Cadillac of shoes in those days. (Some shoe companies made these ridiculous styles for sale only in the black ghettoes, where ignorant Negroes like me would pay the big-name price for something that we associated with being rich.)" (78).

The metamorphosis from Detroit Red to Malcolm X requires the pro-tagonist of the *Autobiography* to deny a part of himself for every piece of knowledge he gains from the Nation of Islam: "'You don't even know who you are,' Reginald said. 'You don't even know, the white devil has hidden it from you, that you are of a race of people of ancient civilizations, and riches in gold, and kings. You don't even know your true family name, you wouldn't recognize your true language if you heard it" (160). Conver-sionists of the religious or political kind are particularly prone to self-de-nial. At one point, in Ghana, at a party given in his honor, Malcolm X says to his hosts: "You wonder why I don't dance? Because I want you to remember twenty-two million Afro-Americans in the U.S.!" At the same time, he tells the reader: "But I sure felt like dancing! The Ghanaians performed the high-life as if possessed. One pretty African girl sang 'Blue Moon' like Sarah Vaughan. Sometimes the band sounded like Milt Jackson, sometimes like Charlie Parker" (358).

Through conversion, Malcolm X not only attempts to abandon expressive styles in language, dress, and hair associated with black ghetto life; he also speaks of Detroit Red as if he were a different person: "I still marvel at how swiftly my previous life's thinking pattern slid away from me, like snow off a roof. It is as though someone else I knew of had lived by hustling and crime. I would be startled to catch myself thinking in a remote way of my earlier self as another person" (170). Malcolm X associates Detroit Red with death and now thinks of him as a menace to society: "Awareness came surging up in me—how deeply the religion of Islam had reached down into the mud to lift me up, to save me from being what I inevitably would have been: a dead criminal in a grave, or, if still alive, a flint-hard, bitter, thirty-seven-year-old convict in some penitentiary, or insane asylum" (287).

The first part of the *Autobiography* is carefully crafted to lead up to Detroit Red's transition from unemployed hick to hustler to hardened criminal and drug addict. Even the sequence of chapter titles—"Detroit Red," "Hustler," "Trapped," "Caught"—presupposes an inevitable descent that, for Malcolm X, can be reversed only through conversion: "Today, when everything that I do has an urgency, I would not spend one hour in the preparation of a book which had the ambition to perhaps titillate some readers. But I am spending many hours because the full story is the best way that I know to have it seen, and understood, that I had sunk to the very bottom of the American white man's society when—soon now, in prison—I found Allah and the religion of Islam and it completely transformed my life" (150). Malcolm X attempts to account for the rough edges in the text, such as the places where the reader identifies with Detroit Red's love for black culture, by assimilating them to a state of alienation. Against Detroit Red, he asserts that "what makes the ghetto hustler yet more dangerous is his 'glamour' image to the school-dropout youth in the ghetto" (311).

Toward the end of the first part of the *Autobiography*, Detroit Red sinks to the bottom, and the narrator with him, as if black culture has died with them. The black cultural figure most vividly present in the chapter entitled "Trapped" is Billie Holiday, whose end as a drug addict bears a strong resemblance to Detroit Red's last days in Harlem. It is interesting from a stylistic standpoint that Malcolm X and Alex Haley put Billie Holiday and other tragic figures at the end of the first part of the book. Presenting culture as a dead end helps the conversionists' case. Malcolm X traps Detroit Red in a hole and leaves him no choice but to convert, inducing the reader as well to identify with the sermon of change. Crucially, when Detroit Red returns to Harlem as Malcolm X, he wants to change it completely. This occurs at the time the jazz clubs are moving from Harlem to 52nd Street, leaving hustlers and prostitutes without jobs.

Malcolm X makes an important contribution to the art of autobiography by exploring the alienation which enables him to distance himself from Detroit Red. Malcolm X often refers to Detroit Red as another person—a stylistic device that generates an autobiographical text in the form of a sermon. Malcolm X and Alex Haley have shaped the *Autobiography* as a preacher would a sermon. They do not intend the reader to be entertained by Detroit Red's story; they want the reader to understand the symbolism behind it and take it as a lesson. With Malcolm X and Alex Haley, autobiography ceases to be an intimate and personal story, and becomes a public and conversionist essay.

The frequent reference to change in conversionist discourse echoes the modernist impulse toward constant renewal. Every conversionist discourse addresses an epistemological crisis which requires the author's contemplation for a solution. Malcolm X's autobiography includes moving scenes in which he ponders situations of crisis and imagines ways of getting out of them. Such reflections always mark him as an outsider to culture, a philosopher burdened with the desire to change things, a utopian reconstructionist.

The most widely quoted lines from the *Autobiography* dealing with an epistemological crisis come at the point where Malcolm's English teacher, Mr. Ostrowski, tells him: "A lawyer—that's no realistic goal for a nigger. You need to think about something you can be. You're good with your hands—making things. Everybody admires your carpentry shop work. Why don't you plan on carpentry?" (36). In this passage, the young Malcolm is asked to accept a stereotype of himself and his people as a reality. Malcolm's reaction to it sums up why young blacks call into question the fairness of the system and identify with a lawbreaker ideology, through which they feel that they can overcome the obstacles placed in front of them by the likes of Mr. Ostrowski.

But for me, Malcolm X describes his distress at epistemological crises more effectively when he delineates them as a coming-to-consciousness from a state of innocence, a process by which new knowledge displaces business as usual and enables forward movement. These are the moments of discovery in the *Autobiography,* moments when Malcolm X is with a group but feels lonely, lost in contemplation of a better future for black people. For instance, there is a lovely passage in the opening chapter of the book where Malcolm X reflects about the satisfaction he derives from working in the family garden: "I loved especially to grow peas. I was proud when we had them on our table. I would pull out the grass in my garden by hand when the first little blades came up. I would patrol the rows on my hands and knees for any worms and bugs and I would kill and bury them. And sometimes when I had everything straight and clean for my things to grow, I would lie down on my back between two rows, and I would gaze up in the blue sky at the clouds moving and think all kinds of things" (8).

The clouds moving on the horizon are leitmotifs for change in the *Autobiography.* For instance, years later, during his trip to Mecca, Malcolm X thinks of his break with Elijah Muhammad and pictures his new predicament using the sky as a setting: "I remember one night at Muzadalifa with nothing but the sky overhead I lay awake amid sleeping Muslim brothers and I learned that pilgrims from every land—every color, and class, and rank; high officials and the beggar alike—all snored in the same language" (344). The leitmotif occurs for the third time when Malcolm X returns to the States: "I remember there in the holy world how I used to lie on the top of Hector's Hill, and look up at the sky, at the clouds moving over me, and daydream, all kinds of things. And then, in a funny contrast of recollection, I remember how years later, when I was in prison, I used to lie on my cell bunk—this would be especially when I was in solitary: what we convicts called 'The Hole'—and I would picture myself talking to large crowds" (365).

Malcolm X makes this last allusion to the sky and clouds in 1965. The epistemological crisis in question concerns how to build a black nationalist organization that would welcome Christians, Jews, Buddhists, Hindus, agnostics, and atheists. As Malcolm X puts it at the time: "I have friends who are called capitalists, Socialists, and Communists! Some of my friends are moderates, conservatives, extremists—some are even Uncle Toms! My friends today are black, brown, red, yellow, and white!" (375).

Malcolm X was a complex man who constantly revised his thinking. As the recurrence of cloud and sky imagery shows, he was very American in his dreams: he was impatient with the obstacles placed in front of black people. Like the Founding Fathers, he was prepared to remove these obstacles by any means necessary in order to move ahead, toward better and better societies. Malcolm X was also a modernist, as revealed in the way he used cloud imagery to reflect his concerns, and in the way he kept revising his style in order to build larger audiences for his ideas.

Other conversionists since Malcolm X have resorted to Marxism, Afrocentrism, liberation theology, and black nationalism as frameworks for the construction of a public sphere among black people. In fact, Malcolm X's *Autobiography* stands out as an inspiration for these conversionist schools, with its detailed discussions of identity politics, class struggle, black self-determination, and religion. Conversionists continue to ring the wake-up bell for black people, and—much in the manner of Malcolm X (312–314)—to treat black culture as pathology.

Yet there is a good deal of evidence that Malcolm X the modernist feels ambivalent about his thoroughgoing embrace of a conversionist stance. He emphasizes in the *Autobiography* that his success as a public speaker depends on the fact that he is a "homeboy" who "never left the ghetto in spirit, . . . [who] could speak and understand the ghetto's language" (310), and who has been schooled as a hustler like most ghetto kids (296). But one could argue that Malcolm X's purist philosophy is too demanding, in the sense that it incorporates only black people who have left their culture behind. Malcolm X's philosophy in the second part of the *Autobiography* does not, to borrow an expression from a critic of the Black Arts movement, "address itself to the mythology and life style of black people" (Harper, 1996: 46). Malcolm X himself repeatedly ponders the shortcomings of his purist philosophy: "my old so-called 'Black Muslim' image kept blocking me" (375); "Numerous people said that the Nation of Islam's stringent moral restrictions had repelled them—and they wanted to join me" (316). Still, Malcolm X remains a conversionist who believes that "it was a big order—the organization I was creating in my mind, one which would help to challenge the American black man to gain his human rights, and to cure his mental, spiritual, economic, and political sicknesses" (315). But the conversionists of today are the culturalists of tomorrow.

Culturalists

Then, suddenly, we were in the Roseland's jostling lobby. And I was
getting waves and smiles and greetings. They shouted, "My man!"
and "Hey, Red!" and I answered, "Daddy-o."
—The Autobiography of Malcolm X

There is another way to look at the epistemological crisis Malcolm X
shared with other black people, without reverting to a view of black
culture as pathology. This demands a partisan identification with culture,
a belief that *culture* knows and that it can be channeled to create and
capitalize on epistemological breaks. My culturalist approach stipulates
that—contrary to the conversionists' view of "authentic black culture" as
an emanation of the church, or of a true revolutionary consciousness, or of
a separatist gesture toward Africa—black religion, revolutionary theories,
and political economy are all specific expressions of black culture.

The view that conversionist discourses are but enunciations of particular aspects of black culture enables us, first of all, to distinguish culture
from its particular manifestations in the church, the arts, and politics. I
shall define "culture" here as a way of life aimed at producing the black
good life. A major part of black culture in America is created through
attempts to liberate everyday life from colonizing systems. Blacks often
derive the good life by systematically reversing the signification of the
institutions built against them. They test the limits of modern institutions
for inclusion and emancipation of multicultural ways of life. Hence, black
culture is the last frontier of American modernism.

Second, a view of culture as that which encompasses the church, the
black nationalist tradition, and other ideological movements not only
liberates us from the monopoly that these institutions place on black
culture, but also legitimizes other elements of culture such as economic
narratives, art in the context of international politics, and other cultural
forms engendered through black people's relation to more and more
complex systems. In other words, we can no longer afford to locate and fix
black culture in a specific ideological institution, lest we run the risk of
overlooking newer manifestations of culture which are more effective in
producing a black good life and ethics within the political economy of the
so-called global village.

Malcolm X's popularity today resides as much in his elucidation of black culture, through his personal transformation and his description of the economics of Harlem high life in the 1940s, as in his conversionist discourse in favor of black self-determination.

Homeboy

I still was country, I know now, but it all felt so great because I was accepted.
—*The Autobiography of Malcolm X*

People would watch for clues from Bird and Dizzy, and if they smiled when you finished playing, then that meant that your playing was good. They smiled when I finished playing that first time, and from then on I was on the inside of what was happening in New York's music scene.
—Miles Davis, *Miles: The Autobiography*

The young Malcolm's flight from Lansing, Michigan, to Boston and later to Harlem points toward a rift between the country and the city, which Malcolm X himself characterizes as a protest against white racism and black petit-bourgeois ideals of order and respectability. Malcolm Little makes his break with the country after a crisis that results from his encounter with Mr. Ostrowski. "If I had stayed on in Michigan, I would probably have married one of those Negro girls I knew and liked in Lansing. I might have become one of those state capitol building shoeshine boys, or a Lansing Country Club waiter, or gotten one of the other menial jobs which, in those days, among Lansing Negroes, would have been considered 'successful'" (38).

By 1940, when Malcolm Little leaves Lansing to go to Boston, he has acquired an image of cities from his half-sister, Ella, and from black music. Ella's visit to Lansing helps shape the phantasmagoria of city life for the young Malcolm because she instills in him a sense of pride, freedom, and mobility: "A commanding woman, maybe even bigger than Mrs. Swerlin, Ella wasn't just black, but, like my father, she was jet black. The way she sat, moved, talked, did everything, bespoke somebody who did and got exactly what she wanted. This was the woman my father had boasted of so often for having brought so many of their family out of Georgia to Boston. She owned some property, he would say, and she was in 'society'" (32).

Jazz music and musicians are the other forces beckoning Malcolm Little to the city. In the 1940s, many people associated jazz "with flappers, skyscrapers, and the entire panoply of twentieth-century modernity" (Naremore, 1993: 52). Malcolm Little, too, used music as a means of contemplating the city and of detaching himself from the country: "Sometimes, big bands from New York, out touring the one-night stands in the sticks, would play for big dances in Lansing. Everybody with legs would come out to see any performer who bore the magic name 'New York.' Which is how I first heard Lucky Thompson and Milt Jackson, both of whom I later got to know well in Harlem" (Malcolm X and Haley, 1992: 28).

By the time Malcolm Little leaves Michigan, he has already developed resentment toward the Jim Crow system that obstructs black people's access to modernity, secularism, and progress. Young Malcolm in the city bears a certain resemblance to the *bohème,* as described by Walter Benjamin in his classic book *Charles Baudelaire: A Lyric Poet in the Era of High Capitalism:* "The brutal, starved, envious, wild Cain . . . has gone to the cities to consume the sediment of rancour which has accumulated in them and participate in the false ideas which experience their triumph there. This characterization expresses exactly what gave Baudelaire solidarity with Dupont. Like Cain, Dupont had 'gone to the cities' and turned away from the idyllic" (Benjamin, 1983: 25).

Malcolm Little, too, has gone to the cities, to get even with the modernists. The chapter dealing with Malcolm's arrival in Boston is appropriately entitled "Homeboy," and it opens with the following words: "I looked like Li'l Abner. Mason, Michigan, was written all over me. My kinky, reddish hair was cut hick style, and I didn't even use grease in it" (39). On one level, a homeboy is understood in the book as a small-town or country dweller who has come to the city through a network of migration in search of the American Dream, with other migrants from the same region. A new form of kinship develops among the homeboys, which leads the members of the group to empathize with one another, to help one another in finding work, and to prepare one another for life in the city. In the words of Malcolm's friend Shorty: "Man, this is a swinging town if you dig it . . . You're my homeboy—I'm going to school you to the happenings" (44).

Malcolm Little, as a homeboy, is part hustler and part cosmopolitan artist. A homeboy is a *bohème* who is angry at the world because he is not getting his fair share. Malcolm Little joins other similarly positioned homeboys to take revenge on the system for standing between them and the American Dream. The homeboys—as we see in today's rap music and in the new *films noirs* being made by black directors—form a group of professional conspirators who believe that the most important thing in life is to be paid in full for their work. Today's homeboys, like Malcolm Little, are impatient with the system, and more prone to take power than to receive it from a public sphere that they see as erected against them. In their view, as one homeboy tells Malcolm Little in the *Autobiography,* "the main thing you got to remember is that everything in the world is a hustle" (48).

To empathize with homeboys who are hustlers is to concur with black cultural criticism of the way in which modern systems colonize the everyday life of black people. There are several places in the *Autobiography* where Malcolm X identifies with lawbreakers, on the grounds that homeboys are not allowed, because of racism, to develop their skills in such productive areas as the sciences, linguistics, and the arts. Concerning an old pickpocket who is given meals and treated respectfully by younger hustlers, he says: "To wolves who still were able to catch some rabbits, it had meaning that an old wolf who had lost his fangs was still eating" (90).

But identification with lawbreakers is not the only way black structures of feeling are expressed in the *Autobiography.* Malcolm's cosmopolitan artistic sensibility is another manifestation of black culture. Malcolm Little is a *flâneur* looking for modernism in the ballrooms, bars, and streets frequented by the world's greatest and hippest musicians. His search for musical expressions of black culture in the 1940s can be compared to Miles Davis' quest during the same period. In his own autobiography, Davis states that he enrolled in the Julliard School of Music in order to be in New York, near Charlie Parker (known as Bird). Later, Davis traveled from New York to Los Angeles, and back to New York, looking for Bird. During those years, he says, he was studying for the "master's degrees and the Ph.D.'s from Minton's University of Bebop under the tutelage of professors Bird and Diz. Man, they was playing so much incredible shit" (Davis and Troupe, 1989: 61).

Malcolm Little spends a good deal of his time looking at and soaking up the styles and worldviews of great musicians like Duke Ellington, Count Basie, and Lionel Hampton: "They'd be up there in my chair, and my shine rag was popping to the beat of all their records, spinning in my head. Musicians never have had, anywhere, a greater shoeshine-boy fan than I was" (50).

It is easy to see why the young Malcolm admires these musicians. They appear to be free, to be in control of their lives at a time when the only lifestyles available to black people are those imposed on them. The musicians—with their zoot suits, conked hair, and music that fascinate both blacks and whites—appear to have more power than people in other spheres. Most of all, they seem like a commodity which is desired by everyone and which therefore enjoys an enviable position in the marketplace. You can guess what's coming: Malcolm X, the conversionist, criticizes this situation in the second half of the book, disparaging it as alienation from the spiritual, economic, and political true course.

Detroit Red, on the other hand, wants to lose himself in the musicians' elaboration of black culture. "Sometimes I would be down there standing inside the door jumping up and down in my gray jacket with the whisk-broom in the pocket, and the manager would have to come and shout at me that I had customers upstairs" (51). In his secular imagination, Detroit Red sees musicians such as Duke Ellington, Lionel Hampton, and Billie Holiday as leading black people toward spiritual, economic, and political fulfillment. The revolution presupposed by Malcolm X, in which black people would cease to identify with commodification and would take control over the modes of production, might have been out of the musicians' reach; but for Detroit Red, music nonetheless helped people to pass the time. As his reading of a song by Lionel Hampton reveals, musicians provided the public sphere with philosophical narratives which defined the culture and the reality of the time: "The people kept shouting for Hamp's 'Flyin' Home,' and finally he did it. (I could believe the story I'd heard in Boston about this number—that once in the Apollo, Hamp's 'Flyin' Home' had made some reefer-smoking Negro in the second balcony believe he could fly, so he tried—and jumped—and broke his leg, an event later immortalized in song when Earl Hines wrote a hit tune called 'Second-Balcony Jump'" (74).

Detroit Red is a homeboy who wants to be intoxicated by the city, and it is in the city's nightlife that he finds black cosmopolitan culture. In the 1920s the best of culture had been located in the work of black writers, but in the 1940s the energy lay in the music scene. Detroit Red becomes a *flâneur* and soaks up the Harlem nightlife like a sponge. When he has been completely modernized, he poses the way "hipsters" wearing their zoots "cool it" and takes a picture of himself to send home, with "hat dangled, knees drawn close together, feet wide apart, both index fingers jabbed toward the floor. The long coat and swing chain and the Punjab pants were more dramatic if you stood that way" (52).

The Periodization of 1940s Harlem

Malcolm's story operates on several levels. It is a personal account of his growth and decline. It also describes the development of the black public sphere and the creation of audiences for black culture in Harlem in the 1940s. And it is an economic narrative that reveals how black art was channeled toward the attainment of greater economic well-being for blacks, and how that channeling came to an end.

In the *Autobiography*, Malcolm X portrays the 1940s as a period when new doors opened for black people in America: "Old Man Roundtree, an elderly Pullman porter and a friend of Ella's, had recommended the railroad job for me. He had told her the war was snatching away railroad men so fast that if I could pass for twenty-one, he could get me on" (70). Nightlife flourished in Harlem during the war years, when servicemen looking for a good time crowded the streets and the bars. "Up and down along and between Lenox and Seventh Avenues, Harlem was like some technicolor bazaar. Hundreds of Negro soldiers and sailors, gawking and young like me, passed by" (74).

It is important to distinguish this attempted resurgence of a black entertainment industry in Harlem, during the war, from the Harlem Renaissance and its nightlife, which came to an end in 1929, after the stock market crash. There were still some of the same clubs and ballrooms, like the Savoy, Small's Paradise, and Minton's, and the same theaters, like the Apollo. But the most obvious difference between the 1920s and the 1940s involves a change in the relative importance of key figures in the black public sphere—a decrease in the influence of writers and political figures (such as W. E. B. Du Bois, Langston Hughes, Marcus Garvey, and Alain Locke) and an increase in the popularity of entertainers (such as Duke Ellington, Dizzy Gillespie, Billy Eckstine, Billie Holiday, Ella Fitzgerald, and Diana Washington).

Detroit Red derives his cultural and political formation from the bars and streets of Harlem, or, to paraphrase Miles Davis, from the universities of Small's Paradise and the Braddock Hotel, where the bars were jampacked with famous black entertainers. The black culture of today bears similarities to that of the 1940s, relying for its essential definition on forms of entertainment—rap music, the films of Spike Lee, and popular novels such as those by Terry McMillan.

Like Detroit Red, I am fascinated by 1940s Harlem, when arts and entertainment were closely linked to economic activity in the community. It is still not clear to me why the jazz clubs moved to 52nd Street around 1945, leaving many Harlemites without jobs. Maybe the imminent end of the war and the desire to return to the status quo had something to do with it. Maybe the cause was racism, as Miles Davis suggests in his autobiography: "If it's one thing white people are united on, it is that they all hate to see black people making the money they think belongs to them. They were beginning to think that they owned these black musicians because they was making money for them" (73).

According to Malcolm X, hustlers like Detroit Red may have turned to armed robbery after the 1943 Harlem riot and the change of music scene from uptown to 52nd Street. "Things had grown so tight in Harlem that some hustlers had been forced to go to work. Even some prostitutes had gotten jobs as domestics, and cleaning office buildings at night. The pimping was so poor, Sammy had gone on the job with me" (114–115). Malcolm's deteriorating economic status coincides with a decline in the audience for black culture and a decline in the stability of the black economic public sphere in Harlem.

In sum, by inverting the relation of culture to materialist and ideological systems such as economics, religion, and politics, I am trying to remove culture from the pathological spaces that these systems reserve for it. If we turn these systems upside down and view them as aspects of black culture, it is easy to see that conversionists themselves enunciate culture even as they call it something else and that they embrace it even as they denigrate it.

My aim here is to open the door to criticism, not to propound a grand theory. A more inclusive view of culture allows us to criticize the black church's monopoly on ethics, even as we recognize its historical importance to black people. It seems to me that the definition of ethics should be tied to culture, and to the creation of audiences. Malcolm's embrace of the Nation of Islam and then Islam itself constituted a move beyond Christian morality, toward a secularization of the just and the true—beyond "black culture is bad," toward a more inclusive ethics. In other words, black people do not divorce ethics from the material conditions that produce the black good life. We should not be afraid to embrace a multiplicity of cultural expressions as we pursue the good life for ourselves and for one another.

5

▲▼▲

The Shape of the Future

Modernity Is in Evil Forest

I woke up as soon as the morning light entered my hotel room in Conakry. My mind was on Malcolm X, Sékou Touré, and Richard Wright—all conversionists, and heroes of our modernity. An old man once told me, "We do not want you to replace us; we want you to continue the work we have started." Are conversion and continuity reconcilable? I pulled back the curtains and saw the ocean, beyond the tall thatched roof covering the bar-restaurant of the Hotel Camayenne. Between the hotel and the bar was a swimming pool surrounded by tables with giant umbrellas. As soon as the sun appeared, white people began crowding around the swimming pool in their bathing suits. I picked up *The Color Curtain* by Richard Wright, left my room, found a table by the pool, and sat with my back to the people, facing the ocean. The water had receded some distance, revealing black rocks; a fishy smell invaded the morning air. As the sun quickly chased the morning away, children came out to stand on the rocks and gaze at the swimsuit-clad whites. I drank my coffee, looking from the children to the white people, who seemed completely oblivious of their presence. The people around the pool were swimming, kissing, or eating; the ones on the rocks were watching, talking, and pointing at them. I was in the middle, neither here nor there.

Suddenly I noticed something that disturbed me for the rest of my stay in Guinea. A man was looking at *me* from the rocks. He wore a sleeveless mud-cloth shirt, and short, baggy pants that were tight-fitting at the knees. He looked like a hunter from a Mande secret society: defiant and angry, with red eyes, and yet a slave to a ritual that had to be performed to the end. When I stared back at him, he quickly looked to the ground, mumbled some words, and pointed a finger at the sky before staring back at me. That made me shiver to the bone. His clothes were dirty and his hair was covered with dust. I concluded that he was crazy.

The man moved a few feet away from me, lowered his pants, and squatted in order to defecate in plain view, on the rocks. I looked away in disgust, but then noticed that there were other people on the rocks who were doing the same thing. I could not believe my eyes at first. Then I told myself that the only reason it seemed unbelievable to me was that the hotel was close by. The people on the rocks were fighting over the space with the hotel guests, who were invading *their* privacy. I remembered that, in childhood, Sidimé Laye and I and our friends had often relieved ourselves by the river.

The futile resistance of the people on the rocks against the hotel guests reminded me of a scene in Chinua Achebe's novel *Things Fall Apart*. The villagers of Mbanta set aside a piece of land they call "Evil Forest." This place is off limits to women and children, because it is peopled with evil spirits and taboos. For example, twins are considered diabolical by the society, so they are thrown at birth into Evil Forest. The same treatment is given to the "Osu," or outcasts, who symbolize everything the tribe abhors. The "Osu" carry the sins of the people; they never shave their hair, which dangles behind them like a nest of snakes. They are forbidden to enter the village. Evil Forest is also the dumping ground for the masks and other idols of powerful medicine-men after their death. Evil Forest thus exists in opposition to Mbanta as civilization exists in opposition to wilderness, order to chaos, and good to evil.

When Christian missionaries arrive in Mbanta and ask for a place to build their church, the villagers gladly offer them Evil Forest, hoping to see the intruders quickly punished by the gods. The missionaries transform Evil Forest into a haven for outcasts, twins, and other marginalized people. Slowly they are joined by respectable and prestigious men from the village. The rest of the story is a metaphor for the history of colonialism and modernity in Africa: the roles are henceforth reversed, as Evil Forest becomes the civilizer of Mbanta.

To this day, the Mbantas of Africa resist Evil Forest—now represented by such establishments as my hotel in Conakry—and still use primitive weapons. Like Richard Wright, I wondered about modernity in Africa. Would it always be an alien, outside thing, or would it penetrate the African body and organize it for competition and success?

Culture and Nationalism as Resistance to Globalization

I still remember my high school entrance exam in Bamako, because of drawing. I had prepared well for the important subjects: math, French, history, geography, and biology. Drawing, physical education, and music were not as important, because the scores in these subjects were not weighted by a multiple factor in the overall final grade, as was the case with math and French. But that year we were asked to draw a blazon, and I did not know what the word meant. I knew that although drawing could not hurt me much, it could help me. We weren't supposed to talk to the examiner, so I looked intently in his eyes to show that I needed help. He came toward me and said to me: "Draw something, just anything, with something on it." I took my chances and drew a fisherman casting a net in the river, with fish visible in the water and the sun glowing in the background. When I went home that day, my uncle asked me how I had done on the exam. I said that everything had gone well, except for drawing. I asked him what a blazon was. He did not know the meaning of the word either. I was disappointed. He told me that he was sure I had done well.

When the exam results were posted, I found out that I had done well in drawing. This surprised me, but I did not think much of it, since I was going on to high school and this was all that mattered. I now associate the event with two other incidents in my life. The first took place around 1968, when Mali's national cigarette factory caught fire. I had a cousin who was very hip then. He was "in the wind," as we used to say, with his Honda motorcycle, his collection of records by Johnny Hallyday and James Brown, his Elvis Presley navy cap, and his white jeans. My cousin attended the Ecole Normale d'Administration in Bamako, where Mali's future leaders were trained. When he heard that the factory was on fire, he rushed there on his Honda. He came back later, all covered with ash and dirt. He kept walking up and down in the yard, and everyone who came by asked him what had happened to his clothes. "I was at the national factory, helping to put out the fire," he said. I wondered why he delayed going to the bathroom to wash up; but I did not make much of that either.

The second incident happened in 1969, after the coup d'état that overthrew Modibo Kéita in November 1968. In reaction to the social-ist policies of the previous eight years, the new military regime un-leashed a campaign of privatization which included an accusation against the national factories for draining the resources of the peasants, inducing drought, famine, and corruption. The soldiers promised that once we privatized everything, the French, the Americans, the World Bank, and the International Monetary Fund would help us, and foreign companies would invest in our country. I was not too bothered by this turn of events, for there were things about the old regime that I hadn't particularly cared for, such as the fact that we'd been unable to buy the latest records by the Beatles, the Jackson Five, and James Brown. I had also been resentful because my peers in Côte d'Ivoire and Senegal had enjoyed access to new movies from Europe and rock concerts. And I definitely had not liked the neighborhood policing, the curfews, and the imposition of Russian- and Chinese-language study in our school curriculum.

I was surprised, therefore, to see people marching toward the National Assembly building with banners and shouting, "Ne touchez pas aux acquis du peuple, Yankee! Go home! Jan Smuts, au poteau!" ("Hands off the people's property, Yankee! Go home! Down with Jan Smuts!" Smuts had been the prime minister of South Africa and was still a potent symbol of injustice.) They were marching against capitalist invasion and appropriation of our national culture and economy. Because it was the thing to do, I joined the march until the tanks came and chased us away. Later, whenever we talked about that march, we linked it to another event—one that took place a bit later, in the National Soccer Stadium. The president of the military regime had appointed one of the organizers of the rally to his cabinet. When the privatization issue came up again, the man waited for a big gathering at the stadium; he stood up and sang the national anthem, declared his opposition to privatization, and handed his resignation to the president. The man's courage made him an instant national hero. According to some versions of the event, tears were flowing from his eyes as he sang the national anthem. That man was Alpha O. Konare, who is today the president of Mali. Looking back at my high school drawing, I realized that, by creating my blazon, I had been participating in the creation of a national structure of feeling. The fisherman with his net full of fish symbolized our desire for self-determination. I had unconsciously absorbed the elements of independence as an everyday fact. My drawing, just like my cousin's dirty clothes after he had helped put out the factory fire, expressed the deep pride we felt for our nation.

Before the devaluation of the CFA (Communauté Française Africaine) franc on January 20, 1994, globalization was viewed in two ways in West Africa. Some people perceived it as a new form of colonialism—the coopting of cultural life in Africa by transnational corporations, in complicity with Western governments and corrupt African leaders. Others viewed it as an opportunity for African artists and entrepreneurs to leave the periphery and join the metropolitan centers in Europe and America. The first paradigm relies on Fanonian theories of resistance and nationalist consciousness, whereas the second is based on performance and competition in the global market. As restructuring programs began to take their toll on national institutions like education, health care, state-owned factories, and the department of labor, people who felt that these were symbols of national autonomy engaged in cultural and social forms of protest and resistance. The boy scouts movement, which started in the 1960s to build patriotic sentiment among youths and to draft them into the project of nation building, changed in the 1970s and 1980s into social-protest movements in high schools and universities, opposing the government's decreased commitment to education.

In the 1960s, mass education was integral to the independence movements, which presented schools as the road to Africa's development and self-determination. Independence, people thought, meant that everyone would have access to free schools—unlike colonialism, which denied access to education. Schooling therefore has become a necessary symbol of national sovereignty, and students who fight to keep the education from deviating from its original purpose are the new national heroes.

Souleymane Cissé's *Finye* (1982) is a classic example of a narrative that constructs students as national heroes struggling for self-determination, democracy, and equal right to education. The film tells the story of Bah and Oumou, two high school sweethearts from different socioeconomic classes. Oumou's father is a member of the ruling junta and governor of the region. Bah lives with his grandparents in an impoverished section of the city; his parents were presumably killed by the junta. The conflict involves the elite, who are powerful enough to buy high exam scores and scholarships for their children abroad, and the masses, who are victims of educational reforms. Naturally, Oumou passes her exams, but Bah and other poor students fail, an injustice that sparks a student movement against the military dictatorship. The film ends with the mobilization of the whole country and the international press in support of the students. Bah dies a national hero, and a civilian governor replaces the colonel.

Finye, inspired by the many student strikes in Francophone Africa, has become a prophetic film that continues to influence the youth movement against neocolonialism and military dictatorships in West Africa. A few years after the film was released, a student leader known as Cabral was killed by soldiers who were attempting to break a students' strike that had closed the schools. The student had taken his name from Amilcar Cabral, the revolutionary leader of Guinea-Bissau who was assassinated by the Portuguese army. Cabral the student, like his namesake in the liberation struggle, and like Bah, the character in Cissé's film, became a martyr who inspired other Malian students to continue the struggle until the military was defeated. By 1992, democracy had finally arrived in Mali, after a bloody confrontation between the students—who were supported by their parents and other social groups—and the military. Life had imitated art: Cissé's *Finye.*

For those who believe in the second paradigm, good African art means an art that has exiled itself from the continent, in search of eager audiences and economic success in the metropolitan centers of Europe, North America, and Asia. Paris, New York, London, and Brussels become outlets for the latest African music, films, theater, fashion, and literature. After acclaim has been heaped on the artist in Europe and North America, he or she returns to Africa to display the laurels. Some artists return when the metropolis no longer has a use for their work. In other words, Africa is considered a secondary or marginal market for African art.

Like *Finye,* Sembene Ousmane's *Gelwaar* (1993) is another film that summons African youth to revolution. It is a film that is concerned with ensuring a better future for Africa's people in the twenty-first century. It inveighs against corrupt African leaders and the way in which people lose their dignity to victimhood and poverty. The plot of *Gelwaar* revolves around conflicts between Muslims and Christians over the body of Pierre Henry Thioune, a.k.a. Gelwaar (meaning "noble," "truthful," in Wolof), a Christian and a political activist, who is buried in a Muslim cemetery and must be exhumed and given a proper Christian burial. It turns out that Gelwaar was killed because he exposed the negative effects of international aid on his country and incited the people to rebel. For Sembene, political culture in Africa has become so dependent on aid that it has lost the capacity to produce anything but a generation of beggars. In a controversial and powerful scene, the film contrasts begging with prostitution, to illustrate that the prostitute's work is nobler than the beggar's because the prostitute supports herself and the beggar depends on donors. This is new thinking, insofar as it changes the cultural significance of begging in predominantly Muslim and animist West African societies, where beggars are seen as humble, honest people and as intermediaries between God and repentant sinners.

At the end of the film, a group of young people, inspired by Gelwaar's statements, stop a truck full of sacks of flour donated by international organizations and spill the flour on the road. When an elderly man tells them that it is a sacrilege to pour food on the ground, Gelwaar's wife replies that what really constitutes a defilement of culture is to continue receiving this aid from foreigners.

With *Gelwaar,* Sembene returned to the utopian topic of self-determination that he explored in such early novels as *O pays, mon beau peuple (O Country, My Beautiful People)* and *Les bouts de bois de dieu (God's Bits of Wood)* and which he abandoned in his later films in favor of satire, social realism, and criticism of postindependence regimes. By describing itself as a legend of the twenty-first century, *Gelwaar* draws attention to the African fin-de-siècle, when young people will ideally break away from old paradigms of Afro-pessimism and take their destiny into their own hands.

In Africa, national spirit is built through soccer matches and through star musicians, athletes, filmmakers, and writers, whom the nation appropriates. Countries that are predominantly Islamic foster national unity by identifying with Arab nations that claim to be successful through the grace of Allah and that are hostile to Christian demons and imperialists. Christianized Africans, on the other hand, think that they have a monopoly on modernity and create a spirit of unity by labeling Islamic Africans as backward. But external influences aside, Africans themselves have contributed to the shaping of national structures of feeling. Writers such as Sembene Ousmane and Ngugi wa Thiong'o link the rise of national consciousness in Africa to World War II, in which Africans fought alongside white people to resist fascism, xeno-phobia, and racism. In *O pays, mon beau peuple,* one of Sembene's characters argues that the war was more important for Africans than education, because it demystified white men for black people, who traveled to Europe and learned that whites were normal human beings, capable of evil and good, cowardice and courage.

Each nation in Africa has tended to define itself in opposition to other African states. In the 1950s, Guineans despised Malians because they were poor and were emigrating to Guinea to "steal" precious resources. People in Côte d'Ivoire blamed Ghanaians for the increase in prostitution and other crimes in their country. During my boyhood in Guinea at the time of independence, whenever the Malian national soccer team won a game, Malians' joy was mixed with fear. There were fights in the streets, and for a time my young friends would refuse to play with me.

West African Markets and Currency Devaluation

The markets of West Africa, traditionally centers of international con-sumption and cross-cultural fertilization, pose a serious challenge to globalization and to the structural adjustments advocated by the World Bank and other multinational corporations that are vying to recolonize Africa. Merchandise from all over the world is on display in these traditional markets, which makes it impossible for the nation-states to control the flow of goods, currency exchange rates, and the net worth of the markets. Everything—from computers and fax machines to brand-name shoes and gold jewelry—can be found, covered with dust, in the marketplace. Merchants who specialize in currency exchange carry large bundles of Japanese yen, German marks, British pounds, French francs, and U.S. dollars in the deep pockets of the billowing trousers they wear under their long, loose gowns. The markets are also visited by numerous well-traveled businessmen and businesswomen who speak English, Spanish, and German, in addition to French and various African languages.

Markets occupy an important place in the collective unconscious of West Africans. Every market is surrounded by legends and ghost stories. West African folklore abounds with market stories in which human beings conduct transactions during the daytime and the spirits take over at night. For some criminals and vandals, such lore functions as a powerful deterrent. They view modern shops, with their electronic alarm systems, as safer targets than the markets, which they believe to be crowded with ghosts at night. There are at least two other reasons people keep away from traditional markets at night: merchants are thought to use the magic power of medicine men and marabouts to protect themselves and their belongings; and markets provide a night-time refuge for outcasts and deranged people.

The history of markets in West Africa is also the history of the slave trade and of the movement beyond tribal isolationism toward the mixing of cultures, customs, and languages—in other words, the movement toward globalization. Medieval towns in West Africa—such as Timbuctu, Ganem, Araouane, Kumbi Salle, Bornou, and Niani—prospered through their markets, where Arab traders bartered salt, beads, dates, and livestock for slaves and gold. The disappearance or decline of some of these historic cities may have resulted from the ban on slave trading or the displacement of some commodities by others in the marketplace.

West African markets continued to develop and support cities during the centuries of European slave trade and colonialism, cementing ties among diverse tribes around market goods and commercial languages such as Dioula and Hausa. The long journeys of kola merchants from Mali to Côte d'Ivoire, the regional roaming of Hausa spice and medicine dealers, and the expeditions of the slave traders between the interior of the continent and the coasts constitute the first efforts at creating a regional imaginary, with faithful consumers waiting to receive commodities and cultural novelties from greedy and crafty merchants. What makes these traditional schemes of globalization special is the structural continuity they maintained with contemporary markets—in contrast to the modernist forms and structures that nation-states have put in place in West Africa since the 1960s. It is for this reason that some dismiss the markets as conservative and primitive forms of transaction which are opposed to the structured development plans of the nation-states.

What strikes the visitor to a market in West Africa is the seemingly haphazard display of commodities: tomatoes and lettuce sit next to colorful fabrics from Holland and Hong Kong. The markets are honeycombed with curving paths that seem to lead out of the confusion rather than take one to the merchandise of one's choice. If there is a vendor of mangoes, bananas, and oranges at the east entrance of the market, there are likely to be others at the north, west, and south entrances as well. In fact, most merchants prefer to be dispersed throughout the market or located at the entryways, instead of being grouped according to merchandise or affinity, or concentrated in the center area. Another—merely apparent—symptom of disorder is the way in which merchants fight over shoppers and reduce prices to undercut one another. The visitor to these markets may also be a little startled by the sight of deranged people, nearly naked, moving naturally among the crowd.

In West Africa today, traditional markets still pose the greatest obstacle to nation-states and their plans for modernization. The markets also challenge the World Bank and other global institutions that consider nation-states the only legitimate structures with which they can do business. Local banks and treasuries compete with the markets for institutional funds, and it is not uncommon nowadays to hear that all the money has vanished into the markets and that the banks and the government coffers are empty.

Many state officials depend on the markets when coping with financial crises. Government employees often withdraw foreign currency from banks and take it to merchants in the market, where they get a better rate of exchange. Customs officers and tax collectors supplant their low wages with bribes from merchants, consisting of new cars, villas, and large sums in cash. Government ministers and army generals receive equally valuable gifts in return for their friendship and protection.

Traditional markets can also serve as sources of emergency cash for politicians in power. Merchants are often asked to contribute when the president's office needs money for a prestige trip to the United Nations or the Organization of African Unity. In the worst-case scenario, when the banks run out of money and the president's office must have it, the government may suddenly remember an uncollected tax and threaten to close the markets until the amount needed is collected. To the outsider, all of this may seem grotesque or at least an abuse of the merchants by the state; but the markets accept it as normal because it increases the state's indebtedness to a system that is dismissed in official statements as artisanal, primitive, and corrupt.

The markets' competition with the nation-states and their multinational allies over the control of economic culture in West Africa has led to the politicization of merchants, who see in the new schemes of democratization and globalization nothing more than a means of taking business away from the markets and delivering it to Lebanese-run and French-run stores. On the other hand, African governments and the World Bank blame the failure of development projects on the markets, where corrupt merchants peddle smuggled goods at very low prices and prevent the rise of legitimate entrepreneurs who pay taxes.

Recently, the World Bank threatened to suspend a loan to Mali until the government was able to reduce significantly the flow of illegal merchandise in Bamako's largest market. The market subsequently caught fire, which led people to speculate whether this had been the work of officially sanctioned arsonists. The Kermel market in Dakar burned under similarly suspicious circumstances in 1993, and it was rumored that the state fire department, which had been alerted at two in the morning, had not arrived at the site until six, by which time the place was completely engulfed in flame and smoke.

One must bear in mind that after the Arab and European conquests of Africa, many aristocrats from declining empires transformed themselves into powerful merchants and created a link between the court nobility and economic capital, not to mention cultural capital. They elevated commerce to the highest social levels, and brought modern merchants a distinction comparable to that of medieval warriors and powerful landlords. Their "authentic" nobility contrasted with the dubious status of colonial army officers and state functionaries, who were relegated to the lower classes.

Clearly, therefore, West African markets have structured economic fields of power, as well as social spaces in the cities and provinces, that engaged the colonial system in a competition for the development of public spheres. At the time of independence the nation-states, like the colonial system, regarded the markets as backward, and failed to share with them the responsibility for producing the elites of the modern state. Thus, right from independence West Africa has had two antagonistic systems, the market and the nation-state, competing for economic and cultural capital.

The fact that markets have long been associated with the nobility is evident not only in the distinction of the richest merchants, but also in the accumulation of what Pierre Bourdieu calls symbolic capital—that is, a set of behaviors (such as lowering prices for certain people, helping the needy, living the life of a good Muslim, remembering one's origins, refusing to be blinded by money, maintaining personal cleanliness, dressing well, respecting the rules of courtesy) which mask their monetary motivations by linking themselves to recognizable and accepted practices of the family, kinship, and the market. In accordance with the aristocratic values of the markets, state functionaries are viewed with distrust because they always come to the market to take something and never give anything back. They are men without honor; they feed off the merchants' sweat. Students are also regarded with suspicion because, like baby snakes that grow into big and dangerous snakes, students will turn into functionaries one day. In West Africa, the majority of pickpockets and other petty criminals are school dropouts. They are alienated from the values of the market, yet are not adept or educated enough to become functionaries of the nation-state.

In contrast to the market aristocracy, members of the state nobility are selected from among those who can read and speak French. Schools and armies are the principal sources of this new type of African elite, which considers the merchants highly uncivilized, corrupt, and backward. Any self-interested project of nation building would do well to revise the dichotomized relation between the state and the market in West Africa. A more productive approach would put the traditional market economy at the base of the state's political culture, and progressively transform the merchants into modern businessmen and entrepreneurs. In other words, the West African governments would do well to further the interests of the markets, with their age-old amalgam of Hausa, Soninke, Yoruba, Fulani, Sérère, Mandinka, and Dioula traders.

But from their inception, the West African states entered into complicity with their European partners and not with the merchants of the marketplace, who were considered too primitive to be included in the category of the "new man," as Frantz Fanon conceived him. The problem here, contrary to what Axel Kabou and others seem to believe, is not that African traditions are closed to the outside influences that are necessary to modernization. Indeed, West African merchants were familiar with faraway and forbidden metropolises like Paris, New York, Hong Kong, Tokyo, and Johannesburg long before African students set foot in those places. (There is a saying in West Africa that when the Americans reached the moon, they found Soninkes and Hausas, looking for diamonds.) The problem is that the nation-state put too much faith in the "new man" and confused him with European man and his culture, which could be acquired in West Africa at the expense of the market man and woman and their cultures.

The concept of Western technology involves a masked essentialism and immanence that cement the relationship between European man and modern technology and posit that any participation in the techno-logical revolution must necessarily import European culture. The im-plications of this ideology, which refuses to place science in a historical context and to see the evolution of Europe as a particular moment in that history, have been devastating to cultures in Africa, which are normally seen in binary opposition to Western culture and technology. African states have surrendered to the notion of the superiority of European rationality, and have internalized the stereotypical idea that African experience in the market is incongruent with the interest of the "new man." Yet if the Japanese had listened to the Europeans, they would be laughing at themselves today, and the scientific world would be worse off.

West African merchants are struggling against this homogenization of world markets and cultures by doing what they have done ever since the Middle Ages: traveling to faraway places to bring back goods that will keep them competitive in the market; resisting attempts at takeover by Lebanese and Europeans; resorting to culturally sanctioned strate-gies of price cutting, tax evasion, and corruption of state agents, while denigrating the same civil servants for being too Westernized and for opposing the prosperity of the market. Far from remaining closed to outside influences, the merchants have been the first to introduce radios, sunglasses, watches, televisions, and Mercedes Benzes to the remote regions of West Africa. They revitalize traditional cultures by introducing these new elements into the market, resist multinational corporations that try to take over businesses, and compete with the agents of the state for the role of cultural modernizer of the masses.

African intellectuals and European expatriates, blinded by an essen-
tialized notion of Western technology versus African traditions, consider the consumer culture of the market alienating. They unleash a
plethora of arguments, drawing on anthropology, Marxism, and nationalism, against Muslim and Christian fundamentalism, which attempt to shield Africans in their authenticity, their pure relation to
production, and their uncorrupted communion with God from the
exploitation, alienation, and identity crises brought on by Western
consumer culture. Although the alienation thesis may have been a
meaningful argument during the early phases of nation building in
Africa, or during colonialism, it has lost some of its explanatory power
in the era of globalization. For instance, it is possible to see a valid
theory of alienation in Fanon's discovery that the French used culture-
specific radio dramas (enticing love stories and so on) to destabilize the
Algerian family structure during Algeria's war of liberation. To
Fanon's mind, the French deliberately used the radio to strike at the
core of the Algerian resistance movement. Fanon's critique of alienation was extended to television and newspapers, to show that Africans
use European culture as their reference for news, fashion, and definitions of reality.

African filmmakers have unsparingly deployed this Fanonian concept of alienation to define their own positions against cultural imperialism. Films denounce it under whatever form it appears. *Xala* (1974)
and *Gelwaar,* by Sembene Ousmane, decry the way in which some
Africans prefer French to local languages. *The Garbage Boys* (1986),
by Cheick Oumar Sissoko; *The Shadow of the Earth* (1978), by Taieb
Louhichi; *Zan Boko* (1988), by Gaston Kabore; and *Bab El Oued City*
(1994), by Merzak Alouache, a powerful film about Muslim fundamentalism in Algeria, all criticize the growing habit among Africans of
watching television as an escape and of using broadcast Western images as a source for identity formation. *Bab El Oued City* opens with a
scene in which words of resistance emanate from a loudspeaker: "We
must clean our city of the filth coming from outside." The allusion is to

European cultural imperialism, which stands between Algerians and their Muslim identity. Imported goods—particularly those associated with France, such as Camembert cheese, alcoholic beverages, television soap operas, and cosmetics—come under attack, forcing people to buy and enjoy these commodities in secret. But as the film shows, with globalization and the homogenization of taste, goods imported from Europe and elsewhere may be the only goods that some Algerians know. Clearly, by placing a ban on the consumption of these products, advocates of the alienation thesis may be involved not only in regulating taste and encouraging the consumption of local and culturally authentic goods, but also in a decision that can lead to the people's physical and mental starvation.

The markets in West Africa, on the contrary, give back to people what the state and the multinational corporations take away from them—that is, the right to consume. The slow death of many African nations is the result of the many structural adjustments, including the devaluation of the CFA franc, which exclude the people from the spaces of consumption. As postmodern reality defines historicity and ethics through consumption, those who do not consume are left to die outside history and without human dignity. The traditional markets are the only places where Africans of all ethnic origins and classes, from the country and the city, meet and assert their humanity and historicity through consumption. People find unity in their lives through the consumer culture of the market. If their existences are denied daily by currency devaluation and other structural adjustments, at least in the market they can buy, sell, exchange news about the crisis, help each other out, and, in the process, find themselves. When state functionaries are discharged because of budget cuts, they have the market to turn to for self-renewal; when peasants leave their villages for the city, they get "modernized" in the marketplace; women increase their self-worth in the market, as their entrepreneurial skills raise them to the rank of rich male merchants. Markets thus become a meeting place for the employed and the unemployed, the young and the old, women and men, the intellectual and the peasant. They are a site for new generative forces, for the transfiguration of old concepts, and for revitalization—a place that provides not only the basis for a challenge to structural adjustments, but also, as C. L. R. James discovered in his analysis of the Accra market in 1946, a basis for revolutionary action.

Markets in West Africa clearly undermine official forms of globalization, according to which a nation-state attracts investment by multinational corporations after undergoing a measure of structural adjustment—that is, devaluation. By producing disorder through pricing, pirating, smuggling, and counterfeiting, African markets participate in the resistance to multinational control of the national economy and culture. In this sense, it is possible to argue that they are engaged in a struggle to keep life in Africa from being recolonized by multinational systems which have an eye only for cheap labor, cheap natural resources, and devalued cultures. For example, as a challenge to the monopoly of Thai rice in Senegal, merchants smuggle rice from neighboring countries and sell it on credit to loyal consumers, who are persuaded by necessity and through market gossip that Thai rice is short-grained and sticky and therefore not good for the national dish, *Cebu-jen*.

This brings us to the charge that West African markets resist efforts to systematize them. The nation-states should have given a modern structure to the markets, not by trying to create a tabula rasa "new man" but by channeling the economic and cultural capital of the market into the modern political culture of the state. This would have entailed the transformation of some merchants into new elites of banking, entrepreneurship, and government bureaucracy. Instead, the nation-states turned against merchants and demonized them, labeling them uncivilized tribalists and feudalists. Blinded by their commitment to Euromodernism, which has long regarded African cultures as its polar opposite, African intellectuals and political leaders have no choice but to view markets as chaotic, incoherent, and precapitalist modes of exchange—in other words, as corrupt and conservative.

Clearly, charges that the markets are disordered and their prices arbitrary emanate from a complete misunderstanding of the way markets participate in the African culture of call-and-response and compete to attract a wide variety of consumers, from black American tourists looking for the "real thing" at bargain prices, to African women shopping for the latest "super wax" cloth, to servants buying condiments for middle-class kitchens, to young people trying on the latest Adidas and Nike shoes, to nouveaux riches acquiring sinks and toilets for their new villas. The markets have an order that is one of inclusion, regardless of one's class and origin, regardless of whether one is a buyer or a *flâneur*. Markets, aside from being the best reflection of West African societies, are the places where Africa meets Europe, Asia, and America. As they say in West Africa, "Visit the market and see the world."

What about the charge that the markets are corrupt? I believe that this, too, must be put in the context of the war of position between the markets, on the one hand, and the states and their Eurocentric vision of modernization, on the other. We have already noted the way African markets operate according to values of nobility, and the way in which symbolic capital is accumulated by individuals in the marketplace. This system, like every other system, has its internal and external rules according to which government functionaries, just like the former colonizers, are not to be trusted. From this perspective, the corrupting of civil servants—or, to put it in another way, the "buying" of customs agents, army and police officers, government ministers, and even the president—is a step toward winning the war, or at least prolonging the life of the market.

The nation-states have yet to win the support of the powerless in West Africa, other than by military and police intimidation. Most people cannot send their children to school and do not have access to health services, electricity, running water, and dependable roads. To these disenfranchised people, government seems good for nothing but hosting international organizations and channeling foreign aid through the leaders' own families. Government leaders incessantly sign deals with foreign corporations to exploit gold, oil, and other raw materials. Meanwhile, hard-working merchants and farmers encounter road-blocks throughout the region, designed to prevent them from shopping and selling freely across national borders. It is in this sense that one can argue that "buying" civil servants to circumvent roadblocks and keep the markets alive is a way of resisting the recolonization of life in Africa.

Crucially, therefore, one must distinguish the corruption of the state from that of the market. State corruption is the result of a liberal attitude in favor of bilateral and multilateral relations with Europe and other developed countries, to the detriment of the masses in Africa. Only the elites benefit from this type of corruption, which, in a sense, prevents states from building broad-based and democratic political capital. Aside from undermining the politics of self-determination launched by the independence struggles of the 1960s, state corruption also fosters tribalism and military dictatorship. Market corruption, on the other hand, benefits the masses by increasing the variety of goods in the marketplace, lowering prices, and making consumption possible. This role of the market is often overlooked by African political scientists, who, in their eagerness to become advisers to the World Bank, ignore the role of European governments and international institutions in the corruption of the state and blame African traditions for failing to embrace modernization, supposedly because of their innate predisposition to debauchery.

One must also consider the particular historical context of Africa today, in order to understand market corruption as a form of retaliation against the nation-states and the World Bank for taking jobs away from people, reducing their power to consume, and devaluing them in society. The markets have survived because the nation-states could not satisfy the people's demand for goods and because they lacked inclusive economic programs. Now that the nation-states are no longer considered the best modernizers of the people and the multinational corporations have assumed this role, the markets are again the focus of attention. Instead of emphasizing the function of markets as agents of globalization and homogenization, the World Bank and other financial and political institutions use nation-states to stem the circulation of goods in the markets. Thus, the marketplace becomes a site of resistance to any globalization that does not take into account social agents in West Africa, whose patterns of consumption and political positions are determined by their social spaces.

On January 20, 1994, European and American financial institutions imposed an expected but long-resisted currency devaluation on Francophone Africa that rendered export goods and labor in the region cheaper and more attractive to international corporations. Nigeria, Zaire, and Ghana had already gone through this process in the 1980s. The World Bank argued that these "structural adjustment programs," by attracting investors to devalued products and people, would create business opportunities for Africans who had been excluded for decades from the global marketplace.

Before the devaluation occurred, countries such as Congo, Côte d'Ivoire, and Cameroon were already suffering from the low prices offered for their exports in Paris, London, and New York. Furthermore, it is difficult for Africa to repeat the economic success of the so-called Asian Tigers (Hong Kong, Taiwan, and South Korea), given the historical differences between the two regions with respect to Western-imposed slavery, forced labor, and colonialism. During the independence movement, Francophone Africans were closely allied with the French Left and the labor unions—a fact that now makes it possible for Africans to take for granted the rights of workers, and that complicates the emergence of organized cheap labor in Africa as a means toward development.

The currency devaluation constitutes, therefore, the most serious economic and cultural crisis in Franco-African relations since the 1960s, when most African countries assumed their independence from

France. It bears on the collective imaginary of Francophone Africans in two ways. First, it identifies France, the World Bank, and "weak" African leaders as enemies of the people, demons that can be blamed for people's daily sufferings. Second, it provides people with a new perspective on their own lives, their relation to their leaders, their political institutions, and globalization. In a sense, one can say that devaluation has united Francophone Africa inside and outside. From within, it mobilizes an inter-African imaginary for self-determination against the recolonization of Africa. From without, it links Africa to the West by lowering the cost of raw material—and this has induced the worst economic crisis yet.

Like an earthquake that destroys the houses of rich and poor alike, and against which there is no insurance policy, people from Dakar (Senegal) to Douala (Cameroon) feel the impact of the devaluation every hour, every day, and every month. Imagine the plight of a farmer who has to plough twice the acreage to obtain the same quantity of meal, or that of a head-of-household who has to feed thirty-two people with the ration that previously fed sixteen. In the urban enclaves, where small entrepreneurs mingle with the middle class and the underclass, the devaluation—or *dévalisation* (a pun on *dévaliser,* meaning to rob)—has the impact of a bush fire in a dry Harmattan season. In Dakar, the price of a sack of rice has doubled, producing a swarm of beggars in the streets. The middle class itself has been devalued and pushed out of the center of the marketplace, joining the underclass on the margins and leaving restaurants, movie theaters, clothing stores, and nightclubs to tourists and expatriates.

Gasoline has become so precious that cab drivers wisely wait in front of hotels for customers. Universities have been closed in Senegal, Mali, Gabon, and Côte d'Ivoire. The fire departments, police forces, and hospitals are barely functioning in these countries, where people seem to be more preoccupied with the arduous search for daily bread for themselves and their families.

Everywhere in Africa new social movements are sprouting, with a view to wresting the nation away from what are perceived as incompetent leaders, or to liberate it from a second colonization by France, the World Bank, and the International Monetary Fund. People in Africa do not take the issue of second colonization lightly. In Dakar recently, I was discussing structural adjustment and Africa's second colonization with crew members of Ethiopian Airlines. Unsurprisingly, a young flight attendant said with pride that Ethiopia, unlike the other African states, had never been colonized. The copilot took issue with the statement by asking rhetorically whether the World Bank or the International Monetary Fund had a presence in Ethiopia. In his view, this was enough to prove that Ethiopia, too, had joined the ranks of colonies.

In Mali, university students, who played the central role in overthrowing the military dictatorship and bringing in a democratic regime, are once again agitating and vowing to overthrow the government. Because of the recent structural adjustment programs and the devaluation, they are faced with reduced scholarships, higher admission standards, school closures, and little prospect of finding jobs after graduation. In Mali, Côte d'Ivoire, and Senegal, there are hints that education may be privatized—something that even military dictators had not dared to do before. Many West Africans are longing for the reappearance of heroes who can turn the tide of misery and humiliation that has resulted from structural adjustments and devaluation.

In 1994 students at the University of Dakar walked out of negotiations to end a year-long protest when they heard that the World Bank was behind the plans to restructure the university. Resistance is also mounting in such Dakar newspapers as *Sopi, Le Sud, Wal Fadjri: L'Aurore,* and *Le Cafard Enchaîné.* Whose side are the International Monetary Fund and the World Bank on, when they look solely at economic factors and insist on closing down state-owned factories and institutions? The press sees the international financial institutions as using structural adjustments to intentionally undermine the nation and to destroy the social and cultural fabric of people's lives.

Many conversations in Dakar's streets involve expert analyses of the

World Bank's investment activities in Africa. An unemployed school-teacher may, for example, hold forth on his pet theory about how the bank has refinanced Africa's debt to industrial countries in order to impose structural adjustment programs on African states, while making sure that they owe an even bigger sum than before. This unfamiliar theory may confuse many of his listeners, which is precisely what the schoolteacher was hoping for. He might then explain that the interest on the bank's loans absorbs revenues from coffee and oil exports that are necessary for the development of the continent. Or that the bank gives only a small portion of the loans at a time, investing the biggest chunk in Western banks and forcing Africans to pay interest on the total package.

A cab driver in Dakar once told me that he had learned one lesson from the devaluation: African leaders are not real presidents—they are mere ambassadors, who do what the "real presidents" in France and the United States tell them to do. He insisted that to be president is not to be ordered around like an ambassador. If African presidents had been in charge, they would have responded to the devaluation by forming a united front and creating their own money. How can you be independent when you do not have your own money? Mali and Senegal, he reminded me, had once been a single country but had been divided all because Senghor had listened too much to de Gaulle.

People in Africa feel that any change must first begin with the leadership: African governments should not be run according to the needs and concerns of Europe and America. People do not understand why such issues as structural adjustment, pollution, environmental concerns, population control, the preservation of "authentic African cultures," and many other obsessions of European specialists have come to dominate the lives of Africans, pushing to the side concerns for survival, modernization, and the good life in Africa. There is much admiration for Japanese and Chinese leaders, and much regret that African leaders have not followed their example. The saying goes that the West respects Japan, Hong Kong, China, and Taiwan today because these countries did not wait for the advice of the white man to devise their own style of modernity. Africans, too, must find their own way in the modern world.

African leaders themselves view the devaluation as closing the era of personal friendship with French presidents. Gone are the days when African leaders could count on France as a strong "father" who would defend them against the "bullies" of the World Bank and the International Monetary Fund. With devaluation, African presidents have been dealt a humiliating blow that can neither be effaced by a promise of economic recovery nor concealed by long speeches on national television. This is all the more devastating because some people associate the power of the leaders with the wholeness of their public image. In Mali the griots used to sing a popular song called "Patron," which reminded the masses that their leader's power could be seen in the fabulously expensive embroidered clothes he wore, in the car he drove, in the villa where he lived, and in the way he spoke French. But since the CFA franc had been devalued, the exchange rate for the president's clothes had also been devalued, damaging his symbolic capital.

Most people in West Africa believe that France approved the devaluation for two reasons. The first was the death of Félix Houphouët-Boigny, commonly known as Le Vieux (the Old Man). Rumors have it that Mitterrand had promised Houphouët not to lower the value of the currency in his lifetime. Such a move would have meant a personal affront to the Old Man, after all that he had done for France. Hadn't Houphouët conspired with de Gaulle to isolate Sékou Touré after the latter's insulting no to France during the referendum of 1958? It was after Guinea's dramatic break with France that de Gaulle used the Old Man and Léopold Sédar Senghor of Senegal to prevent Guinea from participating in the economic and cultural activities of the region. Cornered like a wild animal, Sékou Touré then turned against his own people and became one of the worst dictators of West Africa. Many people believe that such sanctions would not have succeeded without Houphouët, who was respected by everyone in the region.

Because of the Old Man, Côte d'Ivoire became the privileged partner of France, which was eager to hold the country up as a model of success in contrast to Guinea and Mali—nations that had opted for socialism and that looked to the Soviet Union, China, and Cuba for help. For years, France continued to invest in Côte d'Ivoire, making it the envy of the region. In his last years, the Old Man was clearly in a good position to take credit for the rapid and relatively peaceful modernization of his country, while economic crisis, dictatorships, and military coups were rampant throughout the rest of Africa. France remained loyal to Houphouët even during the economic crisis of the 1980s, coming to his rescue when oil and coffee prices fell. The Old Man became an undisputed leader in Francophone Africa, garnering votes for France at the United Nations and buffering the region against American and Soviet influences. It was the Old Man himself who appealed to Mitterrand not to devaluate the CFA franc. The Old Man supposedly believed that, of all the elements of a crisis, devaluation was the one which affected people the most at the individual level, and therefore was the most likely to tarnish the popular image of a president. France wisely waited until the Old Man died to devaluate the CFA franc—to half its former value.

The second reason the CFA franc was devalued had to do with France's position in Europe. France had to choose between a role in the European Union (EU) which had global economic implications, and a role as the lone superpower in Francophone Africa. The emergence of the EU as a European supernation had begun to erode not only France's power to protect certain national rights, like those of its own traditionally strong unions, but also its power to sustain bilateral economic and political relations with Francophone Africa and distance them from the influence of the EU's political culture. To save face, France often attempted to integrate Francophone Africa into the political culture of the EU by shifting projects for African development from Paris to Brussels. The strategy was not only a money-saving device for France, but it also warded off any immediate challenge to the older-brother image of France in Africa and the unequal nature of Franco-African relations. Furthermore, France's role as intermediary between Africa and Europe strengthened Francophony at the European level. This was no small gain in view of the fact that Germany, the United Kingdom, and France were all jockeying for linguistic dominance in the EU.

It became clear that other EU members wanted a distinction drawn between those interests that were germane to the particular identity of France and Francophony, and those that were of consequence for the EU's role in the global market. Some EU members, conscious of the need to foster European economic hegemony throughout Africa (unlike France, which places priority on Francophone Africa), began seeking to diversify aid among Anglophone, Francophone, and Lusophone African countries. Clearly, France could no longer ignore the realities of the global economy and resist injunctions by the EU and the World Bank to stop overrating, for solely political reasons, the value of the currency in Francophone Africa.

In August 1994, seven months after the devaluation of the CFA franc, the prime minister of France, Edouard Balladur, toured Africa's Francophone countries to reassure them that France had not abandoned them. While in Dakar, he stressed the common ties that bind France and Francophone Africa and reiterated France's commitment to those ties. He declared that France was ready to support Africa during this difficult time by giving financial aid that could cushion the impact of the devaluation, and by underwriting the cost of certain pharmaceutical products to keep their price from doubling. Balladur also pointed out that the devaluation was not a bad thing: its aim had been to bring Africa back into the world economy, and it had done just that. Francophone Africa was now exporting more goods to Europe, America, and Asia than before; the lowered value of the currency also had the potential to attract investors and to create jobs in Africa. Visibly, Balladur's optimism was shared by Côte d'Ivoire's new president, Henri Konan Bedié, who believed that his country had put the devaluation behind it and was ready to compete, as the African Elephant, against the Asian Tigers. In Burkina Faso, Mali, and Senegal, the governments began trying to make a patriotic issue out of the devaluation by launching campaigns in favor of consuming national products, and by demonizing imported goods such as cheese, ice cream, certain brands of rice, designer clothes, and perfumes. It is true that these political campaigns on radio and television were greeted by nationalist feelings, but the masses also felt anger toward their leaders and members of the elite, who were the primary consumers of these goods. Some also pointed out that the issue was not consumption but devaluation, which had deprived people of the money to consume local or imported goods.

The argument that the markets are conservative and against the nation-state renders invisible their competitive and revitalizing nature. When the nation-states emerged in Africa in the 1960s, they were greeted as the proper structures of modernization, bringing national education, health care, armed forces, sports systems, national factories, and large-scale cooperative ventures. These nation-states went to war against the markets, which were considered either artisanal or corrupt. In socialist states like Guinea-Conakry, the markets were completely abolished, and the state became the only supplier of goods.

As the twentieth century draws to a close, it becomes clear that the nation-state, for which many Africans still fight, kill, and die, is no longer viable as a cultural and economic unit. For example, with the nation-state as the paradigm of political, cultural, and economic development, Mali, Guinea, Côte d'Ivoire, Burkina Faso, Gambia, and Senegal have been pushed into competition against one another over the production and ownership of "authentic" Mande music and culture. Clearly, West African musicians, filmmakers, and artists are the losers when their arts are confined to just one country. The narrow frontiers and visa requirements of nation-states also affect the merchants and consumers who are not free to drive across borders to shop.

Typically, Malians have relatives in Guinea, Senegal, Burkina Faso, Côte d'Ivoire, and Niger. But the nation-state is built in such a way that Malians define their belonging to Mali through opposition to other nation-states in the same region. To survive in the postmodern world dominated by new regional economic powers and information systems, West African states, too, must adopt a regional imaginary and promote the circulation of goods and cultures that are now sequestered or fragmented by the limits that the nation-state imposes on them.

One can envision a new map of West Africa: it would include Côte d'Ivoire, Burkina Faso, Niger, Nigeria, Ghana, Togo, Mali, Senegal, Guinea-Conakry, Guinea-Bissau, Sierra Leone, Liberia, and Gambia, and it would show English, French, Hausa, Yoruba, and Dioula (also known as Bambara, Mandinka, or Wangara) as the principal languages of business, politics, and culture. What is urgently needed in West Africa today is less a contrived unity based on innate cultural identity and heritage than a regional identity in motion which is based on linguistic affinities, economic reality, and geographic proximity, as defined by similarities in political and cultural dispositions grounded in history and patterns of consumption.

6

▲▼▲

Finding Sidimé Laye

During my childhood in Guinea, Sékou Touré had often said that Guinea's independence was but the beginning of the United States of Africa. In that ideal future, Sidimé Laye and I would be citizens of the same country. The Pan-Africanists had been looking for an Africa without frontiers, one that would be competitive with the rest of the world. These were the thoughts that haunted me in 1996, as I sat in the Hotel Camayenne in Conakry, watching white people go about their business.

And then there was Sidimé Laye. I was reading by the pool, racing against the fading daylight. A few mosquitoes were circling above my head, as if to celebrate the arrival of the evening. I was determined, however, not to let the mosquitoes or even the darkness climbing onto the pages stop me from finishing the passage I was reading in Richard Wright's book *The Color Curtain.* In the episode, which takes place in 1955, Wright arrives in Bandung, West Java, and is on his way to meet one of the leaders of Indonesia's opposition party. The Bandung conference is to bring together Asians, Africans, Central Americans, and South Americans who are mobilized around the issues of decolonization and national culture. Wright sees history in the making in this unprecedented meeting among the nonwhite races of the world, the wretched of the earth, the societies that have been pushed out of

163

▼

modern history by whites. He writes excitedly about the new voices of freedom emerging from Asia, Africa, and the Americas. He also describes vividly the nervousness of the United States and the Soviet Union about the prospect of unity among the nonaligned countries. The people gathered at the meeting—their political support and their national resources—are, after all, the stakes in the Cold War between the CIA and the KGB. News reports in the United States are already labeling the Bandung meeting a communist gathering.

But Wright is also uneasy about the way the conference is enabling the revival of national religions and their placement at the center of the anticolonial struggle. He has just heard a speech delivered by Sukarno, the leader of Indonesia, which linked decolonization to the free and open practice of Islam and other traditional religions throughout the world. Wright's desire for individual freedom and antiracist democracies justifies his anxiety about any attempt to use religion as a basis for national identity. He sympathizes more with progressive social movements that propel the masses of the Third World into modernity and render them uncolonizable than with efforts to restore authentic traditions and religion.

I was in the middle of Wright's book, captivated by his argument, when the hotel's paging system brought me back to reality: "Monsieur Diawara est demandé au comptoir de la réception, s'il vous plaît." They were summoning me to the reception desk. Night had set in by now. Some lights had been turned on around the swimming pool and the bar. Expecting nothing in particular, I walked to the hotel's reception desk. I was informed that a gentleman by the name of Sidimé Laye was looking for me. He was sitting over there, behind me, the receptionist said, pointing to the sitting area in the lobby. Just like that, he had shown up, I said to myself, feeling suddenly victorious. Then I turned and walked toward the sitting area, where several people were seated. Without a second thought, I headed toward the best-dressed man among them. It was then that a man looking more like a hotel employee, clad in a red Lacoste T-shirt and black jeans, walked toward me smiling. But I was focused on the well-dressed man behind him. I almost passed him. Then he said to me, "Maraka den, An Xubare?" ("Soninke boy, how are you?")

I was shocked. I took two steps backward, as if to make the man standing in front of me disappear. He couldn't *really* be Sidimé Laye! His hair was dusty. He was wearing white tennis shoes that were discolored with dust and black spots. His red Lacoste shirt with the green crocodile looked out of place and time. He was slim, deep black—about my height, but looking much younger. Tiny beads of sweat stood out on his forehead. He was still smiling. It was Sidimé Laye, all right. I felt like asking what had happened to him. But we hugged each other instead.

"Burulaye, my little brother," I said, "how have you been?"

"Who're you calling your little brother?" he asked, pointing his finger at me. "You remember the time I saved your ass from Bangali and his gang?"

"Tell me, then, who used to protect you from the girls—Dusu and Fanta particularly—who waylaid you coming from school?"

"Maraka den! You haven't changed a bit. You still have a big mouth."

We both laughed and embraced again. Then I invited him to come with me to the bar outside. I was still a little embarrassed at my reaction toward him, and surprised at myself for my elitist behavior. But how could this be the Sidimé Laye I used to know and admire? How could he be wearing such dirty clothes in a public place?

He must have guessed my thoughts, for as we sat down he said, "Maraka den, I bet you're wondering if I really am Sidimé Laye!"

"Well, I don't think you would have recognized *me* either if you'd met me on a deserted street."

"Are you crazy? With a face like that? I couldn't miss you in a crowded street. And that mark below your right eye—I remember the day you got it. You still look the same, with your bumpy forehead, your slit eyes, and big nose. Like a Dan mask."

We both laughed. He was looking at me with a penetrating gaze. His long face was animated by a playful smile which pulled the whole of his body into the action. He had no gray in his hair; his mustache was thin, like a young boy's; and he was beardless.

"Hey man," I said, "what took you so long to come and see me? Didn't you get my message?"

"I did," he said without changing his smile.

"Were you out of town?"

"No."

"Then what held you back?"

"I was busy."

"Busy doing what?"

"Finishing something."

"What could be more important than seeing your old pal, your big brother, your main man who used to protect you from all those mean and ugly girls?"

I was getting tired of his sly look and his yes and no answers. I wanted to tease him a bit.

"I saw you in the store," he said. "I figured you weren't going anywhere—at least, not until you ran out of money to pay this god-damn hotel. So I figured I'd finish my work first and see you after."

"You saw me in the store?"

"Yes, both times."

"And you let those guys make a fool out of me! I'll get you for this. What were you doing anyway that was so important?"

"Carving a Fang mask."

"What? What do you know about carving? And what do you know about Fang people?"

"I'm pretty good at my work. Some people even think I'm the best in Guinea. But I think my uncle is better than me."

"Your work? Are you an artist? I mean, that's great. I mean, I thought you'd be a politician or a doctor or a lawyer by now!"

"Oh, those were childhood dreams. They weren't real."

"What do you mean? You were the best student I ever saw. I wanted to be like you when we were growing up. You were my role model even in America."

"Very well, then. You, the Maraka boy, have become a white man, and I became a carver like all my family."

"You're an artist. That's great! I'm a writer myself." I was trying to change the direction of the conversation, for I did not like where Laye was taking it.

"No, I make masks. Traditional idols and stuff like that."

"And where did you learn to do that? I mean, did you study at the Ecole des Beaux-Arts here or in Europe?"

"No, I learned it from my uncle. Do you remember him?"

"Yeah! I used to be scared of him because his statues looked so real. I used to think he was a magician. Do you remember being afraid to cross the vestibule at night—the place where he worked?"

"No, Maraka den, you never really knew me. I wasn't afraid of statues the way you were."

Sidimé Laye took out a pack of cigarettes and offered me one. I declined. He lit one for himself.

"You know," he said, "in those days, after walking you to your house, I used to come back to the vestibule to play with my uncle's statues. Some of them were the same height as me, some were taller, some shorter. I used to watch the shadows move across their faces as the sun disappeared. Some of them looked furious, like lions in the dark, and I would hide behind the others for protection. I then felt their warm bodies, with their tight muscles and strong legs. I knew they were not afraid of lions. I used to imagine all sorts of games with them that I could not play with you and the other boys. That's when I started sitting near my uncle in the vestibule and watching him work."

"You're kidding! I thought your father hated your uncle's work because it was evil!"

"That's not true. We've traditionally been a clan of carvers. My ancestors made idols for many tribes in the region. People used to come from very far away to ask my grandfather to carve their ancestral masks. He was the best carver in the whole region. He made masks for the Baga, the Bambara, the Senufo, and the Guro. My father himself was once an excellent carver, though most people don't know it. He stopped carving only after he was married and it was revealed to him in a dream that he had to stop making humanlike figures or lose his family. That's when he started a small school at home and taught the Koran to children."

"So it was because of his religion that he stopped carving?"

"No. It was because of his dream. He was getting too good at it, and his hand was being possessed by the ancestors whose images he was carving. The same thing happens to me sometimes when I am in the middle of a work. I become possessed by the mask I am carving. The finished work sometimes turns out completely differently from what I had intended. My father was afraid of visiting these areas of spiritual creativity. He thought he was going mad. That's why he stopped carving. As for me, I prefer this spiritual moment above all else in the world. I enjoy being lifted out of the present to meet interesting spirits, characters, and shapes that are several centuries old. I love affirming their permanent power and beauty."

"That's interesting, Burulaye. Could we go see your work? I can't wait to see it. That's so fascinating."

"I don't have work that is mine. Once I finish a mask, it is mixed with my uncle's carvings and those of my cousins and nephews, and shipped to different places to be sold. There are some in the store, but I don't consider them as my work. They are sold simply as African masks."

"But if the spirits guide your hand while you're making the statues, why don't you treat the finished product seriously?"

"For me it is just work."

"Yet you're selling not only art, but the bodies and souls of the spirits that possess your hand. I understand now why your father stopped carving."

"For me it's just work. Find me buyers and I'll make you more of them."

"Do you respect the spirits that possess your hand?"

"Oh yes! And they know it. That is why they always visit me."

"But only white people buy the masks. They lock them up in their museums, and they decide what's authentic and what's a fake."

"That's all right. Maybe the masks will do a better job of representing us in Europe than African people like you."

"Nonsense! White people use the masks as a sign of our primitiveness. They deny us a role in modernity. That's why they prefer the masks to us."

"That's not my problem, because I am not dying to be loved by white people. I just want to be paid for my work."

"Burulaye, do you think the masks you make are good?"

"People have said so."

"How good?"

"Good enough for the experts not to know the difference between my work and the idols of which they are a copy."

"But they can tell the difference by looking at the age and the patina of the wood."

"That's what they say. But age alone does not determine the originality of the work. Even today, in remote villages, people break their idols during ritual performances. They simply replace them with new ones. Look at the Dogon, for example: they make new masks every day. I myself have carved idols for clans."

"Then how do you tell a good mask from a bad one?"

"That's not my problem. All I know is that all of my masks are good because they're possessed by the spirit of the idols they're supposed to represent. That's why I am able to sell them."

"Are you troubled by the fact that there are so many bad African masks in the market today?"

"No, because only the ones with a spirit sell for significant money."

"Why?"

"They attract the buyers in the same way they possess my hand when I am carving them."

"Do you collect masks?"

"No. I used to keep some of my uncle's work around until I mastered how to make them. Now I just keep catalogues of museum exhibitions around, and I can make any mask or statue once I see it in a catalogue."

"What are your favorite masks?"

"I don't like to admire the finished work. For me, that's dangerous. I just like working on masks and knowing the character of the spirits that enter them through my hand. I like the fine features of Bambara masks, which have frightening horns on their heads. For me, those features symbolize the refinement of the society and the dangers for those who violate the taboos. That's why I don't like to interact with people once I feel the spirit of a mask entering my hand as I work. I also like the forehead of a Dan mask. For me, the forehead has to have a magnetic force which can suck out the brains of those who refuse to obey it. It's the most difficult part when I make one of those masks. The forehead determines everything there. It's where the spirit resides."

"How about the Chi-wara mask?"

"It's not difficult to make; it just takes too long. It's really for beginners. I don't like to make them anymore."

It was getting livelier on the hotel terrace. Some people were having dinner, and the bar area was crowded with more and more white people. There was a band in the background playing songs like "Guantanamera" and "J'entends siffler le train" ("I Hear the Train Whistle Blow"). The wailing of the guitar in those songs generally used to evoke in me feelings of loneliness, of not belonging to "this place," of a strong desire to travel far away. But today they seemed obtrusive. I did not want to leave this place, now that I had found Sidimé Laye. I realized then, as the noise began to drown out our conversation, that there was a powerful complicity between hotel spaces in Africa and these songs, one which excludes Africa as a viable and livable place and transforms the hotels into the refuge of heroes—that is, romantic and lonely people. The tunes become blues songs whose protagonists are the hotel customers. Funny—the Westerners staying in these hotels had always seemed like passengers on a lost ship, but this was the first time it occurred to me that they could be conceived of as victims of Africa. I asked Sidimé Laye to take me to a quieter place, where we could have dinner and converse in normal voices. We had so much to catch up on.

Laye suggested we go to a small Moroccan restaurant not far from the hotel. He said they had good couscous, which he was sure I would appreciate, seeing as how I was a "Maraka den." We both laughed. When we were little boys, my mother had cooked couscous every night, and my friends had made fun of my people for keeping to their traditional diet even in the big city. They had often joked that no amount of civilization could change the Maraka people.

Laye said he liked to go to this particular restaurant because of a Cuban waitress who worked there. I asked him if he wanted to go home and change his clothes. He laughed and said they already knew him there. He'd often eaten there with an American dealer who ordered a Baule mask from him. I asked him if he was married. He said no, not anymore. His mood suddenly changed. He took out a cigarette and lit it nervously. His permanent smile had disappeared—he now seemed to be avoiding my eyes. I wished that I had not asked the question.

When we arrived at the restaurant, the Moroccan owner and the Cuban waitress were very cordial to us, but Laye no longer seemed to be his usual confident self. He was smiling with downcast eyes as he introduced me to them. The Cuban woman was very beautiful. She looked like a model for Calvin Klein or Levi Strauss, with her tight-fitting jeans and T-shirt. I wondered what a beautiful woman like this was doing in Guinea, ten years after Sékou Touré's death. Well, the country was now pro-French, and the Cold War had ended. When she came to our table, Laye told her that I was from New York. I spoke to her in the bad Spanish I had learned in restaurants in America. She told me to take her to New York with me. The owner of the restaurant saw us talking and called her back to the kitchen. She smiled timidly, revealing her dimples. Laye told me that the owner was very jealous, even though he was married.

"So, Burulaye," I said, "how long have you been living in Conakry?"

"Oh, I just moved here. I was living abroad myself until recently, when my wife left me. I was first in Côte d'Ivoire for a long time, to perfect my carving skills. Then I settled in Nigeria—in Lagos—where I had several orders for Igbo masks and Yoruba ivory carvings. I was there with my wife and five children. Then we received the news of my father-in-law's death. I sent my wife to pay her condolences, and it was then that a rich businessman corrupted her and her mother, with his money. She never again returned to me and the children in Lagos. She simply wrote me a letter asking for a divorce. I was beside myself. I could no longer concentrate on my work or the business I was starting to build. So I returned to Conakry to try to win her back."

"And?"

"Well, it hasn't been easy. The man is very rich. He owns hotels, and he is well-connected with officials in the government. The important thing is that I can work again, and my children live in the big family with my uncle. Maybe one day she will return to me."

"Oh my God, Burulaye! I am truly sorry! It is the same everywhere nowadays. It is so difficult to keep a marriage together."

"Everything was fine until then. If only I had gone with her to pay my condolences."

"Hey, man, don't blame yourself. I swear it isn't easy to keep a marriage together nowadays. There are so many competing interests and competing ways of looking at reality, that marriage as we used to know it, as it was with our parents, is no longer possible."

"But we loved each other, and that should have been the most important thing."

"I know, Burulaye. I just don't want you to keep on blaming yourself. You're still young, and you have a whole life ahead of you."

"You're right, Maraka den. Where did you become so wise? Did the

Americans teach you that, too? I heard they were number one in everything."

We both laughed and ordered more drinks. I remembered the dream that Laye's father had had, warning him to give up carving for the sake of his family. Was there something about Laye's profession that worked against marriage? But, I thought, it would not be wise to return to that conversation. Laye's story had made me uneasy enough as it was. I did not want to get too personal at this stage of our reunion.

"So, Burulaye," I said, "what happened to the other guys we grew up with?"

"Oh, most of them live abroad. You know, there was nothing left to do here under Sékou Touré. Some went to Senegal, some to Côte d'Ivoire, and some to France. Do you remember Lamine Diakité—old 'Fatty'? He was with me in Lagos. He is quite rich today, with an import-export business. Antoine, the son of Monsieur Charles, the mulatto doctor, is in France. He is a French citizen now. You know Bangaly Sidibé, who used to fight like Jack Palance in cowboy flicks? He returned from Mali five years ago to work at the shipyard as a customs officer. His half-sister Dusu got him the job. She is a very wealthy businesswoman here in Conakry, with trucks going from the port to the interior of the country and beyond. You know, in this country you can open all doors with money. Bangaly didn't even have a background in tax law, and now he's one of the most important men in the shipyard. But God help you if you haven't any money or connections! Even your family will forsake you."

"What happened to Lamine Diakité's brother? You know, the one who used to pick people's pockets."

"Salif? He died a long time ago. I think he was in prison for armed robbery. They sent him to Camp Boiro with the political prisoners."

"Wow! Did anybody study to become a schoolteacher, a lawyer, or a doctor? Remember the way we used to dream of one day becoming like Sékou Touré and Diallo Telli?"

"Yes. But those were just childhood dreams. I dropped out of school one year after you and your parents left Guinea, and went to work with my uncle as an apprentice carver. Remember the day you came to say goodbye to us in the schoolyard? I did not want to be seen too much with you, because I was afraid someone would denounce me and my family to the secret police. You see, they had already arrested my other uncle, Mamadou Sidimé, who was in the Office of Political Affairs and was the governor of Kankan. He was accused of smuggling antique masks out of the country. In reality, he had given one of his brother's carvings to an Air Afrique pilot to take to the governor of Freetown, Sierra Leone, who was his friend. Unfortunately, there were some soldiers on the plane who were trying to flee Sékou Touré. They were arrested before the plane took off, and the search revealed the mask that was linked to my uncle. After independence, it was against the law to perform traditional rituals with masks or to smuggle idols out of the country. So my uncle was arrested with the insurrectionist soldiers and accused of attempting to overthrow Sékou Touré and the revolutionary government. After that, my whole family was under surveillance by the secret police. So there was no point for me, or anybody in my family, to stay in Sékou Touré's schools."

7

▲▼▲

Africa's Art of Resistance

Blinded by My Loss

That night, Sidimé Laye and I walked back to my hotel surrounded by
the loss of our childhood innocence, the loss of lives during Sékou
Touré's revolution, the loss of friends and lovers. We were quiet as we
made our way through the darkness that claimed most of Conakry.
The sound of our footsteps competed with that of the ocean waves
tumbling against the black rocks. Sidimé Laye left me in front of the
hotel, promising to meet me in the morning at ten.

When Sékou Touré had expelled my parents and me from Guinea, I
had imagined all the tragedies of the world to be mine alone. I had
loved Sékou Touré and the revolution he was leading. By sending me to
school against my parents' will, and against the odds in favor of
illiteracy among the Soninke, Sékou Touré seemed to have made available to me the role of the modern hero. I could learn to speak French,
write letters for my people, and become the equal of my lettered
Guinean friends. I could even become a doctor or a teacher for the new
nation-state. I had felt then that the expulsion was taking all of this
from me and sending me back to my tribe and its customs. I had envied
my friends who, unlike me, would continue to enlarge their roles as
actors in the Guinea revolution. I confess that the main reason for

coming back to Guinea after all these years was so that I could recapture some of what the expulsion had taken away from me—so that I could be a part of Guinea again.

But how could I have known that Sidimé Laye, of all my friends the object of my greatest envy, had been losing something to the revolution? I had seen only his unwrinkled school uniform, his perfect scores in dictation and math, and his dignified comportment, unusual for a kid our age.

I remember one time we'd been playing soccer and Bangaly had kicked the ball over the wall and into the yard of Musa Diakité, a mean old man with a whip made out of camel hide. We all knew the rule laid down by Musa Diakité for getting the ball back: whoever went into the yard to retrieve it would receive ten lashes from the old man. Sometimes, the bravest among us would quickly climb the wall and bring the ball back before Musa Diakité could get his whip and run after them, hurling foul words at them, their fathers, and their mothers. Musa Diakité had more than four wives. Whenever he was beating one of them with the camel-hide whip, no one dared to interrupt him lest he accuse the meddler of sleeping with his wife and start whipping him, too.

That time, when Bangaly had kicked the ball into the yard, the mean old man, who by then knew how to outsmart us, had gone after it first. When he'd retrieved it, he'd gone inside his *ce-so* (the head male's room in a compound), brought out his whip, and sat by the door. Sidimé Laye had said then that he was going in to get the ball back. What about the whip? I'd asked him. He'd replied simply that it was only a beating and that it would pass. For some reason, Musa Diakité had not whipped him. He'd given the ball back and we'd never kicked it into his yard again.

I had always thought that Sidimé Laye's nobility was inviolable, that no one could touch him, that no one could take anything from him. I had always thought him luckier than I was. He'd been ahead of me in school, and he'd had perfect parents who never embarrassed him in public, unlike mine, who could not even speak good Mandinka. Every-one had wanted to be friends with Sidimé Laye, boys and girls alike. How could I have thought him vulnerable to anything, especially to the revolution that was making heroes out of us? Was it possible that I'd been so involved in my own loss that I'd been unable to see his? My loss had blinded me. I'd thought that, compared to mine, everyone else's life was without suffering.

But in fact I was more fortunate in having left Guinea when I did. My father had escaped Sékou Touré's prisons, and I had continued my schooling in Bamako, Mali. After a short time there, I had made new friends who had taken the place of most of my friends in Guinea. But I'd continued to admire Sékou Touré and to hold on to the memory of my childhood with Sidimé Laye, Bangaly Sidibé, Lamine Diakité, and Antoine Mitterrand. I left Guinea at a time when the revolution had begun to run out of steam, so I can say that I left Guinea during the good old days. I'd had the good fortune to live in Guinea when Sékou Touré had demystified white people, and I'd been personally touched by him. I'd been lucky, too, to have carried with me to Bamako a feeling of myself, created by Sékou Touré, as a new man who could shape the destiny of my Africa.

I can still remember as if it were yesterday the voyage that took us back to Mali. There were more than 350 of us in a boat that they said was designed to hold 150. It was January and the river waters were receding. The boat often ran aground, and we had to camp on shore so that the men could remove the sand that was obstructing the passage. I would take out my Swiss army knife and carve my name on trees next to those of Sékou Touré, Patrice Lumumba, and Kwame Nkrumah. Sometimes we camped near a village, where we would spend the night. There were always policemen and soldiers, who counted us and made sure we returned to the boat in the morning. I used to imagine then that I was Moses, searching for the land that Sékou Touré, Lumumba, and Nkrumah had promised us.

Sidimé Laye had remained in Guinea through the nightmarish years when brother turned against brother, and children sent their own mothers to die in prison. I had lost my childhood to the fantasies of new manhood and decolonization, and Sidimé Laye had lost his to violence, political conspiracies, and betrayals. I still live and am sustained by these fantasies of African liberation, and I returned to Guinea to revisit the birthplace of the dream, the place where I had been born again as a new man. Sidimé Laye had lost his uncle to the incessant political conspiracies, which had also torn his family apart and interrupted his education in Sékou Touré's revolutionary schools. I had left Guinea believing in the revolution, not realizing that the expulsion of Africans like my parents was the first sign of its failure. Sidimé Laye had seen the revolution turn into a nightmare and had struggled to endure it every day until he was old enough to run from it. He had started over in Abidjan, Côte d'Ivoire, and had later moved to Lagos, Nigeria, where he had done well with his carvings. He had now returned to Guinea to win his wife back and to rebuild the life shattered by the legacy of Sékou Touré. It is clear to me now that my Guinea is different from Sidimé Laye's. His is where things went wrong, where dreams were betrayed, and where people were trapped in constant fear. Mine still bears the patina of innocence, beauty, and exuberance.

His father's dream about sculpting masks began to have relevance to me not only because Laye had lost his wife, which in itself is no small matter, but because a mask discovered on a plane had led to the arrest of Laye's uncle and to Laye's leaving school before even completing eighth grade. How could it be that Sidimé Laye now found peace in sculpting masks and statues, when his father's dream was an unmistakable warning of the restlessness they could cause the soul? His uncle's arrest and death under torture, the sudden manner in which he himself had been snatched out of school, his wanderings in West Africa as a Guinean exile, and the loss of his wife—all made it clear that the masks had placed a curse on Sidimé Laye.

In the initial years after independence, Sékou Touré had changed the object of the revolution: he'd turned his rage toward other African ethnic groups and traditions in Guinea. On the one hand, the expulsion of people like my father might have been justified because of their petty-bourgeois values, which undermined the collectivizing efforts of socialism and the efficient and corruption-free management of the nation-state. On the other hand, the expulsion of West Africans from another West African country with a common historical and cultural heritage cast doubt on the meaning of independence and Sékou Touré's belief in Pan-Africanism. I remember how my father used to say that Sékou Touré had gotten rid of the French so that he could be free to kick us around: he wanted to make sure there was no one around to see him when he turned his rage against his own people. My father had never accepted the label of counterrevolutionary as a justification for turning Guinea into a police state. He wanted Sékou Touré to adjust his revolutionary government so that it would include the majority of the population, even if that meant including the counterrevolutionaries.

Another tragic flaw of the Guinean revolution was the way it had continually attacked traditional institutions as reactionary practices. The revolution, Sékou Touré often said, was anchored in African communal systems; it was different from other socialisms because it was an African socialism. Yet Sékou Touré had banned such institutions as tribal masked dances, idol worship, and the clan structure, all of which held communities together. So even as he was asserting the difference between European socialism and his own, he was continuing to judge African traditions with narrow Marxist lenses. Consequently, he had failed to transform the traditional rules and customs of the clans into something dynamic and modern. Like most African leaders, he had succeeded only in temporarily and brutally driving them underground.

The Curse of the Masks

Today, ten years after Sékou Touré's death and the fall of most of the first nationalist regimes in Africa, the masks, statues, and oral traditions—the main supports of tribalism in Africa—have returned with a vengeance. When exhibited in the market by the skilled hands of merchandising experts, masks and statues give an uncanny impression that is the property of kitsch. They look alive, yet derisory and clownish. It is as if at the moment the fact of being alive becomes dramatic, they lose all capacity for seriousness, becoming childish imitations, banal because they appear in such large numbers. It is the very ubiquity of the masks and statues as merchandise that stops one from taking them seriously.

In one corner, there may be fifteen masks, all with horns. Next to them will be fifteen more that represent dangerous animals. There may also be carved faces with nails in their eyes; others with tongues protruding; abstract ones with flat heads, bulging foreheads, elongated jaws, and impossibly long noses; and of course, the obligatory Chiwara (antelope) masks. The statues are usually arranged behind the masks. There are tall ones brandishing rusty knives, with their penises hanging down to their knees, and pot-bellied ones covered all over with tribal scars. There are statues with snakes on their heads; others with lifted arms, with one leg, with three legs; others riding horses or serving as stool bases; others that are part animal and part human, or part man and part woman. Arranged in this way, the masks and statues become the property of the market. Like every other piece of merchandise, they compete for a buyer who alone can restore to them their uniqueness as a Baule mask, a Fang mask, or a Dogon ancestor figure. As they compete aesthetically among themselves, they acquire a dramatic air, as if to say: Buy me, I am more authentic than the rest of them. Buy me, I'm the prettiest mask here. Buy me as a souvenir of this place. Buy me, I'll make a good present.

My father and all the people of my tribe believed in the transformative power of the market. Even those who did not have merchandise to sell would take a shower every morning and put on clean clothes to go to the market. They believed that markets brought good luck to people. My father used to force me to spend my weekends there. I would sell kola nuts from a big tray that I carried on my head between stands, or perhaps sugar cubes, which people needed when they ate food or drank tea in the market. Sometimes I would just sit around and listen to the stories of tribal men.

The merchants always arranged their wares neatly and strategically to attract customers. In the front, they placed the most colorful and least expensive fabrics, hats, shoes, and bags. The fabrics were designed with portraits of Africa's emerging political leaders, such as Lumumba, Nkrumah, and Sékou Touré, or soccer players like Pelé, or with slogans like "Long Live African Unity!" or the independence date of Guinea. The more expensive fabrics, the so-called "Super wax" from Holland, were in the back.

Like the masks, the Super wax fabrics have succeeded in maintaining their symbolic capital in spite of the revolution. People move past the material with big portraits of Sékou Touré and Nkrumah to buy their Super wax from the back of the display. When I was little, I never could understand why Mother, who bought cloth every week, had never bought the kind with Sékou Touré's picture on it. Everybody wore such cloth at political rallies, and to me it seemed the very latest thing because it depicted the major figures of the African revolution. I liked the fabrics with our own African images—the map of the continent, the national currencies, the presidents' faces. My father, on the other hand, hated everything with Sékou Touré's picture or ideas on it. He said Sékou Touré was destroying the market, along with everything that made people happy and free.

By insisting on carving masks for the market, Sidimé Laye showed a certain similarity to my father: they both used the market to say no to the revolution. In a way, the surrender of the masks' dramatic appearance to the market system, which turns them into objects for sale, is not so much a sign of the mortification of the masks' spirit as it is an illustration of Sékou Touré's failure to absorb them into the Guinean revolution, to transform their role in the nation-building effort.

The vengeful return of masks, statues, and oral traditions is also apparent in the survival of secret societies and masquerades in Guinea. Some of these rituals had already been driven underground by the Muslims in the nineteenth and early twentieth centuries. From the early days of his regime, Sékou Touré banned masked rituals and secret societies on the grounds that they were counterrevolutionary reactions against African movements toward progress and unity. Insofar as every leader in Africa needs a religion or a mythic origin to consolidate his image, Sékou Touré chose Islamic mysticism over the masks' magical powers. He added "Ahmed," a shortened version of the prophet's name "Muhammad," to his own name. In this way, Ahmed Sékou Touré became the sworn enemy of clans that worshiped masks and statues.

Sékou Touré's alleged grandfather Almamy Samory Touré had used Islam to unite several tribes across West Africa in a long and bitter resistance to French colonization. Ahmed Sékou Touré himself deployed a blend of Islam and Marxism-Leninism, not only against France but also against those fanatical devotees of masks and tribal idols that posed a threat to the revolution. Many marabouts also saw the revolution as a chance to increase their power beyond the mosque to the rest of their village or even their province, by denouncing the powerful founders and local leaders whom they could not entirely convert to Islam during the colonial era. Their whistle blowing led to corruption and bribery, as the same marabouts soon became rich traders of African masks and statues in New York, Paris, and Geneva. The revolution then banned the masks, both for use in ritual performances and for export to foreign markets. Many innocent people were caught in the net and suffered—even died, like Sidimé Laye's uncle.

Today, like born-again movements, the masked rituals are returning to many villages. And with the zeal and fundamentalism typical of such movements, the villagers look nostalgically to the past, when such rituals were pure, complete, and manly. Senior citizens are asked to remember how the rituals were performed: how many masks were used, what dance steps corresponded to which masks, who was allowed to take part, and how the rituals differed from one another. In reality, some of the rituals died out at the beginning of the twentieth century, and the memory of them survives only through oral traditions. But they are being reconstituted everywhere in Guinea today, as in other parts of Africa, by tribal minorities in search of their ethnic identity.

These minorities are aided in their search by anthropologists, tourists, and historians from the West who are disinclined to look favorably on the nation-state in Africa. Masks have therefore entered global political conflicts as organizers of markets, ethnic identities, and cultures against the nation-states and African unity. In Guinea, for example, the Baga mask performance is an expression of the Baga identity that Sékou Touré's regime repressed. Similarly, the authenticity of Benin traditional art in Nigeria, of Dogon art in Mali, and of Ashanti art in Ghana sets those ethnic groups apart from others as more authentically and originally African.

In fact, ethnicity is in vogue today in Africa, and everyone from the intellectual to the businessman is claiming it against the unity proposed by the nation-state. Some African intellectuals see the new democratic wind blowing in Africa as bringing hope for the future: recognition of ethnic difference within the nation-state. According to this logic, elections are not sufficient in themselves; the winner must, in addition, act like South Africa's Nelson Mandela and appoint tribal representatives to posts in his government.

Masks, even in their kitschiest manifestations in the marketplace, represent the persistence of tribal Africa. Masks are the symbols of clans and therefore the negation of the new nation-state that has tried to suppress them. Soon after independence, the marabouts, Sékou Touré's Marxist ideological advisors, and the educated elites joined forces to eradicate the practice of tribal religions and masked rituals which were continuing to control lives. For this reason, it has proven difficult for Africans, modern intellectuals included, to abandon tribal practices in order to respond to the call of a revolutionary and nationalist identity. When I was growing up, the revolution taught me that clinging to tribal ways was reactionary. I must have believed it because my relatives and I were foreigners in Guinea; we had already moved on, already changed. I was looking for something to belong to, and the revolution held within it the promise of equality. Sidimé Laye and my other friends, in contrast, were in their own element. Change for them entailed a more wrenching effort.

Laye's father had said that the masks place a curse on people who are always around them. This reminds me of the snake god Biida, who put a curse on the people of the Wagadu Empire. When Muslim merchants and slave drivers reached our area, in the early eighteenth century, they declared our gods inappropriate and our customs paganistic. The erosion of our customs and religions by Islam led to the destruction of the Soninke empire of Ghana and its capital, Wagadu.

Ghana was the largest and most powerful empire in West Africa, until Arab traders arrived there at the end of the sixth century and the beginning of the seventh. In those days, it was customary to make an annual sacrifice—the most beautiful maiden of the realm—to Biida, the snake god hiding in the well of wealth. In return, Biida made Ghana the most powerful and fearsome empire, with plenty of gold and silver and abundant harvests.

Then, one year after the Muslims had arrived and had converted the king and the powerful African merchants, a young man by the name of Mamadu Séfé Dokoté—Mamadu the Taciturn—challenged the annual ritual. The chosen maiden that year was named Sira; she was Mamadu's fiancée and the most beautiful girl in Wagadu, even in all of Ghana. When Sira learned of Mamadu's objection to her selection as Biida's maiden, she was deeply embarrassed and hurt. She did not want people to think that she was less beautiful or less dignified than the other young women, or that she was less deserving of being Biida's choice, or that she was afraid of dying. What a dishonor it would be for her if another girl were chosen in her place! And what honor and esteem it would bring her if she could appease Biida's hunger for a maiden, and be the cause of his generosity and love toward the whole empire!

But Mamadu, whose name indicates that he had converted to Islam, was blinded by love and his new religion. He refused to listen to Sira. He sharpened his saber, mounted his horse, and rode to the well of wealth, where he hid himself in the bush until the ritual that brought Sira to the mouth of the well had ended. After everyone had dispersed and left Sira to her fate, Mamadu came out of the bush. Sira was enveloped from head to toe in a white wedding gown, and she did not see Mamadu coming. How could she? This was a sacred place, and no human was supposed to be present when Biida emerged from the well of wealth. Whatever noise she heard, she would have attributed to Biida himself.

Mamadu waited by the well, his saber ready for Biida. From morning till evening, Sira and Mamadu waited in silence. Biida came out at midnight. He emitted a deafening sound, warning the people of Wagadu to stay in their homes and lock their doors. The sound was also a sign of his acceptance of the sacrifice. But Mamadu, too, had taken up his position. As soon as Biida's head emerged, Mamadu slashed at it with his saber and sent it flying off to the north of the empire. To Mamadu's surprise, another head emerged. He chopped that one off, too, this time sending it toward the south. Another followed, which was sent toward the east. Another was flung toward the west. Thus, Mamadu repeated the saber movement four times. Each time a head flew off, it put a curse on Ghana. And ever since that night, gold, silver, salt, rain—all vanished from Ghana. The empire was destroyed, and the people became the slaves of the Moors. Those Soninkes who escaped slavery scattered in search of gold, silver, salt, water, and other forms of wealth. Even today, the Soninke are known for traveling long distances in search of wealth. Perhaps it was the curse of Biida, the snake god, that took my parents to Guinea in the first place and drove them out, too.

After the Muslims came Christian missionaries and colonial expeditions. They raided entire towns and villages, burned masks and statues, and shackled men and women for the Atlantic slave trade. The story has become known through its tellings and retellings by historians, writers, and artists. Chinua Achebe's *Things Fall Apart* is an important account of the way in which Christian missionaries, accompanied by colonial armies, destroyed African shrines and burned the masks and statues which served as symbols of the gods. By telling the story of the fictional Igbo village of Umuofia, Achebe shows how easily people abandoned their resistance to colonization once their gods and customs had been desacralized and dismissed. Like the Muslims in Wagadu, the white missionaries knew that the best way to conquer Africans was to conquer their gods, and that the best way to possess them was to possess their masks and statues. As one village after another fell in Africa, the missionaries burned some of the masks and saved other as trophies to be placed in museums in Europe.

The victory of the Muslims and the Christian missionaries over our gods left the gods angry with us. We had exposed them to foreign judgment and blasphemy. We had been unable to protect them against doubt coming from outside. We had let the Muslims and Christians kill our totems like Biida, and burn and kidnap the masks and statues containing the spirits of the gods. Now we are left with a religious void that neither Islam nor Christianity can fill.

The Fang Byeri Statue as Primitive Art

But the masks, statues, and oral traditions refused to die. They resurfaced in Marseilles, Paris, Berlin, Brussels, and London with former colonial administrators, anthropological expeditions, and artists—all heirs to and beneficiaries of the same enlightenment that had fired its cannons against innocent African cultures. The masks and statues served as raw material for the refined primitivist art of Picasso, Derain, Vlaminck, Lhote, and Magnelli. These modernists treated the masks and statues as a child does its mother's breast milk. They used them not only as a source of nourishment and inspiration, but also as protection against the anxieties of modernity and its grand narratives. The masks and statues found new altars in the homes of these artists, as well as in museums, next to the paintings and sculptures of the same artists.

But as the masks and statues became detribalized and ceased to be the property of a clan or a village, they began to owe their symbolic value to the European artists with whom they were associated. As if by proxy, they carried the signatures of the modernist artists, and therefore were modernist works of art themselves.

In retrospect, I understand Sidimé Laye's reluctance to sign his carvings, for no contemporary African artist is in a position to compete with the primitive and anonymous African art which is associated with the likes of Vlaminck, Derain, and Picasso. Here is another way in which masks and statues have taken their revenge on Africans: they have blocked the recognition of contemporary African artists in the West, and have deprived artists like Sidimé Laye of the ability to sign their artwork. Laye himself said that the masks and statues represent Africa better than African intellectuals and artists. The West likes the masks and statues because intermediaries like Derain and Picasso—who are Westerners themselves, and endowed with a symbolic power to define art—have declared them to be *objets d'art*. Ironically, the more Africans themselves continue to take Picasso as a witness to the aesthetic quality of the masks and statues, the more they help render invisible the contemporary artists who take modern Africa as their aesthetic point-of-reference. Thus, as long as the West holds a monopoly on defining African art, Sidimé Laye's interest lies in carving masks and statues from which he withholds his signature.

The masks and statues serve another strong clientele in the West which has nothing but contempt for African artists and their signatures. This clientele is constituted by powerful art dealers, collectors, merchants, and museums. Like artists in the West, they became interested in African masks and statues in the early twentieth century. Some of the first collectors, such as Pierre Guerre from Marseilles and Jean-

Pierre Jernander from Belgium, came from families with colonial experience in Africa. Jernander, for example, used his former colonial contacts in the Belgian Congo to smuggle out masks and statues, which were sold to museums and collectors in North America (de Roux, 1996). Charles Ratton, an important French collector and dealer, collaborated with the Nazis during World War II. His tainted reputation forced the Louvre to decline important gifts—masks and statues that he wanted to donate to the museum in 1986. The best part of Ratton's collection can be found today in a new museum of African art called the Musée Dapper, in Paris.

Like Western artists, dealers and collectors in the West usurp the authorship of African masks and statues. They themselves have become the most important sources of valorization for African objects. They set the terms of authentication and aesthetic judgment. Thus, when African masks and statues are auctioned at Christie's and Sotheby's in New York, or at Drouot-Montaigne and Drouot-Richelieu in Paris, it has become the convention to list their previous European owners and the museums that have exhibited them in the West. The fact that a mask or statue once formed part of the collection of a Charles Ratton, a Van Bussel, or a Pierre Guerre is a stronger confirmation of authenticity than the statement of any African clan member.

In 1996, a Fang statue was auctioned for more than a million dollars at Drouot-Montaigne, an event that inspired *Le Monde* to hail Paris the new European capital of primitive art (de Roux, 1996). The originality of the statue was confirmed not by the signature of the Fang artist but by the fact that it had once belonged to a Doctor Bergier (who had acquired it from a sailor in 1846) and had then joined the collection of Pierre Guerre. The statue's provenance was deemed all the more distinguished as it had been displayed in numerous Western exhibitions, including the *Exposition internationale des arts d'Afrique et d'Océanie* (Palais Miramar, Cannes, 1957), *Arts Africains* (Musée Caution, Marseilles, 1970), and *Art Fang* (Musée Dapper, Paris, 1991). It was also a feather in its cap to have been the subject of analyses and appreciations by such Western Africanists as Michel Leiris, Louis Perrois, and Raoul Lehuard. Fang masks and statues in general are famous in the West for having been in the collections of Leo Frobenius, Jacob Epstein, Pablo Picasso, Raoul Guillaume, and Charles Ratton.

The statue that was auctioned in Paris is a Fang reliquary figure, about forty centimeters tall and made of hardwood. It is naked and brown, with the face, parts of the neck, the arms, and the navel painted with a black patina that causes it to gleam and sweat like a human being. The face is carved in the shape of a heart beneath a large round forehead. The eyebrows join the line that forms the nose and divides the left side of the face from the right. The eyelids are closed and painted over, connoting blindness caused by old age. The statue must have been an ancestor figure; its shiny forehead is bare, like a skull. Similar family reliquary statues have wide-open eyes which seem to be gazing intensely at someone or something. Some even have round metal plates, beads, or nails in the eye sockets to make their gaze more fearsome. But in spite of its closed eyes, this statue seems to return the viewer's gaze and creates an aura of omniscience.

In contrast to the eyes and the nose, over which hang the rounded forehead and long eyebrows, the mouth protrudes, occupying most of the chin and suggesting a resemblance to an oval-faced Neanderthal man. The statue is also notable because of the remarkable coiffure neatly arranged at the back of the head in symmetrical patterns, like palm fronds. Indeed, the hairdo of this Byeri statue, like that of many statues from Gabon, Angola, and the Congo, is so perfect that it forms an entity separate from the face. Compared to the face, which is geometric in its primitive simplicity, the coiffure exhibits a complexity of design that calls attention to its aesthetic autonomy. The face is as primitive—connotative of religion and vital forces from the ancestors—as the hairdo is beautiful and self-referential.

The neck not only supports the head but forms a smooth cylinder joining the face, which terminates in a pointed mouth with chiseled

Three views of the Fang statue that was sold in Paris in June 1996. (Photo courtesy of Gérard Bonnet, Marseilles, France.)

teeth, and the hairdo, which seems to be attached to the spine. The long, powerful neck also links the head to the square shoulders and the rest of the body, setting up a rhythmic movement between the face and the hands, which hold a bowl underneath the chin. Thus, the neck delineates the spatial configuration of this sculpture by establishing a relation between the shoulders, which form right-angled lines below, and the face and hairdo, which form a triangle above.

The statue rhythmically marks space and time in other ways as well. The lowered face with its closed eyes, the hands holding up the bowl between shoulders and chin, and the bent knees indicate three movements of the body that mark contrasting rhythms: downward, upward, and downward. The distended navel protruding like a small erection is typical of Fang statues, in which the navel often accentuates the sexual ambiguity of the female breast and the male genitals.

Fang statues are also known for their oversized buttocks, which form a circle around the waist and enhance the roundness of the thighs. What is distinctive about this statue is the fine taste with which the artist carved every part of the body. In most other Fang figures, the wide-open eyes, the interlocking sharp teeth, the three large cornrows forming the hairdo, and the exaggeratedly muscular arms, buttocks, and legs serve to reinforce the statue's role as a reliquary object and to characterize it as an ethnological artifact. But here, these canonical parts are tamed by the artist's hand and subjected to an aesthetic law that elevates the statue beyond ritual and ethnology.

To be in the presence of this statue—which gleams, and seems aware like a human being—is more than a religious experience or a discovery of tribal culture. The viewer is awed by the sense of artistic proportion and interplay between the different parts of the body. As one can see from the back, the shoulder blades extend all the way down to the waist, where they meet in a perfect V. This statue is like an architectural work that creates rhythmic relations among its various parts: in some places it harmonizes the movements, and in others it contrasts them. For example, there is a symmetrical relationship linking the circular waist, the triangular back with its broad shoulders, and the strong cylindrical neck which supports the beautiful coiffure. The symmetry and harmony denote a perfectly shaped and therefore superior body.

The Fang statue is thus an interlocutor with modernist art—that is, art from the late nineteenth and early twentieth centuries, which was preoccupied with geometric shapes and physical power. The statue also exhibits a classic modernist trait: it establishes contrasts among these geometric shapes in order to define space. The oval face, with its finely delineated features, is admirable; whereas the plain, cylindrical neck is aesthetically unremarkable, except for the fact that it helps to reveal the stable spatial relationship between the head and shoulders.

One can understand why modernists like Picasso and Braque placed African art in their ateliers, not only as inspiration but as models.

My concern with the maker's signature and with the aesthetic qualities of African art obliges me here to cite the artistic movement called modernist primitivism as a corroborating reference: its proponents were among the first admirers of African masks and statues. But whereas I stress aesthetics and authorship, critics of modernism stress the important role that African art played in such avant-garde movements as Expressionism, Fauvism, Cubism, and Surrealism.

According to Meyer Schapiro, modernist primitivism was responsive to African masks and statues because they were believed to be "charged with the new valuations of the instinctive, the natural, the mythical as the essentially human . . . The very fact that they were arts of primitive peoples without a recorded history now made them all the more attractive. They acquired the special prestige of the timeless and indistinctive, on the level of spontaneous animal activity, self-contained, unreflective, private, without dates and signatures, without origins or consequences except in the emotions" (Schapiro, 1978: 200–201).

Rosalind Krauss, in contrast, sees in the image of the primitive a "ritual of transgression," and therefore a theory of modern art. Building on Georges Bataille's notion of alteration, Krauss claims that primitive art illustrates the contradictions embedded in language—the transgression of the meanings which human reason wants to insist are unequivocal, univocal, but which the words themselves betray as irresolvably diffuse. According to Krauss, and to many historians of modernity, this conception of the primitive as a theory of our modern condition became a powerful shaping tool, a way of rethinking all of the human sciences. And it is not just a historical phenomenon, since it appears in the work of such writers as Foucault, Lacan, and Derrida and their followers (Krauss, 1984).

From these perspectives on modernist primitivism, it is clear that African art, and Africans themselves, are interesting to the West only if they can supply a theory of how the West sees itself—in other words, if they can be timelessly primitive and thereby a compelling exception to the Western teleological narrative. Two widely reviewed exhibitions held in New York City—the show entitled "Primitivism" organized by the Museum of Modern Art in 1984, and the one entitled "African Art" organized by the Guggenheim Museum in 1996—both took this ahistorical approach to African art. They saw the displayed objects as important only insofar as they bore a resemblance to the modernist art of the late nineteenth and early twentieth centuries, or exerted an influence on it, or made an impression on Western artists. In the words of William Rubin, primitive art was valued because it had "an expressive force deemed missing from the final phases of Western realism, which late nineteenth-century vanguard artists considered over-attenuated and bloodless" (Rubin, 1984: 2).

In each of these considerations of primitivist modernism, the African artist remains invisible. All the praise goes to Western artists for discovering in primitivist modernism a way out of what José Ortega y Gasset called the "dehumanizing" effect of industrialization on the arts. While the aesthetics of African statues and masks supposedly helped modernist artists to counter the alienation of the individual in industrial modernism, the role of African artists in shaping the masks and statues is passed over in silence, and the aesthetic intentions of these artists are devalued in favor of the ritualistic function of the objects. What is emphasized in both primitivist modernism and the statues and masks is their ability to redeem the individual within the community—in other words, to make art into ritual, and ritual into art. Both make present at the same time the beautiful and the ugly, the exotic and the ordinary, the traditional and the innovative. Rubin notes that the Dan people of Côte d'Ivoire "not only explicitly appreciated diversity [in their masks] but recognized the value of a certain originality" (3).

But although we know plenty about why modernists like Picasso, Nolde, and Kandinsky favored inventiveness and multiformity in their art, we are less inclined to accord an artistic temperament to African sculptors. It is in this sense that Rubin arrogantly dismisses the majority of the African pieces in Picasso's collection for their "poor-quality carving": they are "unauthentic 'tourist' works" that were "made by tribal artists for sale rather than for ritual purposes" (14). The fact that Picasso himself turned out numerous works *en série* specifically for the market is, in contrast, of little consequence to their aesthetic evaluation. Clearly for Rubin, as for many other critics, production for the market indicates the separation of African artists from their works, so that these works can better serve the artists and art world of Europe.

The primitivist modernists, by valorizing African statues and masks as inspirers of their movement, also froze them in time. Simultaneously, they condemned in the work of African artists the very inventiveness and diversity that constituted its originality. Rubin both praises and damns African art when he finds modernist style in the variety of Dan masks, and at the same time snubs African carvers for feeding the tourist market. Most of the world's artists work to satisfy a certain demand. It seems to me that the African artist, too, achieves innovation through a response to market demands, the most important of which today happens to be tourism. Unlike Picasso, who collected "unauthentic" African art made for tourists, Rubin reveals his disregard for innovation on the part of African artists by insisting on ritual authenticity as the only criterion for judging their work.

Marcel Griaule, in an important article entitled "Gunshot," has criticized this desire for authenticity in African art, noting "the white's absurdity in declaring a Baule drum impure under the pretext that it's decorated with a man bearing a rifle." (Griaule, 1992: 41). Since the rifle is considered European, its presence in African art spoils its authenticity. For Griaule, it is the height of absurdity "when the other party refuses the African the right to 'make art' with a European motif, claiming first that it is European—a somewhat amusingly self-castrating remark—and, second, that it looks 'modern'" (41). When European artists borrow from Africa, this does not detract from the originality of their work, whereas African artists cannot borrow from Europe without being considered inauthentic. In other words, if Western artists can depict Africa exotically, why can't Africans represent Europe exotically—that is, with rifles?

The fact remains that, as absurd as Rubin's depiction of authentic African art may seem, it is the standard by which African art continues to be judged. African artists like Sidimé Laye must remain anonymous in order to give to their works a chance in the "primitive" marketplace. Modern painters, sculptors, and even some filmmakers and musicians from Africa and its diaspora must completely accept the stereotype of themselves as "primitive" to stand a chance of being considered artists.

This fact is often obscured by the Negritude movement's characterization of African art as the bearer of vital force. Léopold Senghor, in his famous essay "L'esprit de la civilisation ou les lois de la culture négro-africaine" ("The Spirit of Civilization or the Laws of Negro-African Culture"), is more interested in the symbolic interpretation of the images represented by African masks and statues. He is trapped in an ethnological reading of African art which considers only its functional role in society. For Senghor, rhythm and movement in African art can be understood only in terms of ritual—that is, the collective participation of musicians, dancers, elders, and ancestors in masquerade. In such a context, it is inconceivable for the masks and statues to have an autonomous identity as works of art. Senghor fails to note that the works' color and symmetry of design can reveal the artists' preoccupation with space and time.

The Fang statue discussed above is a classic modern sculpture with more textual similarities to Picasso's *Les Demoiselles d'Avignon* or Joyce's *Ulysses* than to ethnological texts. Contrary to the Negritude view that African art is complete only in performance, this statue has an autonomy that is challenged only by the assertiveness of some of its constitutive parts. One of the characteristics of the modern text is its tendency to fragment—the ability of its components to form narrative entities separate from the whole. This is obvious not only in modern painting and sculpture, where different parts of a work may compete for the observer's attention and analysis, but also in literary texts like

Ulysses, in which different characters play with time and space to make themselves the center of focalizations that digress from the main narrative.

From the shoulders up, the Fang statue looks like the bust of an Egyptian pharaoh with a dynastic hairstyle. A narrative enigma is also evident when the statue is considered as a whole, with its downcast eyes, hands holding up a bowl underneath the chin, and bent knees. What action is being denoted here? The downcast eyes suggest that this reliquary figure is getting ready to drink from the bowl. The bent knees participate in this narrative by connoting the statue's submission to the contents of the bowl: water, milk, or some potion with a supernatural power. The bowl, in this sense, becomes the most powerful locus of interpretation in the sculpture, forcing the whole body to obey it and creating unfulfilled curiosity on the part of the spectator as to its contents and significance.

It is also possible to read the Fang statue's posture as a gesture of offering: the bowl and its contents are being proffered to someone or something outside the field occupied by the sculpture. From this perspective, the downcast eyes and bent knees signify the reliquary figure's submission to a separate entity that is clearly in a position of power—a god, a king, an audience, or the artist. One of the qualities of the Fang statue is its ability to create by this gesture an off-field that is as pregnant with meaning as what is represented in its own field. In the absence of a signature by a Fang artist, the position off-field is represented by Western artists like Picasso and Braque, who appropriate for themselves the ideal spectator-position vis-à-vis African art.

By inscribing in the design of the statue an off-field audience, or a relation between the statue and an unseen presence, the sculptor anticipated an aesthetic judgment of the object by the beholder. It is true that most Fang reliquary figures seem to act as if they are in communication with an unseen presence. While many Fang statues, like the one under scrutiny here, seem to be holding out a bowl to this presence, others are proffering a horn in lieu of the bowl or brandishing a knife in the right hand as if ready to attack. A few keep their arms down by their side. The intensity of the energy in all of them seems to partake of both submission and resistance. The ones with wide-open eyes and grinding teeth give the impression that they would rather attack the force giving the order than execute its dictates. The ones with closed eyes and the bowl or horn in their hands, like this one, register a "negative" energy that defines the quality of their resistance to submission. Their tense faces and muscles embody contradictory attitudes of surrender and resistance, gentleness and revolt.

Among colonial chroniclers, the Fang tribes had a reputation for cannibalism. The aesthetic features of Fang reliquary figures—their fixed gaze, their sharp teeth, their fists clenching rusted knives, their bulging bare foreheads symbolizing the skulls of the ancestors—were used to support the tribes' cannibalistic rituals. But, as I have shown, the resistance that is implied in the statues' gestures, and their seeming gentleness even when they are holding a knife, contradict the ethnological discourse on the Fang as warmongers and cannibals. This is not to deny that the Fang were cannibals, or to say that they did not like war; for as Ouologuem says, who among us can declare that his or her teeth are not red with "tomatoes"? Who among us, whether European or African, can sincerely say that he or she hates war? The point is that anthropological discourse has fixed the interpretation of Fang statues, masks, and oral traditions, as it has fixed the meaning of life and art in other African societies.

It becomes necessary, therefore, to remove African reliquary figures from their ritual space and function in order to reveal the marks of the hands of the artists who created them. The "negative" energy that I called the quality of resistance in the Fang statues constitutes the expression of the carver's subversion of their original ritual function. By being beautiful and discreet, in contrast to other Fang reliquary figures with their exaggerated organs, a statue such as the one examined here enables the artistic genius of the carver to interfere with the performance of the ritual. It calls attention to itself and mirrors the presence of the artist off-field, instead of participating submissively in the ritual, be it ancestor worship, war, or cannibalism.

The modern African elite, reacting to the confinement of reliquary figures in Western museums, invokes the role of the statues and masks in their original cultist setting, and claims that without this setting they lose their aesthetic value. While this argument decries the pillage and rape of African traditions by the West, it precludes any serious discussion of the embedded signatures of individual carvers on the reliquary figures, or any consideration of the real nature of the indebtedness of modernist artists such as Picasso to nineteenth- and early twentieth-century African carvers. As we have noted, the presence of these reliquary figures in the studios of European artists indicated more than just artistic influence, or an infusion of the vital force of African religious objects into Western art. The geometric lines and abstract renderings of Fang, Dan, and Dogon statues and masks formed the basis of a range of modern artistic revolutions.

In addition to manifesting interethnic relations and influences, African carvers, in their encounters with European slave traders and colonial expeditions, must have, of necessity, sought to surpass the aesthetics of local rituals and their binding conventions. It goes without saying that African carvings bear the imprint of myriad changes that have taken place in Africa over the centuries, from the beginning of the slave trade to the present. Jean Rouch's film documentary *Les maîtres fous* (1955) presents obvious examples: reliquary figures on an altar and actors in a ritual performance are intended to represent colonial administrators; elsewhere, reliquary figures are holding rifles or riding bicycles, or are painted white with long hair to represent white people. What is important here is that these works indicate the readiness of African carvers earlier in the twentieth century, as now, to reflect social changes in their art and to break away from tradition. Western anthropological discourse and the apologists of colonialism ignore the African artist's openness to change when they emphasize only tribal autonomy and authenticity. When African elites insist that African art is not art because it has been taken out of its original context, mightn't they be internalizing the stereotype of themselves as people who view art as functional? It seems to me that a concept of art criticism which stresses the artistic changes in the history of Fang, Dan, and Dogon statues and masks is more important than one that seeks an understanding of the original rituals for which they were created. By following the artistic changes, we learn more about the artists and the societies in which they lived.

The removal of the work of art from its original ritual space raises a "Benjaminian" question that, I believe, is partially answered by the Fang statue discussed above. In his well-known essay "The Work of Art in the Age of Mechanical Reproduction," Walter Benjamin argues that a work of art finds its expression in the service of ritual, whether religious or magical. For Benjamin, the artistic object loses its aura when it is divorced from ritual practice. Even though Benjamin's argument refers to the mechanical reproduction of images—as exists in the relation between original prints and their photocopies, between theater and film, and between other art objects and the industrial means of (re)producing them—it is relevant to the issues that concern us here. Benjamin's nostalgic view of art, similar to the view of the hero and heroic acts in Romantic literature, relies too heavily on tradition and its axes of originality and authenticity, to the detriment of change and innovation. Like Benjamin, collectors and dealers of African art, and even some African artists, argue that authenticity and originality are expressions of artistic aura, and inveigh against the copying of statues and masks, which diminishes their aura.

What African artworks achieve in this respect is the aura of artifice. Their carvers, like Sidimé Laye, allowed their hands to be possessed not only by tradition but also by the love of artifice. They can thus be said to have subverted the idea of an unchanging Africa and the West's monopoly on the universal tenets of modernity. By following the changing patterns of African art, we discover a new aesthetic and an artistic aura proper to its history. We are reminded of the artists that tradition attempted to render invisible: we uncover the role of the individual talent in reshaping tradition. Finally, we discover artists like Sidimé Laye and their signatures.

There is some urgency in this matter. As African artists move away from ritual practice and accumulate artifice around the value of the ritual work, they must deal with profound tensions. The energy brooding behind the closed eyes and raised arms of the Fang statue is an expression of two forces coming into conflict.

It is in this sense that Benjamin's claim for the superiority of the original over the copy reveals its Platonic limitations. Neither the quantity of copies reproduced nor the identity of the object in its ritual context suffices as a basis for a concept of aesthetic criticism. In order for the original and the ritual to maintain their integrity, every copy made of the original would have to be canonically ugly—that is, undistinctive. The minute the artist secretly enhances the copy, he or she risks subverting the original. Tradition thus attempts to prevent material and historical change by rendering the artist anonymous and by denying a particular identity to the copy.

The African artist is particularly vulnerable to the tyranny of ritual in tradition. Whereas in the West the mechanical reproduction of the work of art threatens the aura of the individual artist and the symbolic capital of the work, in Africa the reproduction of masks and statues valorizes the carvers by focusing attention on the artistic signature. It is clear not only that artistic signatures operate to the detriment of the authenticity of traditional ritual, and of the Western collectors who have invested so much in the objects attached to this ritual, but that they are also the precondition for the emergence of African modernity and individual genius in tradition.

Chéri Samba: The Stereotype Strikes Back

In the summer of 1997, I had the opportunity to see an exhibition of Chéri Samba's works at the Musée National des Arts d'Afrique et d'Océanie in Paris. Ever since the show entitled "Magiciens de la terre" ("Magicians of the Earth") had been held in Paris in 1989, Chéri Samba—a painter from Kinshasa—had continued to surprise Western-ers and to tease their imagination with his "naive" paintings. The timing of the recent show could not have been better for him, his clients, the art dealers, and the Musée National des Arts d'Afrique et d'Océanie. One of my filmmaker friends said to me enviously that Samba had become the new "chouchou de la ville" ("darling of the city"). Paris brags about being the capital of African art, ahead of London, Tokyo, and New York, and about its role as arbiter of taste for the rest of the world. The Musée National des Arts d'Afrique et d'Océanie had simultaneously mounted an immense display of tradi-tional arts from Nigeria. African art was also flourishing on the Left Bank, with a show of Ouatara's work at the Galerie Boulakia on the rue Bonaparte, an exhibition of masks and photography entitled "Les Dogons" on the rue des Beaux-Arts, and many artifacts for sale in the antique shops on the rue de la Seine. Never mind the fact that the French have shut the door on African immigration, or that the image of undesirable Africans disembarking at French airports is one of the themes of Chéri Samba's narrative paintings.

Chéri Samba emerged as a street artist in Kinshasa in the late 1970s, painting market scenes, prostitutes, and anecdotes about power and corruption. In 1982 Ngangura Mweze made a short film, *Kin Kiesé* (*Kinshasa the Beautiful*), in which he used Chéri Samba and his works to reveal the contradictory colors of the city. The music of Papa Wemba, another icon of popular culture in Kinshasa, was also used in the film.

In fact, market artists like Chéri Samba abound in such cities as Dakar, Lagos, and Kinshasa. Basing their art on the *faits divers* of modernity and its humorous impact on life in Africa, they combine a form of narrative prose with images that are accessible to a wide audience. Chéri Samba's paintings incorporate words from Lingala and from colloquial French. Like signs in advertising, they combine and multiply meanings through allusions and puns. For example, a popular term like *conjoncture* means at the same time economic crisis, belt tightening, and being resourceful. The audience for these paintings consists of the African elite and of tourists and anthropologists in search of the *mot juste* or the right image to describe Africa. It is also important to distinguish popular market artists who are influenced by the narrative techniques of comic books, movie posters, and cartoons from university-trained artists who want to make it in the modernist and postmodernist canons.

Chéri Samba's art, particularly the paintings included in the 1997 exhibition, contain the secret of how he made it to the top as the most popular African artist. To begin with, for the Musée National des Arts d'Afrique et d'Océanie, African art had previously consisted only of primitive masks, statues, and traditional batik. Chéri Samba was the first "modern" African artist to have an entire room of the museum devoted to his art. Even so, one had to go to the second floor and traverse an arresting and stunning exhibition of Nigerian masks and statues before reaching the Chéri Samba room. The 276 pieces in that Nigerian show included some of the most beautiful Igbo masks I have ever seen, as well as Benin, Yoruba, and Ogoni statues and masks. The exhibition's size and quality alone made one realize why some people felt that the Guggenheim's 1996 Africa show had been inadequate.

I could not help taking with me impressions of the primitive Nigerian art into the Chéri Samba room. It had always seemed to me that modern African art contained no equivalent of the beautiful, terrifying, abstract symbolism of the tribal Nigerian art; modern artists merely depicted for the West what they thought was within the confines of Western *bienséance* and verisimilitude. But upon entering the Chéri Samba room, I was pleased to find that his art was concerned with the same questions of power, fear, morality, and overt sexuality that were represented in the tribal Nigerian art.

The Chéri Samba room was loud and hot with reds and yellows, which contrasted with life-giving greens, sea blues, and flowery violets.

I found myself transported to Africa through these strong colors and the primacy of their rich and exotic associations. Human beings were rendered in such a dark chocolate hue that they seemed to melt under the light. And I said to myself: This guy is the stereotype who strikes back. Chéri Samba is the Amos Tutuola of African art. Ever since Tutuola wrote *The Palm-Wine Drinkard*, his fantastic tale of the underworld, no other African artist has so strongly and cunningly embraced the African stereotype as Chéri Samba.

It is highly fitting that Chéri Samba's art be exhibited side by side with traditional African masks and statues. One clue to Chéri Samba's success is his reappropriation and affirmation of the stereotype of Africa in the modern imagination. Chéri Samba works within such tribal concepts as witchcraft, ancestor worship, and magic. In *L'espoir fait vivre* (*Hope Allows for Life*; 1989), a painting about the story of his success, he explains that he made it to the top without resorting to witchcraft, through hard work, patience, and the blessing of the ancestors. *Autoportrait* (*Self-Portrait*) is similarly about creativity. Chéri Samba tells his competitors and those artists who accuse him of casting a spell on them that his success is due not to incantations or to witchcraft, but to living simply and working hard.

But of course Chéri Samba is not a simple artist. He raises the question of witchcraft in his paintings not only because power in contemporary Zaire is inextricably linked to it, but also because witchcraft fits in the West's way of knowing Africa. This is, in my opinion, why Chéri Samba's work exerts both local and international appeal. "I am not a witch doctor," he says, yet in his paintings he depicts himself bigger than life, and bragging about his power. He appears stereotypical and literal to Western eyes, yet every one of his paintings is reflexive and narrated from a point of view which is often arrogant. In *Hommage aux anciens créateurs* (*Homage to Past Creators*; 1995), he paints a large portrait of himself behind tribal carvings on a table. The portrait seems to be repossessing the masks and statues, which are now locked up in a Swiss museum in Zurich. Chéri Samba criticizes the museum for isolating the objects, which still have their supernatural powers, from people such as himself who are the reincarnation of the tribal sculptors.

Chéri Samba's strategy also involves artists' reappropriation of their own works. *L'agriculteur sans cerveau* (*The Brainless Planter*; 1990) depicts a banana planter sitting on a hoe with his hands and feet tied together. He is framed by two banana trees laden with ripe fruit, and holds a half-peeled banana which he is unable to eat. Behind him is the man with whom he signed a contract; the man is walking away, eating the planter's bananas. Chéri Samba tells the disgruntled planter to read the contract carefully and not to blame the man. Chéri Samba takes up this metaphor of exploitation in several of his paintings. In *Oreilles au ventre* (*Ears on the Belly*; 1991), it is the artist who is famished, while the dealer has a big stomach with ears. In *Pourquoi ai-je signé un contrat?* (*Why Did I Sign a Contract?* 1990), Chéri Samba, in an elegant blue suit, sits on a red couch by a cliff, with a padlock around his knees and a rope around his neck, which is being pulled on either side by critics, artists, curators, collectors, and dealers. Here, the artist declares himself a winner because the contract seemed a necessary step in his career. Thus, the rope and the padlock, as well as the blue suit and red couch, are part of his style rather than constraints that alienate him from his work.

Finally, in *Une peinture à défendre* (*A Painting To Be Defended*; 1993)—Chéri Samba's masterpiece, in my opinion—the artist raises the ante in the relations between politics and the arts, by using a painting as a metaphor for Africa, which he must defend. The composition bears witness to Chéri Samba's reflexive approach to art, which has won him the esteem of both local and international audiences. Space and movement are delineated by an insertion of frames within frames, repetition of actions, contrasts in colors and gestures. Chéri Samba himself is positioned in the middle, facing the spectator, with a brush in one hand and a can of paint in the other. Around his waist is a red rope which is being pulled on the left by two hands; around his leg is a green rope which is being pulled on the right by two more hands. Two men, one wearing a violet jacket and the other a green one, appear in the foreground. The man with the violet jacket is grabbing the artist by the waist, and the one in the green jacket grasps him by the leg. They all say, "I must defend this painting." In the background is a traditional popular painting, which the artist is trying to protect from the assailants. The painting shows a woman with a baby tied on her back; she is braiding another woman's hair. They are surrounded by houses, a child bathing in a tub, and a wagon. This tableau-within-a-tableau bears the caption: "Ekomi popular painting, a few years later." The background of this busy, well-lit scene shows a still night with trees, overshadowed by a dark sky.

Clearly, Chéri Samba is first of all commenting on the recent demand for his own art, which only a few years ago was just another type of market art in Kinshasa. Now, white critics and dealers are fighting for control of it. They all claim ownership, and force the artist to stand up and defend it with his life. But to me, the most important thing in this image is the way it articulates the artist's vision of his painting, which coincides with his vision of Africa. In other words, Chéri Samba takes his painting for Africa, and proposes a militant action through art to reappropriate it. The same reflexiveness runs through all of Chéri Samba's works, whether they address the planter's relation to his produce, the artist and his art, or Africans and Africa. In the triptych *Grand tort de la colonisation et grosse erreur de l'Afrique indépendante* (*The Great Wrong of Colonization and the Grave Error of Independent Africa;* 1994), Chéri Samba represents precolonial Africa as Edenic, and the colonizers as greedy and evil men who divided up the continent among themselves, with no regard for kinship or tribal unity. The last panel of the triptych shows the error of "independent Africans," who fail to recognize that nation-states are an inheritance from the former colonizers, and that they continue to divide ethnic groups and create a false sense of alliance among people. The Africa which Chéri Samba defends in this triptych is the same as that in the "Ekomi popular painting" described above. It is an Africa beyond nation-states, yet also a stereotypical and romantic Africa without boundaries, and without history. As always, Chéri Samba has the last laugh: he has signed a contract, and everyone worries about him. But by the time we find him, he is elsewhere.

Sidimé Laye's Song of Resistance

The fear of masks and statues that Sidimé Laye's father felt constitutes a desire to repress them and the paganistic drive they represent. In his dream, Laye's father was able to see clearly the danger that the return of masks in the public sphere could pose to the Muslim order. The Christian areas in Africa are still afraid of the eruption of the masks' authority in daily life. After all, religious conflict in Africa is not between Islam and Christianity, but between these faiths and the masks that rule the African's unconscious. Thus, carving masks can bring nothing but trouble to Sidimé Laye and all those like him who submit to their power, because the very presence of masks in the modern world is an indication of the failure of Islam and Christianity to conquer pagan Africa.

Sidimé Laye's insistence on carving masks, and his claim that he is possessed by them as he works, manifest the resistance of such pagan forms to repressive orders put in place not only by monotheistic religions but also by monolithic dictatorial regimes.

Sidimé Laye has continued to carve masks in spite of the warning in his father's dream, his uncle's death in the dungeons of Camp Boiro, and his own perils during his years in exile. Could it be that he was resisting Sékou Touré's oppressive regime through his prolific creation of masks and statues? How could the masks' presence have constituted a threat to Sékou Touré's revolution?

Looking back now, I believe that the revolution dealt too harshly with masks, statues, and oral traditions. They should have been placed in national museums instead of being banned. The revolution should have injected itself into the masked rituals and celebrated them as newer expressions of national identity—that is, it should have brought the rituals to the center of society for everyone to participate in, instead of marginalizing them as backward secret societies. This form of valorization not only would have elevated rituals to the status of national ceremonies, but also would have changed their backward orientation into a forward and more inclusive one. Most traditions change by opening up to the outside world and by looking toward the future. The masks, statues, and oral traditions, treated as they were, prevented the revolution from submitting conservative social and religious forms to openness and change.

Sidimé Laye left school and carved masks and statues throughout the revolution, strengthening the resistance of the margins against the center. In this sense, his actions resembled those of many educated Africans, who gave up on the revolution because it lacked the ingredients of traditional structures of feeling. It became commonplace to point to the repression of masks, statues, and tribal ways as evidence of the revolution's un-African and inauthentic modes of thought. Ways of reclaiming tradition became symbols of resistance to Sékou Touré's attempt to homogenize society. For example, some people in the middle class began to wear hunter-style mud-cloth outfits in public, rather than the short white-percale *doloki* that Sékou Touré popularized at the beginning of the revolution. Masks, carved elephant tusks, and statues, previously intended solely for foreign export, made their appearance in the living rooms of the African middle class. The postcolonial era also saw the revalorization of witchcraft, magic, and amulets as traditional means to protect one from the revolution or endear one to Sékou Touré. I find it difficult to imagine Sidimé Laye as a sorcerer or magician whose art numbed the effect of the revolution on people.

The middle class's resistance to the revolution, it seems to me, is much like its reluctance to go along with the new democratic wind in Africa today. The last time I was in West Africa, in January 1997, I had an interesting conversation about African democracies with a Senegalese colleague, whom I'll call Clarence Delgado. I lamented the poor judgment of General Sani Abacha's regime in hanging the writer-activist Ken Saro Wiwa, and expected Delgado to agree with me. Instead, he admonished me for looking at everything through American ethnocentric lenses. People in America, he said, expected the whole world to see life their way, to accept their definition of democracy, human rights, and culture. But Africans had their own ways of doing things, and they had traditions and cultures older than America's to support them in their behavior. Delgado pointed to the empires of Ghana, Mali, and Songhai, which had built world-class civilizations long before America had been born. Who were Americans to think they could teach the world about democracy and human rights? In Delgado's opinion, the main thing wrong with the current democratic movement in Africa was that it was being imposed from outside. Democracy was not an African concept; too much freedom in Africa was bound to create disorder and even anarchy. Take Ken Saro Wiwa, for example: he had had no respect for the Nigerian government, which he'd continually tried to malign in front of the international community, human rights organizations, and environmentalists. How would Americans feel if Africans meddled in their internal affairs, such as their racist treatment of Louis Farrakhan and the Nation of Islam? Delgado said that Ken Saro Wiwa had broken the laws of his own country and had been tried and sentenced to death. Capital punishment existed not only in Nigeria, but in America too.

But—I replied—how about the exploitation of the Nigerian people by Shell Oil, the situation that Ken Saro Wiwa had been protesting? Delgado answered that Shell was English and American and French. How could Americans accept Shell as a household name and make a pariah out of Nigeria? I told Delgado that he was ignoring the responsibility of African leaders to their people by putting the blame on the West alone. We Africans could not waver from our commitment to fundamental democratic values, such as open electoral participation, freedom of expression, and the right to civil education and a safe environment.

For me, the fact that globalization, like a totalitarian regime, continues to obliterate cultural differences in favor of the market's hegemony justifies a form of vigilance and resistance that leads us to protest undemocratic treatment of our own people. It is also too easy to dismiss democracy and multiparty systems as un-African. Lest we forget, the concept is not native to America either. But it is behind Americans' drive to win more equality for blacks and other people who are the victims of oppression and discrimination. Africans, too, must seize democracy, as a tool both for demanding equal treatment in world institutions and market systems, and for eliminating their own archaic practices such as one-party rule and the oppression of women through polygamy and clitoridectomy. No amount of hiding behind tradition can provide sufficient excuse for blocking the new wave of democracy in Africa.

Finally, as forms of art, Africa's masks, statues, and oral traditions made another kind of demand on the revolution. They set in motion dreams and aspirations that the revolution could not satisfy. They encouraged people to identify with models that lay in a realm denied by the revolution, and challenged Sékou Touré to deal with his people's needs and desires. Sidimé Laye's masks and statues were telling the truth to the revolution: they were saying that people were uncomfortable with it and that the regime had turned against its own population. The artist's masks and statues were banned because their very presence in the nation-state constituted an implicit criticism of the regime. When conceived as art that challenged the repressiveness of the revolution, the masks, statues, and oral traditions exhibited a new energy and magic that empowered people against their oppressors. In this sense, resistance became a transformative ritual, a renewal of the revolution by means of these positive energies.

Moreover, escaping Sékou Touré's revolution was another way of escaping the twentieth century and its record of ineptitude, cruelty, and human suffering. We cannot be complacent about the main themes that have characterized power relations in the twentieth century. As the new century approaches, we need to forge new languages and methods with which to replace decolonization, alienation, racial oppression, primitivism, Afro-pessimism, Francophony, tribalism, narrow nationalism, deconstruction, and other poststructuralist approaches to Africa and the black diaspora. We cannot afford to enter the new millennium as unprepared as our predecessors were when they made the transition from colonialism to independence. Many of them never even realized that the white man had left. Consequently, they did not know how to make adjustments, so as to become autonomous citizens.

The Soninke of the Empire of Ghana experienced the same misery and longing for change at the end of the sixth century that Africans are feeling now. One man, a prince named Gassire, was more impatient than the others. According to legend, his longing for change was so strong that he felt as if a jackal were constantly gnawing at his heart. The tradition in those days was war. Every day Gassire went to war and slaughtered fifty men all by himself. He was the strongest and bravest warrior in the empire. In the evening, other warriors praised him for his courage and strength. But Gassire was always unhappy. He wondered when his father would die and leave him the crown. But the king refused to die. Gassire was getting older and older. He now had seven sons, who joined him on the battlefield. They, too, had become brave warriors and were growing older and older. Yet the king was still alive.

One day, Gassire went to see a wise old man who lived at the gates of Wagadu, the capital of Ghana. He explained his predicament to the wise man, who was a sort of prophet. Gassire said that he was tired of fighting and killing, and that he wanted his father to die so he could become king. The wise man, after thinking about Gassire's problem, informed him that his father was not going to die anytime soon. He told Gassire that he had to choose: either be a warrior for the rest of his life, or change his world. "But how?" asked Gassire. The wise man told him to make himself a ngoni, a lute-like instrument, and play it. At first Gassire was angry with the wise man for failing to predict his future as a king. He was disappointed, because he wanted so much to replace his father.

Gassire went to a blacksmith and asked him to make the ngoni for him. When the instrument was ready he played it, but the ngoni produced no sound. Gassire was angry. He went back to the wise man and said, "Look, wise man, the ngoni does not sing!" The wise man said to him, "You have to give it a heart. The ngoni cannot sing without a heart."

Gassire went back to fighting and killing his enemies—fifty a day. Gassire's seven sons died one by one on the battlefield. Each time, Gassire wept and carried his son home. Each time, the victim's blood dripped onto the ngoni. After the seventh son was slain, Gassire no longer had the heart for battle. But he nonetheless rose early the next morning to go to war. On the way, he saw a parrot perched on a baobab tree, singing. Gassire stopped and listened to the parrot's songs, which were about wars and the heroes who had fought them thousands of years before, about lovers whose stories survived long after their own death, and about the deeds of revolutionaries who created great societies and cultures that outlived them.

Gassire then took out his ngoni from its goatskin pouch and began to play and sing. He sang his own praise and the praise of the Empire of Ghana. At that moment, he realized his own immortality and the immortality of Ghana. His story would live on in songs and in people's hearts long after his death.

I understand what Sidimé Laye means when he says that masks, statues, and oral traditions represent Africa abroad better than intellectuals and politicians. Art lives forever, while men and women come and go. Art transcends history, while men and women are bound to the passions of the moment. Art makes visible the need for change and social transformation. That is why Sidimé Laye, like Gassire, trusts art to redeem him, trusts it to carve a way out of the ineptitude of the twentieth century and Sékou Touré's revolution.

Among the Mande, there is a traditional song called "Baninde," which means being in the mood to say no to oppression, to refuse categorically, to defy the oppressor. Griot women sing this song to exhort young people to resist injustice the way their forebears did, in order to make the world a better place. The song keeps returning to the refrain, "Ban ye dunya la dyala," or "Resistance brings joy to the world." Then come the names of heroes whose resistance transformed Africans' lives for the better. A modern version of the song would go like this: "Say no! Martin Luther King said no! And he brought joy to the world. Say no! Malcolm X said no! And it brought joy to the world. Say no! Mandela said no! And it brought joy to the world. Say no! The African people said no! And it brought joy to the world. Say no! Black women said no to sexism and racism! And it brought joy to the world."

In Mande cultures, we refer to this form of resistance as negation with a positive value—as, for example, when Sékou Touré said no to General de Gaulle, thus transforming Guinea into the first independent country in Francophone Africa; or when Samory Touré said no to French colonial penetration, uniting West Africa against European racism and fascism; or when Sundiata Kéita said no to Sumanguru Kante, leading to the creation of the Empire of Mali; or when Malian women said no to the dictatorship of Moussa Traoré, thus laying the groundwork for the rise of democracy in Mali. I say to myself: May the rest of the world be inspired by these heroic acts. Sidimé Laye has given me wisdom through his vigilant and fragile art.

8

▲▼▲

Sidimé Laye One Year Later

In August 1997 I paid Sidimé Laye another visit. He seemed happier than he'd been the year before. He agreed to take me on a tour of the Sidimé family's main shop—where they make and sell masks, statues, and jewelry—and to be interviewed on camera with Nkai, his paternal cousin, who is also a fine sculptor. Laye really welcomed me this time. He introduced me to two of his children, a daughter and a son who were as tall as we were. The daughter was on her way to Dakar for the summer vacation. She would be traveling by herself, taking a bus from Conakry to Bamako, then a train to Dakar. "She loves traveling," Laye said. "We have grown old," I replied. And we laughed.

I was thinking of the boat trip I'd made more than thirty years earlier, between Kankan and Bamako. How funny history is. Like Laye's daughter, I loved traveling. When I was her age, I often traveled during the summer to Côte d'Ivoire and Liberia. I would visit my brothers, cousins, and uncles, who were traders. In Liberia, I would practice my high school English and learn new words. At the end of my stay, I would buy nice clothes and the latest albums by James Brown and Wilson Pickett. When the school year began, I would always have plenty of new friends who admired me. That had been the pleasure of travel for me.

But now I wondered whether the road between Conakry and

Bamako was in good condition. As for the train between Bamako and Dakar, I'd always wanted to take it. I'd heard so much about the scenic route—the markets of Kayes and Kaolack, the rivers it passed over, and the pleasures of night rides, with the sky full of stars and the moon that seemed to travel with the train. But I'd been warned against taking such a trip, because the tracks were in a bad state and hadn't been replaced since World War II.

Conakry, too, had changed since my visit the previous year. The roads were in better condition, the electricity was running most of the time, and the traffic lights were working again. The streets and the markets were full of people, who seemed happy as they went about their business. It was the rainy season and some of the streets were flooded, but that did not appear to be dampening the newfound life and energy in the city. Oddly, even the country's tense political climate was not visibly affecting the political and cultural life of the city. At least, not in the daytime.

The government had imposed a curfew from ten at night till six in the morning, to clamp down on crime and reduce the possibility of a coup d'état. The city was full of refugees from Sierra Leone, victims of yet another military takeover. Rumor had it that they'd brought with them not only crime, but also the potential for destabilizing the regime in Guinea.

When I'd been in Dakar a few days before, Guinea-Conakry had been the cover story of the weekly magazine *L'Autre Afrique,* which claimed to have information that a coup d'état would take place there soon. The friend who showed me the story had said I was crazy to be going to Conakry just then. I'd read the story carefully and thrown the magazine into the trash, but not without some apprehension and heartfelt trepidation. Arriving in Conakry, I found that everyone was talking about the magazine story. The newsstands had run out of copies. Some people were saying that the government had bought all the copies to keep people in the dark about the country's true situation. Others were saying that the story had never really existed—that it was a rumor spread by the opposition to further destabilize the government. I was often caught in the middle of such discussions, as an eyewitness who had bought the magazine in Dakar. People would ask me to let them see it, and when I told them that I'd thrown it in the trash before leaving Dakar, they would continue voicing doubts about the story's truth. That, too, made me nervous. I became even more so when Sidimé Laye reminded me that soon after I'd left Conakry in 1996, there was a coup attempt during which the Palais du Peuple, famous for the long speeches Sékou Touré had given there, was burned to the ground.

People otherwise go about their daily business oblivious to political strife. I learned a long time ago not to confuse political crises with economic and cultural crises in Africa. For example, when I was in Dakar the economic situation was dire, and there were rumors that this could cause a political crisis at any time. My friends told me that the population was particularly angry at the government for taking the side of a French sugar company, which was based in Senegal, against *Le Sud,* one of the main newspapers. *Le Sud* reported that the managers of the sugar company were importing manufactured sugar from France and claiming that it was made in Senegal. This way, they could claim a surplus supply and lay off workers. The company sued *Le Sud* for maligning its good name, and won. My friends said this was one more example of their government's siding with transnational corporations against the population. They warned me not to be fooled by the apparent calm of the people or by the deceptive talk of democracy in the press. Things could blow up at any time, because of the insensitivity of the government to the people's misery.

When I left Conakry a few days later for Abidjan, I was surprised again by the disjunction between politics on the one hand and the economy and culture on the other. From the rooftop restaurant of the Hotel Ivoire, Abidjan looks like any modern city in the West, with a skyline of tall buildings along the Laguna, highways and overpasses, a cathedral, and business centers. Côte d'Ivoire is called the "African

Elephant," because of the economic boom and political stability it experienced under Houphouët-Boigny. The country leads Africa in coffee and cacao exports. Abidjan has a stock market and many transnational services, which keep it permanently connected with the rest of the modern world. Yet the sociocultural crisis in Abidjan is the worst and most brutal in the region. The universities are often on strike, and for the first time professors are envying their counterparts elsewhere in the region. More than one market has caught fire and burned. Armed gangs attack gas stations in broad daylight.

I was walking with my wife in a neighborhood of Treichville—taken over by vendors since the market was burned down—when a policeman stopped us. I was carrying my video camera, and Regina was wearing some gold jewelry. The officer said we were taking too much of a risk walking down the street with such valuables. He escorted us to the jewelry store we were looking for and advised us to take a taxi once we had finished shopping. He told us that the place was too dangerous: there were thieves on the lookout for easy prey like us. They could easily snatch a gold chain and disappear into the crowd.

It wasn't until we were safely in a cab heading back to our hotel that I began to feel the impact of the encounter that had just taken place between the police officer and us. And then I was reluctant to believe him, because I'd often visited Abidjan in my youth and felt that I still belonged to this society and culture. I felt safe because I did not think of myself as a tourist in West Africa. I went along with the police officer's account because I did not feel like arguing with him in front of Regina. I'd said to him in Dioula that Treichville had changed a lot since I last saw it. My intention was to let him know that I was not a tourist. But he'd responded in French that we were making the job of the police more difficult by being so careless and carrying our camera so openly. I felt vulnerable during the cab ride—and every time I told the story to someone in Abidjan who could not contradict the police officer's portrait of Treichville.

It is at times like this that I feel Africa rapidly slipping away from me.

I feel like a permanent outsider, a tourist caught between the alienation of hotel rooms and voyeurism. How many times I have retreated from Africa into my hotel room! From a window of the Hotel Teranga in Dakar, I have looked at Goree Island and then turned my head away, to gaze at where there is only the naked Atlantic Ocean. From a window of the Hotel Independence in Conakry, I have watched fishermen and the mighty Atlantic beyond. At the Hotel du Golf in Abidjan, coconut trees and a blue swimming pool soothed my view and appeased my anger at Africa. Then I would go out again with my camera, in search of exotic images—in search of the Africa that is not me, the Africa that will confirm my identity as a tourist. As I've said, my tourist activity is not devoid of voyeurism. Sometimes I spent hours looking at people who were unaware of being watched. I expected them to do unexpected things that could become the sole possession of my camera. Sometimes I just wander through markets, which I have always loved. My father used to say, "Get up and go to the market. Nothing will get to you lying around the house like this. Go to the market, and maybe you will encounter your luck there." So everywhere I go in the world, I visit the market first, afraid that my luck will abandon me otherwise. I also come to know, by walking through a market, how well a city or an entire country is doing.

Once I saw an extraordinary thing while visiting the Kumasi market in Abidjan. There in the middle was a brand-new, enclosed, three-story market built in the style of a modern mall, and all around it were vendors sitting at their makeshift wooden stands of vegetables, auto and bicycle parts, meat, tissues, and rice. There was garbage everywhere. The market building itself was empty, because the vendors refused to rent space inside it. Why? I am not sure. Some people say that vendors like to be at the entrance of a market because this brings good luck. Some say they don't like the European way the new market arranges and compartmentalizes everything. They prefer the African system of mixing different merchandise in one place, so as to ensure that one of the vendors will get the customer's money. Some say that the vendors just don't like order, because they are corrupt—don't want to pay taxes—and they don't want the government to know where they are getting their merchandise. While there is something to all these traveling theories, I believe that this is a clear case of the right hand not knowing what the left hand is doing, and a product of the alienation of the population from the government's policies.

The dissociation of politics from culture and society makes me want to be a postcolonial subject who can make a virtue out of living in contradictory spaces, in the here and there at the same time, in the in-between and hybrid spaces—neither African nor American, and African American at the same time. To be able to say things like, "Africa does not exist," or "Africa is an invention." To be able to make my "creolity" a pure poetic statement, where rootlessness becomes the only grammar. To find the pleasure of the text in Deleuze, Foucault, and Barthes, and to be able to commit myself to denouncing the essentialism of black people everywhere—their retrograde national-ism, sexism, and homophobia. I say hooray for the coalition of pro-gressive forces, for the rainbow children. Césaire said there is no second blackness without an original blackness. But my creolity is anti-essen-tialist. I prefer the blackness of black British, like Soul II Soul—it is more chic.

But hard as I try, I cannot find peace and satisfaction in living in these contradictory spaces. I feel as if I am being forced to accept an exotic image of myself, to remain nonthreatening to the very logic that made a fixed stereotype out of me. It is like saying: "I cannot understand Africa, but that's all right because it is my postcolonial condition. I see people killed and maimed every day by the dictator politicians backed by the West, and by multinational corporations, and I celebrate this as globalization and the postmodern condition. I am an African who cannot understand Africa, so I enter into complicity with a small group of people who say that Africa does not exist anyway."

Or I can try to find the solution to Africa's problems in Afrocentric-ity, or in nativism. Watch me go all the way back to Egypt, and show

how we Soninkes descended from Assouan, where our ancestors were kings and queens—and neglect to add that the reason we came all the way to West Africa was to escape oppression at the hands of those same kings and queens. Watch me take pains to rediscover the Ashanti divinity system, the Sigi ritual as performed by the Dogons, and the meaning of the Orishas among the Yoruba. Never mind that my primary sources are Arabic and Western. I want to use ancient Mali as my antiquity, just as the Europeans use Rome as their antiquity. It is the only way out. I will teach people to take African names, learn African kinship and government systems, and free themselves of the slave mentality. Never mind that monarchy depends on the premise that we cannot all be kings and queens—that some of us must be subjugated to others. Never mind also that the rest of the world is moving fast, driven by market economies and the desire for open and democratic systems. We are taking our own time.

But in my frustration with Africa's failure to catch up with the modern world, I most want to be a conversionist like Richard Wright, Sékou Touré, Frantz Fanon, and Malcolm X. I want a revolutionary change that will include mass education and more discipline, so people can be productive and economical of their resources. We must unite West Africa against petty-bourgeois nationalists and tribalists who only serve the interest of our enemies. European countries are forming a union; the Asian countries are coming together; the North American states already have an economic union; we, too, must come together. We must not let distinctions like Francophone Africa, Anglophone Africa, and Lusophone Africa divide us. We are first and foremost Africans. If we are to count in the twenty-first century, we must immediately open the frontiers in West Africa, and let people travel freely and do business wherever they choose. To avoid coups d'état and arbitrary abuses of state power, we need a single regional army that reports to a central council elected by the people. We need a single security system in the region, in addition to local police, not only for the prevention of interstate crime, but also to prevent abuses of power and violations of human rights in any state. We must have our own currency, completely delinked from that of France or any other foreign country. We must have equality between men and women, and we must have multiparty political systems. I know that these measures will be painful to implement, and that they will be detrimental to many of our existing cultural practices. But they are the only conditions that will make possible our passage into the twenty-first century as the masters and mistresses of our own destinies.

Luckily for me, this time Sidimé Laye did not leave me hanging out alone, searching for Africa all by myself. It was really easy to connect with him. The people at the main shop recognized me right away. Some even teased me: "Aren't you Laye's friend who was looking for him last year?" Laye's uncle welcomed me with a long, warm greeting. He offered me a chair behind the counter, out of the customers' way. He told one of the young men at the shop to go to Laye's atelier and inform him of my arrival. Then he proceeded to tell me how much Laye had enjoyed seeing me the last time I'd been there. He was sure that Laye would be very happy to see me again. He asked me which hotel I was staying at. The Hotel Independence, I replied. He said, "Ah, you're not staying at the Camayenne this time?" I explained that I had not had a good experience the last time. Then he said calmly, "Fine. I've sent a messenger to get Laye. Go back to your hotel and rest. He will meet you there." I could not help saying to myself, "Not again!"

But Laye came to my hotel that same afternoon. After we'd chitchatted for a while—saying how glad we were to see each other, and exchanging news about our health and the health of our families—I asked Laye what he was working on. "A Baga bird mask known as the 'Kono,'" he said. I asked if I could come and watch him work on it. "Okay," he said, "but don't you have anything better to do while you're here?" I told him that I was in Conakry mainly to see him and to interview some people about Sékou Touré for my documentary. In that case, he replied, we would have to include his cousin Sidimé Nkai.

I could talk to his cousin while he worked. Sidimé Laye himself preferred to concentrate on his masks and leave the talking to others. But he told me not to worry: Sidimé Nkai was one of the best artists in Guinea, if not the best; and just like me, he loved talking about how art is made.

We went to the outdoor restaurant at the Camayenne. I wanted to revisit it with Laye because of the impact it had made on me the first time. We found a table in the bar area, under the thatched roof, and started talking about my previous visit to Conakry. Laye said that things had been really looking up for him lately. He and his ex-wife might soon be reunited. At this point, only formalities were keeping them apart. They had to marry all over again, which meant that his relatives had to take the dowry and kola nuts to her relatives in Kankan. Laye said that he had paid for everything, and it was now up to the Sidimé clan to do their job as ambassadors.

Business, too, had been good for Laye and Sidimé Nkai. They worked as a team, and since the beginning of the year they had received a steady stream of orders for statues and masks from American visitors and African dealers. Laye told me that Sidimé Nkai was the one who took the orders. He was a skilled businessman as well as a fine artist. He knew more about African tribal art than most of the dealers. Sometimes Nkai would buy a mask or statue from a dealer and keep it for a long time, before selling it to a more experienced dealer. Meanwhile, he and Laye would admire the craftsmanship of the artist who had done the work. They kept some masks and statues, which they acquired from small dealers, for more than two years. Laye and Nkai also collected catalogues of art exhibitions, and used the photographed works as models. Nkai sometimes relied on his own imagination to make abstract sculptures. But Laye always worked within the tradition, making masks. Whenever he made one that he liked, he felt that he was contributing to African tradition and to his own culture.

I looked at the black rocks on the shore, where on my last visit I'd seen the madman. They were empty—not a soul was visible as far as I

221
▼

could see. Laye said, "Do you remember your writer friend, the one you went to see when you were here?" I knew he was taking about Williams Sassine. "He's dead, you know." I said, "Yes, I know." I was still gazing at the black rocks. I wondered what had happened to the crazy man who had stared at me until I became afraid. Was he dead, too? I felt my muscles tensing and rage mounting to my heart and my throat. I told Laye about my last conversation with Sassine. When I'd pleaded with him to stop drinking cheap wine from the carton or it would be the death of him, he must have already known that he was dying. He'd said that he was drinking to keep himself from becoming a terrorist. He'd been unable to see this country that he loved so much going to ruin at the hands of one dictator after another. He'd said that he would rather kill himself than become an assassin. To me, Sassine had been an angel who was watching out for Africa. He'd never been afraid to tell the truth as he saw it; but like most angels, he'd been innocent, and vulnerable to the kind of violence we know in Africa. Laye said that Sassine had been given a good funeral in Conakry. It had been televised, and the French ambassador and other important dignitaries had attended. "But," Laye continued, "it is as they say: too much alcohol makes one lose perspective. Do you know Salif Kéita's song 'Primpen'? It says: 'If you don't kill alcohol, alcohol will kill you,' or something like that."

I tried my best to elevate Sassine in Laye's esteem. I told him that to understand Williams Sassine one had to go back to the time of Guinea's independence. He'd been one of the student supporters of Sékou Touré, until the 1962 school reform had turned the student movement in Conakry against the government. The reform had involved extracurricular activities such as manual labor in the fields, ideological training, and the Africanization of the scientific disciplines, all of which many students felt were diluting the content of their education. They'd marched in protest, and some had been jailed as reactionaries and enemies of the revolution. Williams Sassine had eventually escaped and gone into exile. He'd returned to Guinea after Sékou Touré's death, only to find that the new regime was even more corrupt. Sassine had been a creature of the Sixties, a romantic and a perpetual rebel. Perhaps that was why I'd loved him even when I disagreed with him. I told Laye that Williams, whose parents had owned a movie theater in Kankan, also reminded me of the romantic characters in a book by Tierno Monénembo, another friend of mine from here.

During a visit to Paris in March 1997, soon after Williams Sassine's death, I'd had a conversation with Tierno Monénembo, another Guinean writer exiled during Sékou Touré's time. We'd both talked lovingly about Williams as an older brother and as a sweet and funny man. We'd both agreed that Williams, like millions of others who had died unjustly, had been a victim of the inept conduct of African leaders over the previous thirty-five years. Tierno Monénembo had just published a new novel entitled *Cinéma*. I'd accompanied him to the book fair at the Porte de Versailles, where he'd dedicated a reading to Williams' memory.

Tierno Monénembo had read from the first chapter of his novel, which introduces Binguel, alias "the Man from the West," and his sidekick Benté, also known as "the Oklahoma Kid." The story takes place in Mamou, a small town at the end of the world in Guinea in the late 1950s. Binguel has climbed to the top of a flagpole at the center of the public square, which serves at the same time as marketplace, truck stop, bus station for service between this El Dorado and other cities in Guinea, and gathering place for political events or just the daily performances by Sarsan and his troupe of musicians and dancers. Binguel, with one hand on his revolver, has a bird's-eye view of the town, observing every detail and movement. But the Man from the West actually has his mind on the Oklahoma Kid, who has been wandering back and forth between the market and the station looking for him. Binguel has been on the flagpole for hours, and has seen Benté arrive in the market and walk by the garbage dump. King Kong, the town's madman, is sitting on the dump, but Benté passes without showering him with stones. This makes Binguel realize that the Oklahoma Kid must have something else on his mind today. He is nervous; he has lost his cool, which no good cowboy does. Should the Man from the West come down from his hiding place and confront his friend? No, he'll let him suffer a little longer. Sarsan and his troupe are out now, playing their popular tunes and dancing acrobatically in the dust. They are surrounded by a crowd, to the delight of the town's pickpockets. Another extraordinary thing: Binguel sees the Oklahoma Kid responding to Sarsan's melodies. Another violation of the cowboy's code of honor. One should never show emotion, and one should never let oneself be distracted by things like music. The Oklahoma Kid must be losing it. Binguel comes down from the pole, which he says was carrying the French flag two years ago during the celebration of the fourteenth of July, and is displaying the Guinean flag today in commemoration of October second, the day Sékou Touré said no to de Gaulle. The game of hide-and-seek is over, and the Man from the West considers himself the winner over the Oklahoma Kid.

At the end of the reading, Tierno Monénembo, said that he considered the most perfect government in the world to be a cowboy film, in which the characters, dressed as politicians, win towns, or card games, or war games by using the element of surprise, or by being more daring and confident than their opponents, or by always being cool and reacting with precision at the right moment. He said that the novel, appropriately titled *Cinéma*, was about the events immediately preceding and following the dramatic confrontation between Sékou Touré, referred to in the book as Boubou Blanc (White Gown), and Charles de Gaulle, referred to as Le Général—a confrontation which led to the independence of Guinea. Sékou Touré, like the Man from the West, watched the approach of Charles de Gaulle, who was as sure of himself as the Oklahoma Kid. Sékou Touré was able to use the element of surprise against de Gaulle, since he had detected de Gaulle's weakness. Sékou Touré embarrassed him publicly.

Binguel and Benté are young, innocent, and full of life. They go every night to the movies and to bars, to learn scenarios that they reenact in the marketplace. School no longer holds their interest; they prefer the more modern and individualistic world of the movies to the boring reality of life in Mamou, where tradition is repressive, opportunities are limited, and conflict between the Africans and the French colonials is less interesting than a remake of *Albela,* an Indian film. Benté, the older of the two and Binguel's mentor, likes tough-guy actors such as Jack Palance, Kirk Douglas, Rod Steiger, Arthur Kennedy, and Eddie Constantine. Binguel, who is only fourteen, identifies with actors who are introspective and shy, but actually tougher than they look: Gary Cooper, James Stewart, Gregory Peck, Burt Lancaster.

The novel spans twenty-four action-packed hours, from the morning on which the story opens with Binguel on the flagpole, to the next morning, when the townspeople thank Binguel for ridding them of the bad guy Bambado. The action in between includes the gathering of the crowd around Sarsan's performance; a stopover at a joint owned by the Widow Sawdatou, where Binguel has his first beer and his first encounter with Bambado, who is wanted by the authorities; and a confrontation at Sow Bela's nightclub, where he has his final, fatal showdown with Bambado, who has killed the Oklahoma Kid. Thus, the novel describes the coming-of-age ritual of Binguel, the Man from the West. He approaches everything like a scene from one of his favorite films, which he cites incessantly throughout the novel. *Cinéma* is like a knitting-together of scenes from *High Noon, The Searchers, The Virginian,* and *The Man Who Shot Liberty Valance.* The narrator—Binguel himself—makes reference to more than twenty movie titles in the book.

It takes a skilled storyteller like Tierno Monénembo to weave these twenty-four hours of Binguel's life with threads of an equally exciting moment of Guinean history—the period between 1957 and 1960. Going back and forth between the past and present, with his mastery of magic realism and stream-of-consciousness, Tierno Monénembo interlaces voices and temporal layers to create some of the most interesting characters in African literature. Among these is Ardo, the shoeshine man who dreams of changing his life after the country becomes independent from France. Ardo is Binguel's other mentor; he teaches him to read people, to see different colors in the market, and to survive the beatings by his teachers. Ardo is a wonderful storyteller who is able to entertain Binguel for hours at his shoeshine stand. Between Ardo and the Oklahoma Kid, Binguel is not sure who has taught him more about life.

Then there is Mody Djinna, Binguel's father, who opposes independence for Guinea because he fears that it will become a communist state and take his business from him. Besides, how can the Guineans ask for their independence when they can't even make so much as a needle on their own? But as independence becomes imminent after Le Général's unsuccessful visit, Mody Djinna changes his position. He hangs a picture of Boubou Blanc in his living room, between a Muslim calendar and a picture of the Mosque of Al-Azar. After independence, he winds up at the head of the national business that distributes goods. Mody Djinna is one of the most manipulative characters in the novel, moving between the Africans and the French, religion and politics, tradition and modernity.

Finally, there are stories about the relations between blacks and whites that are interesting from the perspective of psychology and history. For example, the French expatriate community is thrown into an uproar when Mademoiselle Saval, Binguel's teacher, chooses Cellou, an African, as her lover over Massalloux, a Frenchman. The white community gossips about Mademoiselle Saval, calling her a whore and a nigger-lover. The whites go so far as to ask the police chief to investigate her background, suspecting that her professional degrees are forgeries. Why else would a single woman like her come all the way to a dead-end place like Mamou to work? They also get angry at Cellou for acting like a white man and forgetting his place. Cellou is a poet and loves Mallarmé, whose poetry he reads to Mademoiselle Saval while they drink red wine. He introduces the youth of Mamou to many new styles, and is the first black to dare to enter an all-white bar. At the

Bastille Day celebration, he is shot dead—for dating Mademoiselle Saval, for going to the all-white bar, and for supporting Guinean independence. After independence, all the white people leave Guinea except for Massalloux, who marries a black woman and has a child with her.

At the end of the novel, Binguel strolls by King Kong on the garbage dump and, as the Oklahoma Kid used to do, throws stones at him to show he's tough, like a real cowboy. But what one actually comes to realize is that King Kong is the toughest and coolest of all the characters in the novel. Binguel compares him to a shadow, a church, and a cemetery in the way in which he remains unimpressed by what is going on around him. He pivots at the top of the dump like the second-hand of a watch, but moves at a much slower pace, sometimes facing in one direction for years. King Kong is said to be a black American sailor whose ship sank off the coast of Haiphong or Manila and who ended up in Mamou, no one knows how. He was persecuted during the period of colonialism; his situation is even worse now that Guinea is independent. But King Kong is the one who survives colonialism and the regime of Boubou Blanc, like the solitary hero in a cowboy film. Even Binguel is coopted at the end as a popular hero.

Without a doubt, Tierno Monénembo will be among the very best writers of Africa in the twenty-first century. In his stories, the individual emerges powerfully—and this constitutes the biggest difference between *Cinéma* and many African novels, which turn away from the hero in favor of the group. Also, Tierno Monénembo's book is not a sad story about Afro-pessimism, or tradition against modernity. The distinguishing traits of *Cinéma* include its well-crafted story, which evokes pleasure in the reader; its willingness to participate in the evolution of the novel that has occurred in other parts of the world; and the skillful way it enters into conversation with other genres and media like movies. Africans who grew up in the 1950s and after can identify with Tierno Monénembo's characters and the popular culture they refer to. One gets the sense that Africans, too, see themselves as part of the world—influenced, just as people on other continents are, by movies, advertising, and consumer goods. It's this humanism and this fragility of Monénembo's characters that remind me of Williams Sassine.

It was dark by the time Sidimé Laye and I left the terrace restaurant at the Hotel Camayenne. I took one last look at the shore for signs of that crazy man, but there was no one there. The white waves of the ocean beating against the black rocks defied the falling darkness of the night.

The next morning, I packed my video camera, tripod, and sound equipment in a canvas bag and went down to the hotel lobby. Mr. Diao, a cameraman from the Guinean Film Center, was waiting for me. I made a deal with him to tape my interviews while I asked the questions. Mr. Diao had his own car, so we did not need a chauffeur. It was better that way. For some reason, I did not feel the need to look for Cémoko, who had been my driver before. I guess this time I wanted a strictly professional relationship with the people who worked for me. Mr. Diao had been trained as a cameraman in Czechoslovakia in the mid-1970s, during Sékou Touré's reign, when the Guinean army had needed its own cameramen; Mr. Diao had been serving in the army then. He was a discreet man who loved making films and appreciated the opportunity to work with me, even though he did not seem to share my enthusiasm for Sékou Touré.

I was excited and nervous, like a little boy. Finally I was going to see Laye's atelier and film him with Sidimé Nkai. I went over the equipment with Mr. Diao, who reassured me again and again that he had everything under control. I handed him the directions to the atelier, which was in the suburbs of Conakry, north of the airport. He knew the way, because he was familiar with the two little African art kiosks that were situated across the street from the atelier.

We were there by ten o'clock. We stopped in front of the two kiosks, and I got out of the car to ask where Laye's atelier was. A man pointed across the street, where I could see nothing but tall trees with thick foliage. The sun was already hot and bright. There was no traffic light or stop sign in the vicinity. Cars and trucks were passing at full speed, which forced me to wait a while before crossing the street. I realized that we were standing on a hill which was masked by tall trees. To get to Laye's place, I had to cross a small bridge and go down the hill into a space completely covered by trees. Laye was sitting there, working on a mask, under the tallest and thickest tree. He was shirtless, and his upper body and arms were covered with wood chips that flew from the mask he was carving. Sweat was running down his body, carrying tiny chips in its flow. When he saw me, he stood up to greet me.

"So this is where you work!" I said.

"Yeah!" he replied, lighting a cigarette.

He told me that Sidimé Nkai would soon be there and we could start the interview. Then he went back to work. I told Mr. Diao to bring the equipment while I looked around. There was a little stream further down, behind the trees, where young girls and boys were busy washing clothes or playing. A few yards away from Laye, near the small bridge, there was a house, and construction workers were building another one behind it. Other than that, the place seemed completely under the spell of the trees, which enchanted me. It amazed me that we were only a few feet away from the traffic and shops, yet we were plunged into a deep, sacred forest. It was just like Laye to call such a shrine-like place as this his atelier. I had been thinking of a somewhat modern place, with electric tools and what not. Instead of using the machines at the main shop in Conakry, Laye worked with his hands, as the tribal carvers used to do. I understood now what he meant when he said he retreated into his atelier until his work was done, and when he spoke of his hand's being possessed by the mask he was working on.

By the time Sidimé Nkai arrived, the mask Laye was working on was already taking shape. It had the forehead of a human being, but the small eyes and elongated beak of a bird. It was the Kono mask he had mentioned. We set up the camera and began taping. I was worried

Sidimé Laye at work in his atelier, August 1997. (From the video *In Search of Africa*, by Manthia Diawara.)

more about the din from the construction workers than about the traffic noise, which was muffled by the thick foliage. Sidimé Nkai did most of the talking, while Laye continued to work, giving only short answers to my questions.

I started with the question of authenticity in African art. Sidimé Nkai said there were several ways of responding to that. First of all, you had to see who was making a big deal out of the issue—collectors, museum curators, and elite art dealers in Europe who were interested in exclusivity and higher prices for their masks and statues. For this reason,

Sidimé Laye shaping the Kono mask. In the background is his cousin Sidimé Nkai; in the foreground is the author. (From the video *In Search of Africa*, by Manthia Diawara.)

they declared that all the original masks and statues had been taken out of Africa by the 1950s. They established this cutoff date to raise the value of their own collections and to maintain Europe as the chief source and venue of African art. In other words, anything coming out of Africa today was a worthless fake. Did that mean that every single African had stopped worshiping masks and statues since the 1950s? Of course not. Traditionally, people worshiped a reliquary figure, or continued using a mask for ritual dances until it was old or eaten by termites. Then they buried it and made themselves a new statue or a new mask in the same spirit, which they kept for fifteen or twenty years, and so on. Did this mean the new one was not authentic or original? Of course not. It was authentic because the same tribes still danced with it and idolized it.

I could see now why Sidimé Laye wanted Nkai to discuss the subject with me. Like me, Nkai loved talking about art and criticism. Laye, on the other hand, kept on working. I attempted to interrupt him by asking, "Laye, what do you think?" Without taking his eyes off his work or stopping the up-and-down movement of his sharp-pointed chisel, he replied: "It's like he said. I agree with him."

Sidimé Nkai lit a cigarette and continued, with the air of a man pleased with himself. But even if for the sake of argument we were to accept the 1950s as the cutoff date for defining authentic African art, another problem arose: that of the desacralization of African village cemeteries and the theft of their masks. At first, the dealers went to villages known for their worship of certain reliquary figures, and bribed informants or elders into opening up the graves of the chiefs, who had been buried with such religious objects. Since the 1960s—with independence, the loss of traditions, and the rise of spiritual alienation—the villagers themselves have gone to the city to sell their oldest religious figures, their most precious gods, all in an effort to be part of a market invented by European dealers and museum curators. Of course, the African carvers vied for their share of the market as well. They used special methods of aging wood, soaking it in the juice of certain leaves, rubbing it in a special oil, painting it, and burying it for a certain amount of time. Some of these counterfeits were better than the so-called originals, because more work went into them. No museum could tell the difference.

As Sidimé Nkai spoke, I was reminded of Chinua Achebe's classic novel *Things Fall Apart*. I wondered about all the graves that might have been opened up in Igbo villages because of that book. It contains so many detailed accounts of Igbo rituals with masks and statues: who wore what, where they were kept, where they were buried. And I thought of a notorious act of thievery by Michel Leiris and Marcel Griaule that took place during the Dakar-Djibouti Expedition of 1931. As Mamadou Diawara tells the story, Leiris and Griaule wanted a Kono mask that was kept in the hut of a Baga high priest. First they asked the priest to bring out the mask and show it to them. Both the priest and the village chief refused to comply with their request. Then Griaule offered to buy the mask for ten francs. Again they refused. Griaule threatened to take the chief and the priest to the colonial authorities. He lied to them, saying that the police were hiding in the truck. Thoroughly frightened, the chief and the priest said that the Frenchmen could go in and take the mask. None of the natives would enter the hut for fear of punishment by the gods. Griaule went in himself. He emerged not only with a majestic mask covered with blood, but also with two flutes which he had slipped into his boots (Diawara, 1994–1995: 228).

I asked Sidimé Nkai what he thought of museums. He said he had no problem with museums, as long as they were ethnological or artistic. The former type should keep only restored objects that had been damaged by termites or abandoned by tribes because of modern-ization. Thus, museums could help to preserve the memory of African traditions. But museums should not contribute to the mummification of living cultures, religions, and artifacts. "Look at the Dogons," I agreed. "They are considered primitive because of the high value placed on their art in museums. So the only authentic Dogon is one who lives the way his ancestors did, hundreds of years ago. There's a case of art in museums influencing reality."

Sidimé Nkai said that he could also see museums devoted to masks and statues because of their aesthetic beauty. He himself had restored some Baga masks that were in the museum in Conakry—displayed not only for their ethnological value, but also for the aesthetic value of the restoration. He said that some African statues and masks "speak to you through their beauty." Such art objects should be in museums just for that reason. He himself had made some statues which to this day he regretted selling.

I then changed the subject to the question of signatures in African art. First I asked Sidimé Laye if he remembered our having had this same discussion the previous year. Had he changed his mind? No, he said. He saw no reason to sign his art, because the ancestors did not

Sidimé Laye trying on the Kono mask. (From the video *In Search of Africa*, by Manthia Diawara.)

sign theirs. He worked in the tradition of ancient sculptors; therefore, he could not affix his signature to a traditional mask.

But how did he feel when he made and sold a mask that he himself liked a lot? He said it gave him pleasure and satisfaction because this meant that he had contributed to the world's knowledge of Africa, and that he had created a place for his own culture in the general knowledge of Africa. This was the reason he did not see any need to sign his masks.

Sidimé Nkai, on the other hand, said that there were circumstances in which he could see himself signing his sculptures. When, for example, he finished restoring a statue that had been gnawed away by termites or had rotted underground, he liked to put his name on it as the artist who had repaired it. Sometimes he created abstract statues that belonged to no tribe in particular, and in this case, too, he would sign his name. Finally, tourist art of all types could be signed without

Sidimé Laye (left) and Sidimé Nkai in the main shop in Conakry, August 1997. (From the video *In Search of Africa*, by Manthia Diawara.)

any problem. Then Sidimé Nkai said that there were signatures in traditional art; it was just that people could not decipher them. They were tribal marks.

With my interview finished, we went back to the main shop in downtown Conakry. Sidimé Nkai showed me some of the statues he had made, and some that he had collected from dealers. He and Laye let me videotape the store, the workshop, and the yard, where there were piles of wood and unfinished and abandoned statues. I bought two little statues from Sidimé Nkai, and he agreed to put his signature on them. Outside, the rain began coming down in torrents. Then I realized that I had found Sidimé Laye. I was in his abode, protected from the rain.

I looked at the piles of wood and the unfinished and abandoned statues outside, under the heavy rain. Suddenly I found myself praying,

Twin Congo fertility figures carved by Sidimé Nkai, Sidimé Laye's cousin. (Photo by Elisabeth van der Heijden; courtesy of *October* magazine.)

as my mother and father used to do. May this year's rains bring us a good harvest; may we prosper and fructify; may we be protected from famine and shame at the hands of our enemies; may Africa be the continent of the new millennium. I have found Sidimé Laye. May the gods, the masks, and the statues keep us together; may our children grow up proud, self-sufficient, and generous toward the rest of the world.

SITUATION IV

▲▼▲

HOMEBOY COSMOPOLITAN

The same transformative energy at play in Sidimé Laye's work is found in hip-hop, a transnational cultural form that started with young African Americans. Just as Sidimé Laye comes out of Sékou Touré's revolution, and just as his stubborn insistence on carving masks and statues reveals the limitations of such work, young black Americans coming out of the civil rights movement have used hip-hop culture in the 1980s and 1990s to show the limitations of that movement—its inability to satisfy the aspirations of the masses. Up to now in this book, I have been concerned with the need to overcome Afro-pessimism. In this concluding chapter, too, I would like to help change a prevailing attitude: the perception that black people and their culture are pathological.

When I moved from Philadelphia to New York in 1992, the main elements of hip-hop had already permeated the youth culture of both blacks and whites. By "hip-hop" I mean the youth culture associated with rap musicians, their dress styles, 'hood movies, and spoken-word poetry and graffiti art (Rose, 1994). It seemed to me right away that, like rock-and-roll, hip-hop was infused with rebellion and driven by the market economy. But the fundamental difference between the two movements lies in the fact that young whites have been able to coopt and dominate rock-and-roll by making it reflect their social concerns and aesthetics, while young blacks have retained financial control over hip-hop, reducing the rest of the world to consumers of its social concerns. Like rock-and-roll, hip-hop is vigorously opposed by conservatives because it romanticizes violence, lawbreakers, and gangs. To a greater extent than rock-and-roll, however, hip-hop is criticized by feminists for its misogyny, by the Left for its black nationalistic viewpoint, and by nationalists for allowing the cutting edge of its resistance to be dulled—an edge that was associated with the early songs of the groups Public Enemy and Africa Bambata. Some denounce it for promoting violence and misogyny; others, for falling away from the ideals of the civil rights struggle.

Still, I was uneasy when I saw the convergence of attacks against hip-hop by otherwise oppositional camps. After all, the late twentieth century places a premium value on systems with the potential for globalization. Rap music, and other forms of entertainment which were packaged as hip-hop ('hood movies, homeboy fashion, basketball), were assuming a dominant place in the world market, challenged only by Hollywood blockbuster films, their accompanying toy industry, and computers and other tools of the information highway. Hip-hop also created and maintained a heroic space for the wretched of the earth, which should have endeared its message to leftists and others concerned with issues of human rights.

The packaging of hip-hop as a commodity in the marketplace, and the worldwide spread of hip-hop as a market revolution, are an expression of poor people's desire for the good life. It seems to me that the search for the good life not only is in keeping with the nationalist struggle for citizenship and belonging, but also reveals the need to go beyond such struggles and celebrate the redemption of the black individual through tradition.

Thus, the unrelenting criticism of hip-hop from the Left, the Right, feminists, and nationalists kept me wondering about W. E. B. Du Bois's powerful indictment of Western society, when he stated that the problem of the twentieth century was the problem of the color line. The convergence of these attacks on black people through attacks on hip-hop and the attempts to remove it from the marketplace are symptomatic of the problems that the twentieth century has had with race. They are scarcely justified by the sexism and dehumanization that characterize certain segments of hip-hop culture.

After all, Hollywood action movies, the information highway, and the toy industry are equally sexist and dehumanizing, yet they have not provoked nearly as much protest and indignation from civil society and the state. Indeed, President Ronald Reagan liked to compare himself with Rambo, one of the antisocial, lawbreaking, macho protagonists of the blockbuster action films of the 1980s. Furthermore, gangster rap, as the name indicates, inherited its sexist attitudes and dehumanizing violence from such films as *The Godfather.* Why do we still consider action flicks and computers as valuable commodities, yet try to exclude hip-hop from the marketplace?

Perhaps the answer to this question will get us beyond Du Bois's dictum, which seems to have prefigured and determined most of the discussions, policies, and events involving black people in the twentieth century. But first, let's look at one method that young blacks use to escape the Du Boisian dilemma and the trap of racial immanence—their exclusion from all social roles not conventionally associated with blackness. I call this method "homeboy cosmopolitanism," and have observed it most closely in my neighborhood of Greenwich Village in New York City.

The physical mobility of young blacks, which is aimed at removing obstacles to black Americans' pursuit of material wealth and pleasure, has been represented in the media as pathological and a menace to society. At the same time, residents in predominantly white urban areas tend to be suspicious of young blacks who move into their neighborhoods, viewing them as homeless loafers, drug dealers, and felons of other sorts whose presence brings down property values. In 1993, white residents of Greenwich Village, in order to curtail the influx of hip-hop culture, began linking the fluid activism and *flâneur* styles of homeboys to whites' received notions of criminals and drug dealers.

An August cover story in *New York Magazine,* "The Village under Siege," invoked racial stereotypes to scare naive white people and to justify militarizing the police so as to stop the free movement, strolling, and shopping of young blacks and Latinos in the Village. The cover of the magazine was itself revealing. The camera had been placed in front of the arch in Washington Square Park; the World Trade Center towers and other downtown skyscrapers were illuminated in the background, and a dark Washington Square Park occupied the middle ground. The arch was enlivened with colored lights: its top was green, and its bottom, where the statues of George Washington stood, was ivory. The name of Michael Gross, the author of the article, was printed in red in the middle of the cover. The play of red, green, and white on the dark middle ground of the illustration suggested the fear of what Gross called "other urban pathologies": the menace of darkness against civilization—or, simply put, the fear of black men. In the article, Gross stated that a "battle for a civil Village" was being waged. The residents "are afraid of the drug dealers who set up shop in the streets around Washington Square Park. They're afraid of the hip-hoppers from outer-borough neighborhoods whose urban update on *American Graffiti* finds them cruising the Village streets in expensive cars fitted out with trunk-mounted speakers blasting rap music" (Gross, 1993: 32).

Gross concluded by invoking the image of a war zone in which New York's police force prevailed over the intruding homeboys. He celebrated the militarization of the police: "The last word this evening belongs to the cops of the Sixth [Precinct]. A few moments before, I'd left a whole roomful of them singing the stirring Wagner passage that Francis Coppola used as music for the helicopter assault in *Apocalypse Now*" (37). Gross described the young blacks and Latinos as "denizens of rap culture" and characterized them as street peddlers, vagrants, drug dealers, armed robbers, and people who defecated and urinated on the sidewalks.

Gross left out the fact that white youths from New Jersey had always converged in the Village to drink beer in the streets and occasionally urinate on the sidewalks. He also avoided mentioning young blacks' consumer habits, which at that time accounted for the most energetic cultural life in the Village. Had Gross considered the way in which they diffused hip-hop culture through clothing styles, street art, basketball in the parks, and multiculturalism in this predominantly white enclave of the city, the homeboys' image would have been quite different in his article.

By the summer of 1993, black youth culture was becoming quite visible in the Village. Every afternoon there were vibrant gatherings of homeboys around parks, stores, restaurants, vending stands, and subway stations between Sixth Avenue and Broadway. It became clear that stores like Tower Records, the Wiz, Footlocker, the Gap, and Urban Outfitters, restaurants such as BBQ, the convenient subway stops, and the basketball courts were doing more to attract young blacks and Latinos to the Village than the drug dealers and the incense vendors. Young Asians and whites also came dressed like homeboys to participate in the strolling and to take back new sounds, slang, and styles to the suburbs.

Consumption around these new public focal points made the Village a battleground for integration and multiculturalism, to the dismay of property-owning residents. The shops tailored their merchandise to the tastes of the hip-hop generation. Stores and restaurants owned by new immigrants were proliferating, and were transforming the baby boomer culture of the Village. The traditional book peddlers were replaced by black vendors who were savvy not only about hip-hop culture but about the black intellectual tradition, from Du Bois to Malcolm X. Usually, in front of the NYU library one could buy Hermann Hesse's *Steppenwolf* and *Siddhartha,* or Thomas Mann's *Death in Venice.* Now the Sixth Avenue vendors were displaying the latest works by Cornel West and bell hooks, *The Isis Papers* by Dr. Frances Cress Wesling, and a slew of books describing conspiracies against black people. One such vendor, who told me his name was Hakim, engaged his customers in discussions not only about the content of each book, but also about the plight of black intellectuals, the Senate hearings involving Clarence Thomas and Anita Hill, and the topics of conferences held at NYU. Hakim and other vendors carried works that could not be found in neighboring bookstores like St. Marks, Shakespeare, and Barnes and Noble. They also provided homeboys interested in political and social issues with the latest gossip and theories about antiblack actions taken at City Hall, Columbia University, City College, and NYU.

Hakim's relations with the people strolling along Sixth Avenue revealed other characteristics of the homeboys. He was a book vendor and street intellectual who considered Sixth Avenue, from Bleecker to Eleventh Street, as his turf. He thus knew all the store owners, newcomers, old people, and cops (which of them were good and which were bad). He knew the political differences between the former mayor and the current one, and how these could affect the homeless, the homeboys, and black people in general on Sixth Avenue. He had definite opinions about black intellectuals—which ones were saying things that were relevant to the lives of black people in the city, and which were not, and were therefore simply selected by the white press to maintain the status quo against the homeless and the homeboys. He was convinced that Rudolph Giuliani had been elected mayor to "clean up" the city, which meant that all the homeless and homeboys would soon disappear from Sixth Avenue.

Hakim was the type of professional conspirator who reminded me of what Paris must have been like in the *feuilleton* era, in the nineteenth century. Walter Benjamin described the *flâneur,* one of the types of professional conspirators in Paris at the time, as an unwilling detective with artistic sensibilities: "He only seems to be indolent, for behind this indolence there is the watchfulness of an observer who does not take his eyes off a miscreant . . . He catches things in flight; this enables him to dream that he is like an artist" (Benjamin, 1983: 41).

Hakim often said that he had many powerful lawyer friends in the neighborhood. He constantly looked left and right before talking to people who stopped by his table. He was fond of introducing people to each other by stating that so-and-so was an author, a lawyer, or a professor. He wanted to go back to school at NYU, to take a law degree or a master's in sociology. He addressed me as "Professor Diawara," and told me about his most recent intervention to stop unlawful harassment of black and Latino youths by the police in the Village. He said that something had to be done, because all these blacks and Latinos were coming to the Village and they did not know their rights.

Hakim was also a race man, devoting his life to the uplift of his people. Not only did he address me as "Professor Diawara," but he always spoke in proper English, and never cursed or used an ungrammatical sentence in front of me. He had read every book on his table, and used to tell me how ashamed he was of some of the black authors, whose knowledge and scholarship left a lot to be desired. Hakim read the *New York Times,* the *Wall Street Journal,* and all the book review magazines. He followed with great interest the creation of Harvard's "dream team" of black professors by Henry Louis Gates Jr. He used to ask me whether Robin D. G. Kelley or Michael Eric Dyson was coming to teach at NYU, and if we too were going to create our "dream team." But Hakim reserved his harshest criticism for the Afrocentrists at City College. He did not believe that they were interested in scholarship or that they cared about the real problems facing black people in America. Every once in a while, he would interrupt our conversation to tell me that Stanley Crouch, or bell hooks, or Derrick Bell had recently stopped by his stand.

I began to see the Village through Hakim's eyes. I came to understand, for example, how consumerism related to political activism among young people in the Village. For me, as for Hakim, police actions came to seem a form of aggression by the state against civil society. I realized that the only reason *New York Magazine* and the landlords of the Village were siding with the police was that the youths in question were black and Latino. The young people coming to the Village as *flâneurs*—dudes who dressed up to be seen, and to see themselves being admired by others—were enjoying the black good life: a freedom and energy associated with individual fulfillment that had been denied black people, in spite of the gains of the civil rights movement and integration. The Village provided secular spaces for pleasure—spaces that no longer existed in the homeboys' neighborhoods and that had to be conquered.

242
▼

After *New York Magazine* published Gross's article, my black students at NYU who wore dreadlocks and dressed like homeboys often complained of police harassment. One day, my class on Pan-Africanism was discussing the police's attempts to keep blacks out of the Village. A student with dreadlocks reported that his claim to be an NYU student had been disputed by a policeman. The class then talked for a long time about activism and civil rights, with particular reference to the right to shop and stroll in the Village.

Of course, Greenwich Village has always been considered a gathering place for young people and a haven for avant-garde cultures. Students at NYU, the largest private university in New York City, often intersect with these youth cultures, even participate in them. Compared to people living in other neighborhoods, residents of the Village have traditionally been more willing to embrace youth culture—in spite of the noise it brings, and the seemingly messy and disorderly behavior—because of the vitality that characterizes lifestyles on the cutting edge. New trends are often tested in the Village, where they are either rejected or turned into fashions for the rest of the world to follow. Hip-hop culture, too, is helping to shape the phantasmagoria of life in Greenwich Village.

In 1993 the homeboy look was popular among black, Asian, and white students at NYU. It consisted of a loose shirt, oversized jeans, dreadlocks or a haircut called the "fade," and a baseball cap; a small radio–cassette player with headphones was an essential accessory. Having just arrived at NYU, I was afraid that my white colleagues would subscribe to the stereotype of black masculinity presented in the *New York Magazine* article and would dismiss the homeboys as drug dealers and lawbreakers. At that time, hip-hop was the most important multicultural youth movement in America. The fact that it was being spearheaded by young blacks did not make it less American or less appropriate for the Village. My criticism of the *New York Magazine* article here is intended to persuade people to take a closer look at this youth movement, so that they can distinguish the creative members from those that stagnate, the homeboys from the drug dealers.

The artistic philosophy of hip-hop is reflexive. It produces laughter through ironic and parodic re-representation of black history and desire from a black point of view. It is as if every image in hip-hop were a retelling of the story of Cain and Abel from Cain's point of view. The "in your face" retelling of the original story with bright colors and laughter nullifies the discursive elements that once kept the black image in captivity.

Since the rise of the hip-hop movement, the word "homeboy" has acquired new currency in popular culture, influencing the meaning of maleness among black and white youth. The image of the homeboy constitutes a shift of the stereotype of black maleness from the margin to the center—from crude criminals in the ghetto to cosmopolitan *flâneurs* and MTV trendsetters. One can see, then, how hip-hop's re-thematization of the myth of Cain has enabled the emergence of new and complex characters, such as Easy Rawlins in Walter Mosley's mystery novels, Doughboy in John Singleton's film *Boyz N the 'Hood,* and new styles and behaviors engendered by the music of Public Enemy, KRS One, and Wu Tang Clan and by the films of Spike Lee and other directors.

The Homeboy and the Myth of Cain

The story of Cain and Abel in the Book of Genesis is interesting because Cain's character is associated not only with fratricide and eternal sin, but also with eternal mobility, invention, and self-fashioning. Yahweh tells Cain that death will be crouching at his door, always ready to catch him. Cain flees from the vicinity of Eden to the distant land of Nod and becomes the first founder of cities. Yet the Bible warns us that there is no peace to be found in cities, because they will never come near the perfection of the City of God. As Saint Paul says, "There is no permanent city for us here. We are looking for the one which is yet to be" (Hebrews, 13:14). Finally, the Bible says that Cain is an angry man, envious of Abel for being the focus of Yahweh's esteem. He is out for revenge.

Writers like Charles Baudelaire and Walter Benjamin have already linked this image of the cursed Cain to modernity and modernism. In Benjamin's view, "Cain, the ancestor of the disinherited, appears as the founder of a race, and this race can be none other than the proletariat" (Benjamin, 1983: 22). He also links Cain's passion for revenge to heroic acts against the race of Abel—the race that, as Baudelaire puts it in "Le vin du chiffonnier," eats and sleeps in peace.

I, too, wish to claim Cain—claim him for the black race, in order to contribute to the Marxist rereading of the story of Cain and Abel, and, in the process, remove blackness from the captivity of negative signs. The resemblance between the situation of Cain and that of black males in American society also helps explain why hip-hop culture creates rebellious art forms that combat racism, calls for more options in life for blacks, and demands the right for blacks to live in peace as individuals in the city. The myth of Cain is a powerful metaphor for the way relations between blacks and whites are represented in the media. In the American imagination, no figure is as evocative of Cain—condemned to be a wanderer and a pariah—as the black man, who struggles to find a home and to participate in the public sphere that whites consider their private property.

It is no exaggeration to say that the modern city has replaced Eden and that the black man has been indelibly marked by the curse of Cain. The image of the hip-hop generation as a group to be feared and avoided is always fixed in the mind of the nation. All young black men are equated with thugs who wear dark sunglasses, gold chains, basketball sneakers, and jeans from the Gap or Urban Outfitters; drag their feet when walking; carry knives, guns, beepers; verbally assault women as bitches, white men as motherfuckers, black men as niggers.

The homeboy's antisocial behavior supposedly justifies society's contempt for him and the police's brutal efforts to control him. The homeboy, like Cain, is reduced to mere appearance, the sum of selected formal signifiers; he is scapegoated for the current crisis in America's cities. The desire by the police and the media to control the homeboy's image keeps relations between blacks and whites at a level of tension which is always threatening to erupt. The black man is always guilty, no matter who perpetrates the crime.

It is thus one of hip-hop's cultural and artistic achievements to have redefined the homeboy. Hip-hop artists create new meanings for the image of the homeboy by providing him with functions that contradict the mainstream media's construction of him. Hip-hop culture gives aesthetic pleasure through ironic and parodic play with mainstream images of black people. It forces us to rethink how Cain and sin exist in our society, to ask who the criminal is and who the victim.

Hip-hop music, literature, and film practice an aesthetic of resistance which disarticulates the meaning of stereotypes through what I call the parodic reclaiming of the stereotype. One could actually extend the history of the re-thematization of the myth of Cain in black culture to black folklore, slave narratives, the Harlem Renaissance, the Black Arts movement, and Blaxploitation films. It is odd that no serious effort has been made in art criticism to link the hip-hop movement to the existential morality of these earlier artistic movements, and hip-hop art to the desire for mobility, revenge, and the reappropriation of the image of black people from racial stereotypes. The inspiration for the homeboy image itself can easily be traced to Malcolm X, who also rebelled against a tradition perceived as ineffectual, and who was a cosmopolitan homeboy in Boston and New York when jazz was a popular art form.

The Construction of Mobility in *Superfly* and *Shaft*

The film *Superfly* (1972), directed by Gordon Parks Jr., is an action-adventure movie typical of the Blaxploitation films popular in the Seventies. Centering on a drug dealer named Priest, who is seeking escape from his life of crime and degradation, the film resonates in a number of ways with the myth of Cain. Like Cain, Priest is a man toughened by his experience as prey and predator, seeking revenge and redemption at the same time. Indeed, the opening sequence of *Superfly* is extraordinary for the way it evokes Cain's envy and resentment of the society that has disinherited and abandoned him. The camera work and the soundtrack help create a magnificent narrative of romantic loneliness and heroism.

The opening shot is a bird's-eye view of a street corner in Harlem, which will later be identified as the intersection of 125th Street and Adam Clayton Powell Boulevard. The camera zooms in slowly, in order to focus on two men meeting on the crowded street corner. One asks, "Did you get it?" The other answers, "No! She wouldn't give it to me." The first man says he hadn't expected her to hand over the money, so he's come up with a second option—and this time he intends to do things his own way. He ends by saying, "You hear me, nigger!" At this point, Curtis Mayfield's song "Little Child, Running Wild" comes on the soundtrack. The two men walk down 125th Street in rhythm with the music, as if they were listening to it. Thus, the music serves right away to naturalize the existence of people at the corner of 125th Street.

The camera follows the men at a distance, from the other side of the street. They pass by cigar shops, clothing stores, a Florsheim shoe store, the Studio Museum of Harlem, and peddlers on the crowded street, before coming to a garbage dump, fenced lots, and abandoned buildings. Men who look like drug dealers are hanging about, and scary people are lurking in the doorways. The two men enter one of the buildings and go down a dark hallway; the camera follows them inside until the screen turns completely black. It then fades to an extreme close-up of a man's hairy chest, on which rests a gold chain with a crucifix pendant. As the camera pulls back, we see a pensive man reclining in bed with a naked white woman. The camera tilts up a bit to frame the man's face in a tight medium close-up, which indicates that he has been thinking and that the previous street scene was filmed from his point of view. He snorts some cocaine with his crucifix pendant, and gets up to dress and to leave.

The soundtrack, meanwhile, has been describing the meaning of street life in Harlem and the philosophy of the pusher (drug dealer). "Little Child, Running Wild" attempts to explain the sociological significance of the images passing before our eyes. As the camera focuses on the two men walking down the street in search of their next victim, the song informs us that the world we are being introduced to is filled with broken homes, children whose fathers have run away, and mothers who are tired of raising them. They are all alone, kind of sad, kind of mad, thinking that they've "been had." They constantly feel the pain of abandonment and betrayal, which they try to take away with drugs. As the camera moves along the street, we are introduced to several characters who look like drug dealers, before we get to the man in the bed. We know by then how dangerous the pusher is. "Finance is all he understands," according to the song.

But the pensive image of Priest, the man in the bed, shows that he is not like the other pushers. He identifies with his victims, and in fact considers himself a victim, too. His victim status is confirmed when he leaves the apartment of his white girlfriend in Greenwich Village and finds the police towing away his car. Back in Harlem, he is mugged by the two men seen previously.

I saw *Superfly, Shaft,* and other Blaxploitation films in Monrovia (Liberia) in the early Seventies. I remember being particularly struck by the opening sequence in *Superfly*—it seemed an extraordinary cinematic event. I had been living in Monrovia for almost a year, and was fascinated by the lifestyle in that West African city, which identified more with America than with Africa. People spoke English with a black American accent like the one I heard in the movies, on television (in shows like *Good Times* and *Sanford and Son*), and in rhythm-and-blues and gospel songs. The cities in Liberia have names like Virginia, Maryland, Greenville, and Harper. I lived on an avenue called Randall Street. All the people in Monrovia liked to trace their family origin to the United States. Most of my friends had already been to America at least once, or were getting ready to join a cousin, a sister, or a friend there. Some referred to America as

"home." It was in Liberia that I first learned to speak English, and developed a yearning to go to America myself one day.

The early Seventies were also a time when many black Americans visited Monrovia. Some were Black Muslims, and some were members of the Black Panthers or the Black Power Party. I was familiar to some degree with the civil rights struggle in the United States. In particular, I'd heard

My friend Yassoun Camara, a.k.a. Blanc, in his *Superfly* outfits, 1975 (left) and 1976. (Photos by Hamidou Diarra; collection of Manthia Diawara.)

about Muhammad Ali's refusal to fight in Vietnam, the incarceration of Angela Davis and the Jackson brothers for political reasons, and the defiance of Malcolm X and the Black Muslims. But I was more fascinated with the movies, the music, the hairstyles, the hats, and the leather jackets that were popular among black Americans.

Looking back now, I can see why the opening of *Superfly* had such an impact on me. First, there was what seemed to be the realism of the street scene: many people wearing leather jackets and hats, a multitude of stores full of merchandise, retail signs and advertisements, and the bustle of urban life. The fact that the street was full of black people also reinforced my identification with the scene. It reminded me of Monrovia's Broadway, where the movie theaters were located, the only difference being that the scene in *Superfly* had a lot more people and neon signs. People were also speaking nearly the same English as people in Monrovia, using expressions like "You hear me, nigger!" and "Dig it!" The focus on the meeting between the two hustlers was also important. For a moment, they were the heroes of the film, moving freely in the crowd, unafraid. I identified with them because they symbolized familiarity with the city, and therefore my own cosmopolitanism in Monrovia.

But Curtis Mayfield's song was the most significant reason for my identification with the film's opening. I was already familiar with Mayfield's work, since he'd sung with a group called the Drifters. His voice pierces one's heart and makes one feel like a warrior, or just puts one in a state of feeling invulnerable. His songs contain the right words for defining situations and images; they evoke nostalgia and create bonds between people, so as to mobilize them in the same groove. Thus, I felt praised and elevated by the song at the beginning of the film. Sitting in the movie theater, I felt enriched for a moment by Curtis Mayfield and believed that, like the two hustlers on 125th Street, I was at home in the city. For a moment, I felt that Monrovia belonged to me.

The opening sequence, to me, was better than some of my favorite spaghetti Westerns—*Once Upon a Time in the West*, *A Fistful of Dollars*, and *The Good, the Bad, and the Ugly*. Like them, *Superfly* was filmed in Technicolor; it was full of the kind of actions that define the loneliness of the romantic hero. But in addition to these narrative pleasures, the opening shots also made Harlem and 125th Street available to me. I already knew that the Apollo Theater, where James Brown had recorded the live versions of "Please, Please, Please!" and "It's a Man's World," was on 125th Street. The opening sequence, along with the songs of James Brown and Aretha Franklin, contributed to my image of Harlem as a desirable city, and of 125th Street as a locus of the black good life, mobility, and heroism.

The long takes and wide camera angles help create the powerful effects at the beginning of *Superfly*. First we see the street corner as if we were looking down on it from the top of a roof—lifelike, in color, and full of the movement of people and cars. A narrative is then created out of this shot, as the camera shifts its focus from the general street scene to zoom in on the meeting between the two men, then turns sideways to follow them in their quest. From here on, a classic linear narrative develops from one long take to another, the camera voyeuristically documenting the journey of the two men in the crowd. I say "voyeuristically" because we are introduced to Harlem by being allowed to follow two of its native sons. Finally, the editing is rhythmically motivated by Mayfield's song, which seems to generate the images the way songs do in music videos.

What I call the realism of this sequence contrasts with the abstract style of a famous scene in *Shaft* that takes place on MacDougal Street in Greenwich Village. Shaft meets a racist Italian at a restaurant called the Café Reggio, in order to be taken to the hotel where kidnappers are holding a woman. The Italian man is dressed like a square, in a blue suit, and cares about nothing but business. Shaft, in contrast, is relaxed and looking cool in a leather jacket—a cosmopolitan. He sits comfortably in the café and drinks a cappuccino. When Shaft and the Italian guy walk out of the café, the camera follows them from the point of view of Ben (Shaft's childhood friend) and his revolutionist gang members, who trail them. The camera peers at them from shopwindows, from inside restaurants, and out of basements. Some of the shots reveal Ben and his men looking like stalkers in the shadows; others are deliberately blurred to make the scene look weird, or as if the view is coming from behind a glass window. The soundtrack is also interesting. In its comical abstraction, it is reminiscent of the fear-inducing sound effects in Alfred Hitchcock's *Psycho*. But this kitsch music also accords with the cosmopolitanism of the film and its *noir* style of rendering Greenwich Village.

Although the scene in *Superfly* and this one in *Shaft* both depict mobility in the city, they made different impressions in me as a spectator in Monrovia. I identified more with the two men in the opening of *Superfly*, because the scene seemed real to me, while the MacDougal Street scene in

Shaft was more cinematic—that is, more formal, more stylized, and better structured as a pursuit scene. These formal aspects of *Shaft* had a distancing effect. Also, the fact that I didn't know Greenwich Village was a famous neighborhood in New York, comparable to Harlem, increased the feeling of distance. Curiously enough, my place in New York was being shaped along racial lines even before I left Africa. I saw myself in the opening frames of *Superfly* because Harlem and 125th Street mirrored my ideal image of Monrovia. The fact that the sequence was also accompanied by Curtis Mayfield's music, which in Monrovia was heard in nightclubs and shops and drifting out of people's windows, helped to naturalize it for me.

Now that I live in New York City, a few blocks from MacDougal Street, and teach *Superfly* and *Shaft* at New York University, I have a different reaction to both films. To my students, these films are at best corny, and at worst celebrations of black men's macho, violence, and misogyny. They also find exotic the fact that although I was living so far away and in a completely different culture, I could identify with Blaxploitation films. I think that they are to some extent right: these films are indeed symptomatic of America's cultural hegemony over the rest of the world, and bear all the negative implications of this imperialism. But my students tend to overlook the elements of empowerment and pleasure and the subversive strategies that these films, and black American culture in general, make available to people oppressed because of the color of their skin. It is also important to point out the influence of Blaxploitation films on directors like Quentin Tarantino, the Hughes brothers, Spike Lee, and John Singleton, and on actors such as Ice Cube, John Travolta, Bruce Willis, and Tupac Shakur.

What interests me today in *Superfly* is the narrative conflict between Priest and his friend Eddy, which centers around the moral satisfactions inherent in the life of a drug dealer. *Superfly,* by glorifying drug dealers as heroes, indirectly criticizes the civil rights movement for failing to provide better opportunities for people in black communities. The stigmatization of blacks as a race trapped in an urban ghetto, with drug dealers controlling their lives, is an indication of the uncompleted mission of efforts toward integration and civil rights. The film derives its moral weight from this indictment of the civil rights movement and black nationalist struggles. At the same time, it reveals to Priest the limitations of his drug-dealer lifestyle.

Priest's problems begin when he becomes conscious of his condition—his role as a commodity—and decides to change it. He is tired of being the pusher who has irrevocably broken the social contract and forever abjured virtue and law. He no longer takes his nice clothes, his Cadillac, his abundant supply of cocaine, and his white girlfriend as signs of security and the good life. His skepticism about the indestructible power of the pusher reveals the irony of the title song: "Superfly, super cool . . . How long can a good thing last? . . . Making money all the time." Priest informs Eddy that he wants to be free of this existence; he want to be able to choose what he wants to do, and "not be forced into things." This means that he is ready for a higher level of social consciousness. He no longer wants to be the man in bondage.

Eddy, on the other hand, is less conscious of the fact that he is trapped in the ghetto, and of the role that race and class play in keeping him there. He is intoxicated with the consumer goods that his "pusher man's" trade affords him, and with which he identifies. Here is how he rationalizes his lifestyle to Priest: "You gonna give all this up? Eight-track stereo, color TV in every room, and you can snort half a piece of dope every day! That's the American dream, nigger! You better come on in, man! I know it's a rotten game. But it's the only game the man left us to play." For Eddy, this is the life. This is what he and his homeboy Priest are supposed to do, and they should enjoy it.

Priest's attempt to open Eddy's eyes to social reality and the commodified nature of their life in the ghetto reminds me of Walter Benjamin's analysis of Baudelaire as a petty bourgeois. Benjamin argues that men like Baudelaire will one day become aware that they are blinded by consumerism, and will run from it. But, Benjamin continues, "the day had not as yet come. Until that day they were permitted, if one may put it this way, to pass the time. The very fact that their share could at best be enjoyment, but never power, made the period which history gave them a space for passing time. Anyone who sets out to while away time seeks enjoyment. It was self-evident, however, that the more this class wanted to have its enjoyment in this society, the more limited this enjoyment would be. The enjoyment promised to be less limited if this class found enjoyment of this society possible" (Benjamin, 1983: 59).

Priest desires precisely the kind of enjoyment that I call the black good life, which rejects the imprisoning and policing of black bodies by a racist and capitalist system. Eddy, in contrast, has learned to enjoy the ghetto; he is content to destroy other people's lives with drugs, and to be destroyed himself one day. Every one of Eddy's relationships with people contains a measure of hurt, betrayal, and vengeance. Yet Priest understands Eddy, because he has been there, in the ghetto, with him; and he knows the power of the external forces that conspire to keep Eddy in bondage. In this sense, *Superfly,* like *The Autobiography of Malcolm X,* captures the real essence of the homeboy. This homeboy, too, is seeking the black good life even when his behavior is most destructive. His pleasures are simultaneously an affirmation of life and a celebration of the ritual of resistance against racism. The homeboy is someone you empathize with, someone you cannot condemn totally without sentencing yourself. Eddy's argument that this is the "only game the man left us to play" expresses the failure of integration, and the lack of opportunity for black people.

Clearly, the homeboy motif is deployed in black films in order to highlight important aspects of the black good life in America. In the first place, the motif is invoked in the spirit of fraternity—to signify the structures of feeling known to characters who share the same background, be it cultural, historical, or racial. For example, the relationship between Malcolm X and his friend Shorty transcends Malcolm's political differences with his homeboy. In fact, Malcolm cannot imagine freedom for himself without freedom for Shorty as well. The same desire to share one's success with a homeboy complicates the decisionmaking of such film characters as Priest, Shaft, Tre (in *Boyz N the 'Hood*), and Cane (in *Menace II Society*). Regardless of the political ideal, to die for one's homeboy is often a revolutionary statement in these narratives.

To look at the relation between Priest and Eddy in terms of the homeboy ethic is also to invoke their affinity with Cain, who built a city and tried to hide in it. Homeboys move through the city bearing the mark of Cain—their very blackness—which they cannot shake off. Interestingly, Priest becomes a conversionist, like the Reverend Jesse Jackson. He gets tired of running and of always watching out for the enemy; he wants a change of life. Thus, Priest is a man who also is tired of his identity—a man who wants to be able to walk the streets without raising suspicion. But it is only after Priest and Eddy reach the top as pushers that Priest feels the need to stop selling drugs in Harlem.

The myth of Cain and the story of the homeboy come together here in a powerful configuration of immanence—of blacks' inability to escape a stereotypical identity. Just as Cain struggles to find the ideal city and free himself of the sin of killing Abel, the upwardly mobile homeboy is always endeavoring to overcome the stigma of racism in America. Homeboys are perpetually on the move, looking to make progress and achieve individual redemption. In this pursuit, they desire what I call transtextuality—that is, transcendence of imposed stereotypes and recognition as individuals in the city, both of which run counter to immanence. They want to assume individual identities which they have shaped themselves, out of bondage, and be acknowledged for their contribution to global civilization.

When I look at *Shaft* today, I focus more on the successful integration of John Shaft into all areas of the city—an integration that is typical of the film's cosmopolitan narrative. In *Superfly,* Priest is confined to Harlem. When he is in Greenwich Village, he seems like a vampire or an urban Apache, passing furtively in his long coat and large hat. He walks the streets under police surveillance, or spends most of his time in his car, which becomes his abode. Shaft, on the other hand, feels at home everywhere, in every crowd, like a *flâneur*. It is significant that the film opens in midtown Manhattan, in the theater district, with Shaft emerging from the subway. The theme song on the soundtrack declares him "the Man," who is solicited by everyone. Shaft moves with ease on the crowded avenues, recognized and appreciated by a wide range of people: a blind newspaper salesman who is white; a barber who is black. In a sense, Shaft is *the* native son of New York, an identity that derives from experience and transcends race.

Shaft's office is located midway between Harlem and the Village. He serves as a mediator between white and black, between the powerful and the disempowered. The plot revolves around Shaft's attempt to prevent a race riot by rescuing the daughter of a black gangster, Bumpy, kidnapped by an Italian Mafia boss who is determined to maintain control of underworld activities in Harlem. Shaft is tough, likable, and committed to fairness in his relations with both blacks and whites. He wants to uphold law and order by cooperating with the police, yet he is determined not to overlook the civil rights and nationalist struggles of the brothers and sisters uptown—people like the Black Panthers and the Young Moors, the latter led by his homeboy, Ben Bufford.

Shaft is a film that seesaws between the black and white points of view. Although Shaft himself seems to have transcended race by being less menacing in attitude and appearance than other black people in the film, or Priest in *Superfly,* the film does not go far enough toward eliminating racial stereotypes. Indeed, one could say that it participates in them, by presenting Shaft as an exceptional and benign black man. The scene in the Café Reggio, for example, in which the Italian mobster says, "I'm looking for a nigger called Shaft," is meant to be read against Shaft's appearance as nonthreatening and cosmopolitan, and therefore unlike that of a "nigger." As viewers, we appreciate Shaft's polished manners, which distance him not only from the uncouth Italian criminal but also from black people uptown. The scene creates a spectator position which associates black people who live uptown (unlike Shaft) with criminality.

In yet another scene, we see the way in which *Shaft* positions white viewers in its narrative of integration. Shaft takes a trip uptown in search of Ben Bufford, who is suspected of playing a role in the kidnapping of Bumpy's daughter. The sequence is reminiscent of the beginning of *Superfly*, where the two hustlers attack Priest and he runs after one of them to retrieve his wallet. Such sequences abound in Blaxploitation films; they function as tourist guides to Harlem. The obligatory soundtrack romantically describes the toughness of Harlem—its drug dealers, prostitutes, and abandoned children. The images always include clichés of 125th Street: churches, nightclubs, people sitting on doorsteps. In *Shaft*, we are treated to the same boring tour of Harlem. Clearly, such scenes are intended for outsiders, and serve only to reinforce the stereotypical image of folks uptown.

When it comes to addressing white people's concern about integration, *Shaft* is a safe film because it tries to balance its treatment of white criminals and that of black people who are unlike Shaft. Shaft's cosmopolitanism is nonthreatening because it presents "the other" as exotic, instead of emphasizing the originality of his identity. What impresses me in this film is less its ability to destabilize racial signs and more its inscription and valorization of the pleasure that is associated with Shaft's own freedom and mobility between Harlem and Greenwich Village.

It is this linearization, or movement from point A to point B, that constitutes the pleasure of recent 'hood films. The influence of *Shaft* and *Superfly* on these films is indisputable, but clearest of all in the way they have established the pattern for constructing mobility in the urban landscape.

Spike Lee's *She's Gotta Have It*

When I first saw *She's Gotta Have It* in 1986, at the Edinburgh International Film Festival, my reaction to it was negative. I was participating in a film conference devoted to the application of the theories of Third Cinema to independent films from Africa, Europe, India, and the United States.

Third Cinema was a movement that had grown out of the work of the Argentinian directors Fernando Solanas and Octavio Gettino in the late Sixties. They believed that the camera was a revolutionary weapon: that every film by a conscientious director should contribute to the liberation of the people of the Third World, and to the demystification of First Cinema (the commercial cinema of Hollywood) and Second Cinema (the bourgeois cinema of Europe). The Edinburgh conference had been organized by intellectuals at the British Film Institute who were seriously invested in Lacanian film theory, feminism, and anti-essentialism.

Spike Lee's reputation had preceded him. *She's Gotta Have It* had already been screened at Cannes, to rave reviews, and the director was being celebrated in the European press as the newest and most talented black kid on the block. It was said that his approach to sexuality was liberating, even though some of my colleagues had warned me about his stereotypical treatment of black women. I saw the film late one evening in the company of filmmakers and specialists in black and Third Cinema. There was total silence during the screening, except for a rare outburst of laughter by some of the women in the room, and the buzzing sound of the projector.

I did not like the film because I could not read it as a Third Cinema project. It was too stereotypical in its representation of black men, and it seemed to condone violence against women. I also—like a number of other people—was uneasy about the way in which the white press had elected Lee as *the* black filmmaker. After all, we who were participating in the Third Cinema conference were supposed to deconstruct stereotypes that had a negative impact on cultural and sexual relations. How could a *ménage à quatre* of the kind depicted in *She's Gotta Have It,* not to mention the reductive title of the film, help us in this endeavor?

I was also in Edinburgh to help promote a film: *The Garbage Boys,* by Cheick Oumar Sissoko. It tells a bittersweet story about children growing up in Bamako, Mali. What had endeared this little film to me was the way it presented its human story against a postcolonial backdrop, demonstrating how African nation-states have been forced to cut spending on education, health care, and other means of protecting citizens against injustice and corruption. *The Garbage Boys* showed young people fighting these obstacles daily—as they carry their own schooldesks to the classroom, pick up garbage to earn a living, play in the streets and learn vices (as do neglected children everywhere in the world), and watch their mothers die in childbirth.

I had seen *The Garbage Boys* several times in Bamako, at different movie theaters. I'd been surprised to notice that, in middle-class neighborhoods, people cried throughout the screening. They identified with the children's pain to such an extent that they felt guilt, fear, and shame, which they expressed through tears. Weeping was also a way for them to show that they understood; it was their way of suffering. At screenings in poor neighborhoods, in contrast, the viewers had interacted with the children on the screen and frequently laughed at their expense. Some had even shouted comments like, "You ain't seen nothing yet!" and won laughs from the audience. I had asked a taxi driver in Bamako why people liked the film so much, and why they laughed instead of being sad and angry. "Because it is a good film," he had told me. "It tells the truth like it is—it is the truth itself." So the film made them laugh because it was, for them, a statement of the truth that must be learned by everyone, like a ritual, in order to exorcise the pain within.

As a Malian myself, I was fascinated by the way this film divided Malian society in two—by the way its popular message made some people cry, while driving others to laugh uncontrollably. I suddenly wanted more films like *The Garbage Boys* for African audiences. For me, it was a watershed film: not only was it ahead of its time, but its fast and exciting narrative meant the death of boring, ahistorical, and culturally unrepresentative films by well-known African directors.

In retrospect, I wonder how I was able to find new cinematic truth in *The Garbage Boys,* but no merit in the equally energetic *She's Gotta Have It.* Was it because I looked at one with practical eyes and at the other with theoretical tools? I'm not sure. But when I look at *She's Gotta Have It* today, I am amazed at how many new elements it contributes to black and popular film language. To begin with, it was the first movie of the 1980s to place the fulfillment of individual desire at the forefront of the black liberation struggle, just as the individual is at the center of the hip-hop revolution. Second, it gave blackness a universal face, through the character of Mars (played by Spike Lee himself), and a universal home, Brooklyn.

She's Gotta Have It is the story of Nola Darling (played by Tracie Camila Johns), a young black woman about whom everybody in the film —and, to judge from its reception, out of the film—has something to say. *She's Gotta Have It* creates its narrative challenge and pleasure from the competing points of view on who Nola Darling is. Who really knows her secret? The film gives us two main sources for narrative points of view: the bedroom, where Nola speaks, and the park, where one of her lovers, Jamie (Redmond Hicks), shows that he is the most reliable of all the male voices.

The whole controversy over Lee's sexism in *She's Gotta Have It* rests on the viewer's reluctance to accept Nola Darling's point of view as authoritative. Trusting Nola entails buying into the coherence of the filmic discourse, which opens with a young and independent black woman with transgressive views about sexuality, who promises to tell everything on camera and on open microphone. Can the black men in the film accept such individuality and sexual freedom on the part of a black woman? And can Lee, a black male author, pull off such a feat? A related question, but different in its intention, is: Can the viewer separate *She's Gotta Have It* from Lee—that is, separate the text from the author?

I now believe that it was hasty on our part in Edinburgh to have dismissed the film as merely the projection of a black male fantasy onto a black woman. Nola is one of the principal contenders for narrative authority in *She's Gotta Have It*. The articulation of her point of view can be supported by a formal analysis of the narrative conventions deployed by Lee in the film. For example, because Nola promises at the beginning to tell us her story, we can say that everything in the film is depicted from her point of view; and that because she has already framed the people who are trying to frame her, her level of narrative consciousness is higher than theirs.

It is clear to me now that a large part of the success of the film depends on the audience's desire for a modern and independent character like Nola in the black community. Nola's role is threatening, yet attractive, because she appropriates the stereotype of the promiscuous black woman and redeploys it as an expression of her modernity. The audience identifies with Nola because she symbolizes the individual against the group; she makes us realize how far behind the black community is when it comes to the sexual revolution. The three principal male characters consider her a "freak" for wanting what men in the black community have always had: multiple sexual partners.

The filmic representation of these ideas also surpasses anything previously seen in black independent cinema. To begin with, there is no female precedent for Nola Darling in black independent cinema. Perhaps Ganja in Bill Gunn's *Ganja and Hess* is as invested in her own sexuality as Nola is. But one has to turn to the jazz scene and to hip-hop to encounter the independent and revolutionary spirit of women like her. The use of space is also novel in *She's Gotta Have It*. Nola's bedroom represents the narrative source of most of the episodes in the film. It is there that she imagines the different types of black men and women who have come into her life. It is also interesting that when the other characters try to construct their image of Nola, they always end up in her bedroom, under her control. The bedroom, in this sense, contrasts with the park not only in terms of male and female spaces, but as narrative spaces, locations of truth and falsehood.

Interestingly, Tracie Camila Johns's career has not gone beyond *She's Gotta Have It*. Does this mean that her character merely reinforced the stereotype of promiscuous black women in viewers' minds? Or that viewers remain uninterested in any black woman who is not a stereotype? It seems to me that Spike Lee's talent has consisted in reclaiming the stereotype and redeploying it in a subversive way. Mars, played by Lee himself, is a stereotype of the homeboy, or the next-door neighbor who re-presents the immanent and unchanging image of blacks in mainstream cinema. As such, Spike Lee reached fame as an actor, just like many of the male actors that Lee-the-director discovered. With regard to black women actresses, the condition of immanence must have even deeper roots in our minds. We categorically refuse them any transtextual capacity; and—as in the case of Nola—if they subvert the stereotype, we ignore their talent.

Nola's attempt to escape labels (and here the myth of Cain and his "mark" comes to mind again) is challenged by the three principal male characters in the film, who undermine her authority and the truth of her narrative. "She's bogus—she's not dependable," Mars tells Jamie. As proof of his statement, Mars says he had a rendezvous with her at a basketball game, but she didn't show up. Greer Child (John Canada Terrell) persuades her to see a therapist, telling her she's a nymphomaniac and a freak. And Jamie accuses her of being incapable of love. In fact, each of the three male characters thinks she's abnormal simply because he cannot keep her to himself.

Jamie's is the most compelling of the three male voices, and therefore the one most capable of exposing Nola as an unreliable narrator. In fact, Nola's sexuality, which is expressed through masturbation, the desire for multiple partners, lesbian relations, and sado-masochism, is so threatening to black male viewers that they automatically identify with Jamie's point of view. He is the nicest guy in the story; he wears simple short-sleeved shirts, and has a deep voice that evokes such screen icons as Tony Curtis and Jeff

Chandler. Indeed, he is Nola's favorite lover; the other two men serve as comic relief.

But the male viewer's identification with Jamie is not without problems. It is an expression of both misogyny and guilt. Jamie, unable to control Nola and keep her for himself, stops being Mister Nice Guy and finds himself another girlfriend. When Nola telephones and asks him to come over, he takes the subway to her house and seethes with rage the entire time. The film depicts the subway ride as a succession of still images in which Jamie's face and movements are distorted in an expressionist way, to make him look monstrous. When he arrives at Nola's home he rapes her, because he believes that it is not love she needs. He commits rape to punish her, and to take his revenge on her.

Male viewers back away from Jamie at this point, feeling guilty and ashamed. Some blame Spike Lee, the director, and some point the finger at black men in general. They leave the text behind to discuss nihilism, violence, and other clichés in American society. Most of them never come close to realizing what is in Nola's mind or what motivates her transgressions, because they are as backward as Jamie.

Nola's integrity is surreptitiously challenged even by the implied author of the film. The most effaced narrator in *She's Gotta Have It* is the person behind the camera, who is carrying out the investigation of Nola's life. But we can feel the presence of this omniscient narrator—for example, when the characters speak facing the camera, as if they were talking to a person beyond the fourth wall of the screen; when Mars makes his first appearance in the film, running toward the camera and thus making us aware of its presence; when Mars joins Jamie sitting in the park and says, "Are you still talking to them about Nola?" We feel it, too, in certain stylistic choices: in the acting, the camera angles and movements, and the use of black-and-white film stock.

These stylistic choices are interesting on more than one level. The black-and-white stock helps to create the effect of a 1940s suspense and psychological drama. Alfred Hitchcock reverted to black-and-white in *Psycho*, to give the film its haunting, primitive, uncanny feeling of *déjà vu*. Sometimes, when Jamie talks in the park about Nola, he uses the past tense, as if she were dead. In one scene, he describes how Nola used to like his poems; then we see a flashback showing Nola reading one of them.

The low-angle camera positions are sometimes used for comedy, as in the love scene with Greer and Nola. But they can also be used for artistic effect, as in a scene where the camera is placed on the ceiling of Nola's bedroom, to give a bird's-eye view of all four main characters on Nola's bed. Nola and Jamie are stretched out on the bed in each other's arms; Greer and Mars are curled up at their feet. The white bedspread serves as the background to what seems like a quote from a black-and-white collage by Romare Bearden. The shot has all the qualities of an improvisational jazz composition: each image assumes a pose in order to communicate in a cool way with the others. All these stylistic devices call attention to the presence of an omniscient narrator in *She's Gotta Have It.*

But Nola's voice is, above all, the most revolutionary element in the film. That I and other black American intellectuals and critics missed it in 1986 in Edinburgh reveals our adherence to certain received ideas, such as the theories of identity politics. Spike Lee understood this only too well. He marketed his film in Europe first, knowing that Americans feared black art and sexuality. Even before he began making films, black Americans had come to rely on liberal European institutions for the display, distribution, and promotion of their art, which was suppressed by racism and discrimination in America. Lee knew that in order for *She's Gotta Have It* to survive, he had to first garner praise and accolades at festivals such as those in Cannes and Edinburgh. It was essential that European critics recognize the innovative aspects of his film before it was released in the United States, where it might have been dismissed or killed by racism—or even by black critics who feared Nola Darling's novel recuperation of sexual stereotypes.

The 'Hood in Spike Lee's Cinema

With *She's Gotta Have It,* Spike Lee created a new kind of cinema, whose visual pleasures are associated with home. From *She's Gotta Have It* to *Do the Right Thing* and *Crooklyn,* Lee's films assign narrative functions to home imageries, symbolism, and metaphors. For Lee, "home" stands for black nationalism, the black community, and black people's celebration and ownership of their cultural products. *She's Gotta Have It* and *Do the Right Thing* describe Lee's attempt to valorize Brooklyn as a vibrant neighborhood—as a black Mecca with as much cosmopolitan and universal appeal as Harlem and Greenwich Village.

With a production company, a house, and a store in the Fort Greene section of the borough, Spike Lee continues to contribute to the mystique of Brooklyn. When young black people move to New York, they are more likely to seek refuge in Brooklyn than in Harlem or the Village. Many people feel that Spike Lee is the black Woody Allen, and that he has done for Brooklyn and black culture what Allen has done for Manhattan and Jewish culture. Like Allen, Lee has embraced the stereotypes of his culture. He himself has usually portrayed one of these in his films: the black man as a heroic, loving, and essential element in the neighborhood's history and everyday life. In the 1980s, Lee's identification with black male stereotypes coincided with the success of the hip-hop movement, which was dominated by these images. His depiction of racial issues showed him to be several years ahead of other black independent filmmakers, and way in advance of Hollywood.

In *She's Gotta Have It,* Lee creates the Brooklyn mystique by using space as a narrative device and by portraying Mars as the quintessential homeboy. As the opening credits roll, we see still-photos of children playing in the park, residents sitting on the steps of brownstones in all kinds of weather, men and women at work, people standing around in front of their houses. We see graffiti on a wall: "Bed-Stuy, Inc. Brooklyn Secedes from Union." These black-and-white stills tell the story of a community that calls attention to itself. They and the epigraph from Zora Neale Hurston, which makes reference to ships, create a romantic visual association between the history of the film's Brooklyn and the experiences that inspired Hurston's book *Their Eyes Were Watching God*. Through one stroke of editing, Lee appropriates the history of black America for his Brooklyn. Some might even say that he reduces the black experience to his history of Brooklyn. But, in truth, Lee has discovered the secret of modernity through editing—taking shortcuts to get to the point, or to get the job done. Other independent films from Africa and the diaspora are painfully long and literal in comparison.

Lee is also able to link associations and spaces by the way he edits the stills, showing children playing, seasons passing, adults working, people strolling. This kind of editing produces the same effect as going through a family album, and positions the spectator to feel a sense of belonging to the place. Lee develops his metaphor of public-space-as-home throughout the film. The most fantastic scene and the only one filmed in color, Nola's birthday celebration, takes place in a park. The sequence begins with Nola and Jamie in her apartment. Jamie, through a deliberately cinematic reference to *The Wizard of Oz,* asks Nola to close her eyes and say, "There's no place like home. There's no place like home. There's no place like home."

When she opens her eyes we are in Fort Greene Park, and the film has changed from black-and-white to color, as if to signal the transition to a dream. The setting contributes to the further privatization of the park: in the background is a monument inscribed with children's graffiti; in the foreground, a couple dances modern ballet to the music of an old-fashioned phonograph. The park thus takes the place of home, becoming the site of a private celebration and adorned with household objects and furniture, such as a phonograph, a table, a flower basket, and edibles.

All of Jamie's interviews take place in the park, where he seems most at ease. Lee also uses the park as the locus of uncensored male gossip about women. It is there that Jamie, Mars, and Greer project their sexual fantasies onto Nola. Mars says to Jamie, "She left me for you because you're taller than me." Greer chimes in, "Nola saw the three of us as one: a three-headed monster. We let her create us." And Jamie adds, "It was bad enough, Nola and all her male friends. But there was one particular female friend that was a bit too much." Jamie and Mars are fans of the New York Knicks and the Brooklyn Dodgers, whereas Greer is mocked because of his admiration for the Boston Celtics—a symbol of his desire to be white. The park in this sense is not only a space for leisure, but also a cultural space for black men.

Lee makes the park inviting for black viewers by representing Jamie comfortably sitting on a bench. Jamie considers himself a poet, and he likes reading to Nola in the park. All of these spatial denotations help define the park as the property of black people, and as a cultural and humanizing space for black males. It is the spot in which people and behaviors are designated "not black enough." To drive home this point, the film sets the Brooklynites Jamie and Mars, who are "down" (genuine, real), in opposition to the Manhattanite Greer, who seems superficial in his obsession with his body, stylish clothes, and white women. The park and, by extension, Brooklyn thus constitute a black nationalist space which is contrasted with Manhattan, across the bridge. According to the myth, black men feel at home in Brooklyn and do not have to resist stereotypes there. In Lee's Brooklyn, blackness is associated with being "real"—with the simple life, the working class, and sports. Greer refers to Mars and Jamie as "ignorant and chain-snatching Negroes from Brooklyn." It is precisely this type of prejudice, which whites have always hurled at blacks, that unites Jamie and Mars: though very different in their sensibility and outlook, they come together in their wish to claim Brooklyn. It becomes the space where the homeboy can freely participate in the black good life, away from the prying eyes of white people.

It is interesting to contrast this space, so welcoming to black viewers, with the claustrophobic and threatening one depicted in *Do the Right Thing,* a film in which Lee uses space choreographically and rhythmically. The whole story takes place in twenty-four hours: tension rises as the sun reaches its zenith, and the culminating tragedy coincides with the red fire of sunset. The action takes place on the hottest day of summer, which has traditionally been associated with rioting and arson in major American cities—a signal that blacks have had enough. In *Do the Right Thing,* Lee skillfully employs the classical notion of the unity of narrative time. He gives every moment its mood and color according to the position of the sun in the sky, and extends the interpretation of the fire at the end of the film to the expression of a historically identifiable black rage.

In contrast to *She's Gotta Have It,* where space is constructed as a neighborhood and a microcosm of black nationalist identity, *Do the Right Thing* presents a contested space: the characters are defined through their attempts to lay claim to their environment. Most of the film is set in one location, an urban neighborhood centered on a particular intersection of streets. The landmarks include a pizzeria, a Korean grocery store, and a red wall. In front of the wall sit three black men under an umbrella. Down the street, between the pizzeria and the grocery store, is a radio station. On the other side of the street, across from the pizzeria, is a large mural. What is remarkable about the setting and the construction of space is that whenever one of these landmarks occupies the foreground, we see the action that is taking place at another landmark in the background. For example, from the windows of Sal's pizzeria we see the sidewalk dwellers go in and out of the Korean grocery store. When Sal's son, Peno, has a fight with a fellow named Smiley, we hear the voices of people across the street interfering. Through this mutual visibility, all four corners of the neighborhood are connected.

The characters are divided by age, race, and class. Each group thinks that it is more entitled to the space than the others. The black men sitting under the umbrella watch a police car go by as if it is intruding in their private space. The police officers, in turn, look at the men with contempt and rage. When Peno looks out of the window of the restaurant and sees the men sitting under the umbrella, he says, "I hate this place." One of the black men accuses the Koreans of having built a business in "our neighborhood." Buggin' Out, one of the characters who organizes a boycott of Sal's pizzeria, confronts a white man who owns a brownstone: "Why don't you go in your own neighborhood?"

The conflict over space is also described in terms of a generational shift (to borrow a concept made famous by Houston Baker Jr.). The younger generation is no longer respectful or tolerant of old black men, such as the character Da Mayor. In one scene, the young men try to run him out of the neighborhood by calling him an old drunkard. Da Mayor endeavors to explain the conditions that led to his present predicament, but he fails to win their esteem. They insist he should have fought to win his dignity back; he should have found a job by any means necessary; he should not have used racism as an excuse.

This scene, which depicts the younger generation's scorn for the achievements of their elders and for traditional values, reminds me of the book *Black Power,* in which Richard Wright has difficulties identifying with African traditions. There is also a nearly identical scene of generational conflict in the film *Menace II Society.* Consider the sequence in which Cane defies his grandparents. The opposition between inside and outside, between Cane and his grandfather, is interesting. "Outside" is secular, dangerous, and characterized by black-on-black crime and police brutality. "Inside" is religious, oriented toward family and survival; but it is also framed by claustrophobic architecture, and colonized by the outside. Cane's grandfather asks him to choose between inside and outside. But knowing that the boy will opt for the outside, he adds, "Do you want to get killed?" To which Cane answers, "I don't know." It is possible to interpret Cane's answer as a critique of what the grandfather considers a better life than the one in the streets. Cane and the other homeboys want more out of life than their grandfathers got, and they will not let high moral authority persuade them to settle for delayed gratification.

In *Do the Right Thing,* space is also reclaimed through close-ups. The film opens with a young woman dancing to a Public Enemy song, "Fight the Power." The volume is high, and most of the shots are extreme close-ups of her body in motion. She is literally in the viewer's face. It is through an extreme MTV-style close-up that we are also introduced to Radio Rahim, a character who goes around with a boom box always playing the same song. In one scene we see territory being contested: Radio Rahim raises the volume of his boom box to cover the sound of a Latin song being played on a radio nearby.

Another instance of the use of sound to appropriate space is seen at the beginning of the film, when the disk jockey Senior Love Daddy wakes the whole neighborhood up with his sound system. The radio station becomes a tool for community building, through the way in which it unites people. It gives them the weather forecast, sends out birthday greetings, and makes music part of their community. Sound is one of the means by which space becomes lovable or hostile.

Images, too, contribute to the definition of space. The character named Smiley walks around with a photograph of Malcolm X and Martin Luther King Jr., heroes who symbolize the struggle of black people for citizenship. At the end of the film, Smiley finally succeeds in putting this picture on the wall of Sal's pizzeria, which previously had displayed photographs only of white Italian heroes.

In sum, the space in *Do the Right Thing* is a negative space: it resists viewers' efforts at identification. As a young boy says toward the end, "It ain't safe in this fucking neighborhood." The characters in the film seem lonely. Most of the time, they are in danger from passing cars, from violent youths, from racism, and from the police. In *She's Gotta Have It*, Lee uses space to make the viewers identify with the black good life. In *Do the Right Thing,* he creates a dangerous space to awaken the viewer to hostile and destructive social conditions.

Homeboys and the Reclaiming of Stereotypes

It is surprising to me that Tracie Camila Johns has not gone on to bigger roles, like all the black males who started their careers in Spike Lee's films. In *She's Gotta Have It,* her character adds a new twist to the stereotype of the sensual black woman. Most of the male characters in Lee's films, including the ones played by the director himself, also embody stereotypes. But this has not prevented the actors from going on to greater success. It is unfortunate not only for Johns's career but also for the future of black film that the hip-hop movement of the 1980s and 1990s has been restricted to the deployment of black male stereotypes.

For—as we have seen with contemporary African masks and statues, and with the Blaxploitation movies—reclaiming stereotypes can be subversive, and therefore redeeming for the individual. By making many masks and putting them on the market, Sidimé Laye not only claims the profits generated by the sale of his art, but also resituates the audience vis-à-vis the meaning and aesthetic of each individual mask. He imparts additional meanings to the stereotype; he gives it mobility and a transtextual value. By carving mask after mask, Sidimé Laye is multiplying himself, and redefining himself as he does so. It is in this sense that I call Sidimé Laye's determination to go on carving a form of resistance: it frees the masks from their old stereotypical immanence.

Similarly, black male actors wear masks when they put themselves in the marketplace, so as to repossess and redefine the stereotypes that they embody in films. Every time actors like Spike Lee and Ice Cube appear on screen, they are not only repeating the stereotype of the homeboy—they are also giving the term new currency. They are making it a fashion statement, a customized item, a familiar element in our living rooms. This is ironic because just around the corner from Spike Lee's films (so to speak), the homeboy is viewed as a chain snatcher. I believe that Lee's films afford a degree of transtextuality to black actors who reclaim the stereotype. But only black males have so far been allowed to enjoy this freedom of movement from text to text inside black culture.

A quick look at Mars in *She's Gotta Have It* and Doughboy (Ice Cube) in John Singleton's *Boyz N the 'Hood* will suffice to show how black artists reclaim and redeploy stereotypes. Mars's status as the stereotypical homeboy in *She's Gotta Have It* is first of all indicated by the characters in the film. Greer calls him a chain snatcher from Brooklyn, a hoodlum, and an ignorant Negro. Mars has all the visible traits of someone who is stuck in childhood, a case of arrested development. He wears loud clothes with writing on them and tennis shoes that look like toys; he rides a bicycle; he is unemployed. Jamie cannot see what Nola sees in Mars; and she herself, toward the end of the film, tells Mars to grow up.

But the old stereotype of the homeboy stops there. Mars comes across in the film as someone we all know as our next-door neighbor. Right away, we see that there are two kinds of stereotypes. First, there is the one that is a stranger to us and that must be avoided at all costs. This meaning of the stereotype has no substance by itself. It can be conjured up in the shape of a bad wolf, a boogie man, or a black man. Then there is the one who is familiar to us—the one we know and love. Nola says to Mars, "There's something funny about you." Clearly, Nola loves Mars because he makes her laugh; he is witty and irreverent. Yet he also seems familiar to her. He is like a brother or a childhood friend. Others may not appreciate Mars or may treat him as a nobody, but Nola identifies with him.

Mars also embodies the community's feelings toward its heroes, history, and culture. His identity is bound up with images of cultural icons and superstars, such as Joe Louis, Jackie Robinson, Michael Jordan, and Bernard King. At one point he says that it was he who gave Jesse Jackson the idea to run for president of the United States. This reference to actual people in the fictional world of the film gives Mars an aura of realness and credibility: he addresses the concerns of black viewers. Lee's subsequent films contain references to political heroes like Nelson Mandela, Malcolm X, and Martin Luther King Jr., and to contemporary social issues such as the Rodney King beating, the Howard Beach incident, Tawana Brawley, Michael Stewart, and Eleanor Bumpurs.

In *She's Gotta Have It,* Lee also uses the character of Mars to engender nostalgia for black culture. Consider the scene in which Mars asks Nola to grease his scalp. We are projected into a romantic black past with quaint forms of courtship, as we watch Nola massaging Mars' head with her oily fingers. As Mars converses with Nola, sitting at the foot of the bed with his head between her knees, the film creates an intimacy between them that surpasses her sexual relations with Jamie and Greer. It is interesting that Lee also has scenes focusing on hair in his other films. In *Do the Right Thing,* for example, a character named Mother Sister has her hair done by a friend in the same old-fashioned way, as she sits on the front steps of her brownstone.

Mars's character sets the stage for Spike Lee to play more homeboy roles. It makes sense, then, to compare Lee to Woody Allen, because both have added new archetypes to the American cinematic repertoire. And in the process, they have created a new film language. Lee has fused his screen personae with his real-life activities as a director, businessman, and cultural figure. He has profoundly transformed black film—and American film in general—through the alteration and dissemination of stereotypes.

Ice Cube, who plays Doughboy in *Boyz N the 'Hood,* also embodies the Homeboy both on screen and off. He combines an ordinary appearance and a scruffy style of dress with the musical flair of a fiery preacher. In his music videos, Ice Cube is known as a rebel who lives (in the words of Todd Boyd) "outside of varying sectors of both black and white society." His antihero persona—not flamboyant, yet capable of getting the job done—binds him to segments of the black community that identify with lawbreakers. Ice Cube's "critical cypher treats both African American and the dominant society as equal culprits in the continual destruction of African American culture" (Boyd, 1997: 52).

In *Boyz N the 'Hood*, Ice Cube is the toughest and most dangerous character, yet the one that spectators identify with most closely. Perhaps this is because he is the older brother in the neighborhood, who defines himself through protecting the younger and weaker ones. The viewer also identifies with the character of Doughboy because he delivers the best lines in the film, and saves the life of Tre at the end. But, more crucially, Doughboy constitutes a new character in the depiction of African Americans on screen. He frees the homeboy from the pathological space reserved for him in mainstream cinema, and creates new possibilities for character development for the black male. With Doughboy, the homeboy becomes a critical intellectual, and a resistance leader in the community.

There is a scene in *Boyz N the 'Hood* where the received image of homeboys as unreflective criminals comes face to face with Singleton's new image of homeboys as struggling to maintain a community. The scene takes place on Crenshaw Boulevard, a popular hangout. It opens with a rap song commenting on the militarization of the police against young blacks in Los Angeles. We see Doughboy in a convertible, interacting with his friends, and many young people hanging out in the background. Doughboy and his friends talk about religion, feminism, prisons, and the existence of God. Then a rival gang passes by and the gathering turns into a shootout, with everybody running for cover.

What is special about this scene is that it is a replay of the stereotype of dominant cinema's representation of black-youth mobility in the city. But Singleton renders it in a metafilmic way—that is, the characters play their roles while reflecting on the cinematic representation of blacks in these same roles. Thus, while remaining within a dominant mode of representation, *Boyz N the 'Hood* deploys a didactic language that is critical of violence, misogyny, religious hypocrisy, and black-on-black crime. It is in this sense that Singleton's depiction of homeboys, and particularly of Doughboy, stands as an original contribution to the black male image in film.

The movement toward linearization and gratifying endings, instead of resistance narratives or narratives of high moral persuasion, characterizes the pleasure of 'hood movies. The characters who wind up as winners achieve aesthetic, political, or economic success by overcoming obstacles placed in their way. A film like *Boyz N the 'Hood* is a good example of black youth culture's propensity toward linearization and the development of secular pleasure structures. When I taught *Boyz* in my film class, most of my black students declared that they knew someone—brother, cousin, friend—just like Doughboy. Now, the question is not whether my students actually knew such a person. Doughboy is only a fictional character. What matters is that my students felt the need to link him to their past, in order to justify their identification with the film and, by extension, their identification with the structures of feeling that his actions create. In a romantic sense, Doughboy symbolizes the 'hood as many people imagine it. He is tough and loving toward other black people; yet, like the heroes of Blaxploitation films, he sells drugs to black people. Most important, he is a street intellectual without a job. Doughboy delivers the best line in the film when, at the end, he states that the media and the system "either don't know, or don't show, or don't care" about black life. Doughboy is a new archetype in black cinema who could not have existed without the hip-hop movement, and without the mobile black lifestyles evident in places like Westwood (in Los Angeles) and Greenwich Village.

White males, too, use black stereotypes as their domain of transtextuality. But transtextuality cannot be examined without also considering immanence. By "transtextuality" I mean the movement of cultural styles from character to character in films, and from text to text in written works. And by "immanence" I refer to the trapping of a character in a cultural role. When black maleness becomes transtextual, as it does in the case of Quentin Tarantino's film *Pulp Fiction* (1994), it is not only a source of amusement and role playing, but also a means of revalorizing white characters' cultural capital. It is interesting that *Pulp Fiction* was widely reviewed as fun—a film in which people are just playing—and therefore not homophobic, misogynistic, or racist.

Pulp Fiction is an important film because it brings into play some of the heavily contested themes and representations of black masculinity. The film provides narrative pleasure by deploying some of the most visible signs of black male pathology, black nihilism, and antisocial black youth. These signs include black male vernacular speech, black styles of dress, the black aesthetic of "cool," and black violence. Quentin Tarantino thought that black men were having all the fun in their films, and said that *Pulp Fiction* was his attempt at having fun. Following this logic, we can say that *Pulp Fiction* is a black male film. The film is full of "nigger this, nigger that," which can refer to both black and white characters. Indeed, Tarantino uses the word "nigger" in an enormous range of contexts in *Pulp Fiction*. Furthermore, many of the white actors in the film were previously known for their roles emulating black manhood: Bruce Willis as a rhythm-and-blues singer in *Die Hard*, Christopher Walken as a drug dealer in *The King of New York*, Travolta as a disco dancer in *Saturday Night Fever*, and Tarantino as a fan of Pam Greer and Blaxploitation films in *Reservoir Dogs*.

Pulp Fiction also brings onto the scene several definitions of "cool," in order to determine who is the master of the black aesthetic of cool. According to the film, to be cool one has to learn to survive without such emotions as fear, confusion, naïveté, and stupidity. Cool, as an aesthetic of death, mimics death itself. In the film, the characters Yolanda and Ringo are the least cool, because they don't know how to play the game; they lose control of the situation. Jimi, played by Tarantino himself, is married to a black woman; but he is not cool because he is afraid of his wife, and he panics in the face of death. Butch, played by Bruce Willis, is cool only as a white boy; it is not cool to revisit the scene of a crime. The new capitalist godfather Marcellus is cool, but he cannot keep his woman from falling for the likes of the hit-man Vincent. Vincent must be cool because Jules, an authentic black man, calls him his homeboy; he is also cool because of his quiet, unshakable demeanor. But he plays with death when he tries to make love to Marcellus' wife. He also dies in the film, killed by Butch. Jules is a gangster-liberation theologist with high moral authority. As a gangster intellectual who derives his rhetorical power from the Bible, he has the best lines in the film. He is very cool because he can control very delicate, potentially explosive situations; he knows when to quit. But Winston Wolf (played by Harvey Keitel) is the coolest of all. Other characters, including Marcellus and Jules, defer to him. Most of all, he does a clean job and leaves no traces behind.

Here we have it—Tarantino's characters playing at being cool and out-cooling each other. In the same spirit, one might say that Orson Welles had a lot of fun playing with the *film noir* genre in *Touch of Evil*. And Jean-Luc Godard and his New Wave colleagues had lots of fun playing with the characters and styles of B-movies. Tarantino's discovery is that white characters can play Blaxploitation roles, and that black maleness, as embodied in the aesthetic of cool, can be transported through white bodies. Black films like *Menace II Society* and *Boyz N the 'Hood* are not accorded the same latitude of playfulness and reflexivity. In fact, to criticize *Pulp Fiction* is to be radically uncool.

This brings me to my other category: immanence. Unlike white characters, black people are trapped in their skin. When they play the role of a gangster or a prostitute, spectators see them as playing themselves. They are locked in pathological identities and are not taken seriously when they try to play white roles. A serious look at recent films by black directors also reveals a preoccupation with wearing masks—with playing different roles and infusing stereotypes with new energies. Nola Darling had the potential for opening the door to inverted stereotypes, ones that would enable black women to wear masks and assume new roles. But it seems that no one wanted to go down that dangerous road.

Toward a New Common Ground

Young blacks today are more aware than their parents were of the political issues surrounding consumption in American society. Thus, they do not view consumption negatively, as a form of alienation. They are less concerned than their parents about the cultural content of their blackness, and more concerned with instant gratification. They do not feel driven to seek success, to advance instantly, to consume in the venues that white people want to reserve for themselves and their children. Homeboy activism places mobility and consumption at the very center of the struggle for the black good life. Homeboys refuse to be restricted to black enclaves or to be defined by racial stereotypes. Instead, they put those very stereotypes of blackness in the marketplace, and obtain the highest prices for them. Mobility and consumption have thus become the vehicle through which young blacks control prevailing stereotypes and regain their individuality in the crowd.

Homeboys under the age of thirty-five are less passionate than their elders about the traditional values of the civil rights struggle. For most of them, Martin Luther King Jr., John F. Kennedy, and Malcolm X seem like legendary television heroes. The messages of these leaders have become so distant from the homeboys' reality that the people who are still preaching their values also seem unreal and out of touch. The reality of today's homeboy is shaped by consumption, movement, and information, which define new rights and which are in turn shaped by globalization and immigration.

Globalization and immigration have complicated the meaning of such civil rights concepts as integration, the melting pot, racism, common ground, and common struggle. Some of the most virulent songs from gangster rap and 'hood movies sell better abroad than in the United States. They thus defy the moral outrage of such civil rights organs as the NAACP and the black church. Recent immigration laws favoring blacks from Africa and the Caribbean have also enabled these new Americans to move into the social space created by the civil rights movement. The Caribbean and African immigrants are black, but they do not share all of the values of African Americans, who came out of the civil rights movement. Unlike African Americans, they arrived in this country as individuals searching for freedom and the American dream.

Africans and Caribbeans may build coalitions with African Americans around certain issues such as racism and discrimination, but they may also differ on issues such as the meaning of history, social justice, moral authority, nationalism, and black people's relation to mainstream culture in America. Africans and Caribbeans are to African Americans what post–Soviet bloc Jewish émigrés are to American Jews. Neither Africans and Caribbeans nor these new Jewish immigrants care seriously about the civil rights coalition against Jim Crow racism. In their disregard for history and their inclination toward individual mobility and profit in the market economy, African and Caribbean immigrants share the same mentality as the hip-hop generation.

There is therefore an emerging common ground defined by the declining significance of history and the increasing importance of global-market ideologies. The hip-hop generation and the new immigrants take for granted the privileges won by the civil rights struggle; and they see no need to continue fighting to further these rights, because they want to use the already-won space to do other things.

The activism of young blacks in the 1990s has its own specificity. Their goals are separate from the mainstream agendas of the Left, but closer to the aspirations of recent immigrants from Africa and the Caribbean and of young Latinos and whites. Their activism is threatening both to whites and to a certain segment of the black middle class, because it does not emphasize upward mobility through the upholding of a higher moral authority as taught by the civil rights Left or the black church. The values of young blacks, like those of new immigrants, are shaped in the public sphere, where performance and competition define the individual's worth.

The common ground shared by homeboys, by young Latinos, Asians, and whites, and by recent immigrants also complicates the American Left's definition of itself in the context of globalization. For example, the Left, like every other movement in the world today, needs to become transnational in order to save itself from narrow nationalism and ethnocentrism. Without this transnational perspective, it is easy to oppose immigration on the grounds that working-class blacks and whites are losing their jobs to low-wage Mexicans, Asians, and Caribbeans; or to argue against imported cheap commodities in favor of domestically made products. In fact, a ban on immigration affects people along racial lines as well as class lines, which are structured by the global economy. Americans are losing their jobs not to immigration, but to the gradual transformation of America from a producing nation into a consuming nation. A genuinely transnational Left, instead of always equating consumption with alienation, would therefore include the new societies structured through consumption as an essential part of its understanding of globalization. The question of who consumes and who cannot is as important today as the working class's relation to production was in the period of American industrialization.

Everything the Left does today seems to be a maneuver to keep white men in their position of leadership and privilege. The much-publicized problem between blacks and Jews is really not an issue between blacks and Jews, but a national problem complicated by globalization and immigration: recent immigrants from the former Soviet bloc and the Caribbean are less sensitive to the history of black and Jewish unity in struggle. Jewish immigrants simply inherit the dominant American tradition of discriminating against blacks, while black Caribbeans may blur the distinction between Jews and whites who block their access to the American dream. In sum, it is naive for blacks to direct all their grievances toward Jews; Jewish people cannot by themselves solve the problems of black America. It is also cynical of Jews to single black people out as the fountainhead of anti-Semitism in America. There are criminals on both sides who should be dealt with by the law. But the real issue is whether globalization, in restructuring systems of domination and racism, has also changed the common ground of Jews and blacks. A real political coalition would thus do well to move away from analyzing racism and anti-Semitism, and toward building economic and cultural alliances between these two groups.

The transnational mentality shared by the hip-hop generation and new immigrants also challenges such traditional liberal ideals as the melting pot and the existence of common ground. Recent immigration and the transnational flow of capital have revealed that to live in the United States and participate in civil society, one need not necessarily share any of the melting-pot philosophy. In fact, as the example of Japanese and Arab landlords and businessmen in America reveals, one can be as different as possible from one's neighbor and still share an interest in the market economy and the state. The civil rights Left shows a facet of its nationalism and ethnocentrism by insisting that all Americans partake of one identity, albeit melted, instead of celebrating difference, be it geographic or cultural. The global situation has appropriately exposed these types of Leftists as the neoconservatives of American society.

Black nationalists, especially, have seen their values labeled archaic by the transnational hip-hop culture and by recent immigrants. Let's face it: blacks have not been any better consumers in the new global market system than they were previously, because both the black church and the Left, the two institutions most privileged by black intellectuals and political institutions, are suspicious of the market economy and consumption. The hip-hop movement has done a better job than anyone of explaining the needs and wants of the homeboys.

In this global context, racism too has been redefined. Today, it is not so much regarded as a withholding of citizenship and voting rights, or a denial of other types of entitlement such as housing discrimination. Rather, it is seen as the denial of access to competitive tools in the marketplace, the stigmatization and demonization of young blacks in search of individual identities, and the refusal to see that black people have made and can make a positive contribution to world civilization.

References

Index

▲▼▲

References

▲▼▲

Achebe, Chinua. 1984. *Things Fall Apart*. New York: Fawcett. Orig. pub. 1958.

Appiah, Anthony Kwame. 1992. *In My Father's House: Africa in the Philosophy of Culture*. New York: Oxford University Press.

Asante, Molefi Kete. 1987. *The Afrocentric Idea*. Philadelphia: Temple University Press.

Baker, Houston A., Jr. 1984. *Blues, Ideology, and Afro-American Literature: A Vernacular Theory*. Chicago: University of Chicago Press.

—— 1987. *Modernism and the Harlem Renaissance*. Chicago: University of Chicago Press.

—— 1993. *Black Studies, Rap, and the Academy*. New York: Oxford University Press.

Baldwin, James. 1985. *The Price of the Ticket: Collected Nonfiction, 1948–1985*. New York: St. Martin's.

Benjamin, Walter. 1969. "The Work of Art in the Age of Mechanical Reproduction." In Benjamin, *Illuminations*. Trans. Harry Zohn. New York: Schocken.

—— 1983. *Charles Baudelaire: A Lyric Poet in the Era of High Capitalism*. Trans. Harry Zohn. London: Verso.

—— 1997. *Selected Writings*, vol. I: *1913–1926*. Ed. Marcus Bullock and Michael W. Jennings. Cambridge, Mass.: Harvard University Press.

Bourdieu, Pierre. 1994. *Raisons pratiques: Sur la théorie de l'action*. Paris: Seuil.

Boyd, Todd. 1997. *Am I Black Enough for You? Popular Culture from the 'Hood and Beyond*. Bloomington: Indiana University Press.

Brun, Jean. 1989. "La ville: L'abri et le refuge." *Corps écrit*, 29: 33–38.

Camara Laye. 1976. *L'enfant noir*. Paris: Plon.

Césaire Aimé. 1957. *Lettre à Maurice Thorez*. Paris: Présence Africaine.

—— 1976. *Discours sur le colonialisme*. Paris: Présence Africaine. Orig. pub. 1955.

—— 1983. *Cahier d'un retour au pays natal*. Paris: Présence Africaine. Orig. pub. 1939.

Davis, Angela. 1974. *Angela Davis: An Autobiography*. New York: Random House.

Davis, Miles, with Quincy Troupe. 1989. *Miles: The Autobiography*. New York: Simon and Schuster.

de Roux, Emmanuel. 1996. "Paris, nouvelle capitale européenne des arts primitifs." *Le Monde,* June 23–24.

Diawara, Mamadou. 1994–1995. "Le cimetière des autels, le temple aux trésors: Réflexion sur les musées d'art africain." *Jahrbuch*. Berlin: Wissenschaftskolleg.

——— 1996. "Le griot mande à l'heure de la globalisation." *Cahiers d'études africaines,* 144, no. 36-4: 591–612.

Diawara, Manthia, ed. 1993. *Black American Cinema*. New York: Routledge.

Diop, Cheikh Anta. 1982. *The Cultural Unity of Black Africa: The Domains of Patriarchy and of Matriarchy in Classical Antiquity*. Paris: Présence Africaine.

Du Bois, W. E. B. 1961. *The Souls of Black Folk*. New York: Fawcett.

——— 1965. *The World and Africa: An Inquiry into the Part Which Africa Has Played in World History*. New York: International Publishers.

Eliot, T. S. 1920. "Tradition and the Individual Talent." In Eliot, *The Sacred Wood: Essays on Poetry and Criticism*. London: Methuen. Reprint 1972.

Fabre, Michel. 1993. *The Unfinished Quest of Richard Wright*. Trans. Isabel Barzun. Urbana: University of Illinois Press. Orig. pub. *La quête inachevée*. Paris: Lieu Commun, 1986.

Fanon, Frantz. 1963. *The Wretched of the Earth*. New York: Grove. Orig. pub. *Les damnés de la terre*. Paris: Maspéro, 1961.

Gabriel, Teshome. 1982. *Third Cinema in the Third World: The Aesthetics of Liberation*. Ann Arbor, Mich.: UMI Research Press.

Gilroy, Paul. 1993. *The Black Atlantic: Modernity and Double Consciousness*. Cambridge, Mass.: Harvard University Press.

Griaule, Marcel. 1992. "Gunshot." in *October,* 60 (Spring): 40–41.

Gross, Michael. 1993. "The Village under Siege." *New York Magazine,* August 16: 30–37.

Guerrero, Edward. 1993. *Framing Blackness: The African American Image in Film*. Philadelphia: Temple University Press.

Habermas, Jürgen. 1984. *The Theory of Communicative Action,* vol. I: *Reason and the Rationalization of Society*. Trans. Thomas McCarthy. Boston: Beacon.

Haley, Alex. *Roots*. 1976. Garden City, N.Y.: Doubleday.

Harper, Phillip Brian. 1996. *Are We Not Men? Masculine Anxiety and the Problem of African-American Identity*. New York: Oxford University Press.

hooks, bell. 1992. *Black Looks: Race and Representation*. Boston: South End Press.

James, C. L. R. 1969. *A History of Pan-African Revolt*. Washington D.C.: Drum and Spear.

Kabou, Axelle. 1991. *Et si l'Afrique refusait le développement?* Paris: L'Harmattan.

Kane, Cheikh Hamidou. 1972. *Ambiguous Adventure*. Trans. Katherine Woods. London: Heinemann. Orig. pub. *L'aventure ambiguë*. Paris: Julliard, 1961.

Kelley, Robin. 1994. *Race Rebels: Culture, Politics, and the Black Working Class*. New York: New Press.

Krauss, Rosalind. 1984. "Giacometti." In William Rubin, ed., *"Primitivism" in Twentieth-Century Art: Affinity of the Tribal and the Modern*. New York: Museum of Modern Art.

Leiris, Michel. 1996. *Miroir de l'Afrique*. Paris: Gallimard.

Malcolm X and Alex Haley. 1992. *The Autobiography of Malcolm X*. New York: Grove.

Monénembo, Tierno. 1997. *Cinéma*. Paris: Seuil.

Mudimbe, V. Y. 1988. *The Invention of Africa: Gnosis, Philosophy, and the Order of Knowledge*. Bloomington: Indiana University Press.

Naremore, James. 1993. *The Films of Vincente Minnelli*. New York: Cambridge University Press.

Niane, Djibril T. 1965. *Sundiata: An Epic of Old Mali*. London: Longman. Orig. pub. *Soundjata, ou l'épopée mandingue*. Paris: Présence Africaine, 1960.

Reed, Ishmael. 1993. *Airing Dirty Laundry*. Reading, Mass.: Addison-Wesley.

Reid, Mark. 1993. *Redefining Black Film*. Berkeley: University of California Press.

Robinson, Cedric J. 1983. *Black Marxism: The Making of the Black Radical Tradition*. London: Zed Press.

Rose, Tricia. 1994. *Black Noise: Rap Music and Black Culture in Contemporary America*. Hanover, N.H.: University Press of New England.

Rothenberg, Jerome, ed. 1968. *Technicians of the Sacred: A Range of Poetries from Africa, America, Asia, and Oceania*. Garden City, N.Y.: Doubleday.

Rubin, William, ed. 1984. *"Primitivism" in Twentieth-Century Art: Affinity of the Tribal and the Modern*. 2 vols. New York: Museum of Modern Art.

Sartre, Jean-Paul. 1976. *Black Orpheus*. Trans. S. W. Allen. Paris: Présence Africaine. Orig. pub. "Orphée noir," in Léopold Sédar Senghor, ed., *Anthologie de la nouvelle poésie nègre et malgache de langue française*. Paris: Presses Universitaires de France, 1948.

Sassine, Williams. 1985. *Le zéhéros n'est pas n'importe qui*. Paris: Présence Africaine.

Sembene Ousmane. 1957. *O pays, mon beau peuple!* Paris: Presses Pocket.

Schapiro, Meyer. 1978. *Modern Art: Nineteenth and Twentieth Centuries*. New York: Braziller.

Senghor, Léopold Sédar, ed. 1948. *Anthologie de la nouvelle poésie nègre et malgache de langue française*. Paris: Presses Universitaires de France.

———— 1956. "L'esprit de la civilisation, ou les lois de la culture négro-africaine." *Présence Africaine*, 8–10. Special issue: *Le premier congrès international des écrivains et artistes noirs*.

———— 1996. *Léopold Sédar Senghor et la revue "Présence Africaine."* Paris: Présence Africaine.

Soyinka, Wole. 1970. *The Interpreters*. London: Heinemann.

Touré, Sékou. 1967. *L'Afrique en marche*. Conakry: Imprimerie Nationale Patrice Lumumba.

———— 1969. *La révolution culturelle*. Conakry: Imprimerie Nationale Patrice Lumumba.

Tutuola, Amos. 1953. *The Palm-Wine Drinkard and His Dead Palm-Wine Tapster in the Dead's Town*. New York: Grove.

Wallace, Michele. 1997. "The Prison House of Culture: Why African Art? Why the Guggenheim? Why Now?" in *Black Renaissance / Renaissance Noire*, 1, no. 2: 162–175.

West, Cornel. 1993. *Race Matters*. Boston: Beacon.

Willemen, Paul, and Pines, Jim, eds. 1989. *Questions of Third Cinema*. London: BFI.

Wood, Joe, ed. *Malcolm X in Our Own Image*. 1992. New York: St. Martin's.

Wright, Richard. 1956. "Tradition and Industrialization: The Plight of the Tragic Elite in Africa." *Présence Africaine*, 8–10.

———— 1995a. *Black Power: A Record of Reactions in a Land of Pathos*. New York: Harper Perennial.

———— 1995b. *The Color Curtain: A Report on the Bandung Conference*. New York: Harper Perennial.

Index